Doing What You Know

Doing What You Know: Breaking Through the Invisible Barrier

Movement Edition

By Ray Thigpen

Thigpen Global Press

DOING WHAT YOU KNOW: BREAKING THROUGH THE INVISIBLE BARRIER
Movement Edition

For inquiries, contact:
Ray Thigpen
ray@doingwhatyouknow.com

This is a work of nonfiction. Some names and identifying details have been changed to protect privacy. All stories are true to the best of the author's recollection and intent.

ISBN: **979-8-9999456-0-0**

Cover design by Ray Thigpen
Edited by Ray Thigpen

Movement Edition: 2025
Printed in the United States of America

Published by **Thigpen Global Press**
Distributed worldwide through IngramSpark
www.DoingWhatYouKnow.com

Dedication

To the teams I've had the honor of building.
Thank you for trusting the vision, pushing through the hard days, and reminding me why this work matters.

To the mentors who showed up with truth, grace, and timely wisdom.
A special thank-you to Nancy, whose guidance played a major role in shifting my mindset and helping me see what was truly possible.

And to my wife, Cathy.
Your belief in me, your relentless push for my best, and your willingness to read every single word of this manuscript mean more than I can ever say.

This book is for you.

For all of us who have ever faced the invisible barrier and decided not to back down.

Table of Contents

Preface
Why This Edition Exists

When I first released *Doing What You Know*, my goal was simple: help people finally close the gap between what they *know to do* and what they actually *do*. I believed that if even one person broke through their invisible barrier because of this message, it would be worth it.

That belief hasn't changed, but my vision has.

What began as a personal mission is becoming a movement. I've watched readers overcome lifelong habits, reclaim their God-given dreams, and step boldly into the life they've talked about for years, all because they learned how to flip the switch on the inside.

That's when it hit me:
What if this book isn't just meant to help *someone*? What if it's meant to help *hundreds of thousands*?

That's what this Movement Edition is all about. It's more than a reprint. It's a *call* to anyone who is tired of starting over, who knows deep down they were created for *more*, not *more of the same*, and who believes it's time to finally break free from the invisible resistance that has kept them stuck just shy of success.

As you step into these pages, I want you to do more than read. I want you to **take ownership of the movement**. If this message shifts something in you, if you begin breaking through your own invisible barrier, if you feel God stirring you as you move through these chapters, *don't keep it to yourself.* Share it Gift it. Teach it. **Be one of the people who helps put this message into 100,000 hands by December 31, 2025.**

I'm grateful you're here. Now turn the page. Your breakthrough is waiting.

– *Ray Thigpen*

Introduction

Why You Know What to Do... and Still Don't Do It

I remember standing in my office, staring at the whiteboard. The plan was right there in front of me, clear, strategic, even exciting. I had the tools. I had the training. I knew exactly what to do. But instead of taking action, I froze. Again.

That wasn't the first time. And if you're anything like me or the thousands of people I've mentored, coached, or built businesses with, it wasn't the last time either. You've been there too. That frustrating gap between what you know and what you do. Where your intentions are strong, but your follow-through is weak. Where you've got big dreams and real potential, but feel like something invisible keeps blocking your momentum.

This book is about that barrier.

Not the lack of strategy. Not a shortage of information. Not even fear in the traditional sense. It's about the deeper disconnect. The invisible inner resistance that keeps you playing small, starting over, or spinning your wheels despite knowing better.

I wrote this book because I've lived that struggle. I've built teams, launched companies, experienced breakthroughs, and hit brick walls. I've seen firsthand how powerful knowledge can be and how powerless it feels when we don't act on it.

More than anything, I've seen how lasting change doesn't start with doing more. It starts with becoming more.

That's the heart of this book.

You're going to walk through 15 chapters that will help you move from intention to implementation, from hesitation to action, from surface-level motivation to deep, identity-driven transformation.

Each chapter is built on three pillars:

1. Mindset and identity

Because you won't rise above how you see yourself.

2. Faith and discipline

Because willpower fades, but God's grace doesn't.

3. Practical action

Because breakthrough isn't about hype. It's about habits.

This book isn't filled with hype, fluff, or shallow clichés. It's real. It's grounded in years of business experience, hard-won spiritual insight, personal failures, big wins, and the wisdom of mentors who've walked the walk.

You'll find teachings inspired by voices like Jim Rohn, Bob Proctor, Graham Cooke, and Napoleon Hill. These leaders shaped how I think and how I lead. You'll also see the hand of God throughout every chapter, because for me, faith isn't an afterthought. It's the foundation.

Here's what you can expect:

- Stories that pull back the curtain on what really holds people back (including me)
- Biblical truths and mindset breakthroughs that expose invisible limits
- Action steps, journaling prompts, and exercises to help you live what you're learning

- Encouragement when you hit the dip, because you will, and it's not the end
- A framework for aligning your identity, vision, and daily choices so you can finish strong

This isn't just a book to read. It's a process to engage. A map to help you stop starting over. A guide to finally living like the person you know deep down you were created to be.

Whether you're an entrepreneur, a leader, a parent, a creative, or someone just trying to show up fully for your life, you're not here by accident. Something brought you to this moment.

It's time to break through the invisible barrier.

It's time to stop knowing and start doing.

Let's walk this out together.

Ray Thigpen

Chapter 1 - The Invisible Barrier: Understanding Why We Get Stuck

I. Introduction

I remember standing in my office, staring at my whiteboard, marker in hand. The steps were all laid out. I had written them down with clarity, even enthusiasm. I knew exactly what I needed to do. It wasn't rocket science; it was the same formula I'd heard for years. Reach out, follow up, share the product, and offer the opportunity. I had the scripts. I had the training. I had the tools. And yet... I froze. Again.

That wasn't the first time it happened. And if you're anything like me, or like the thousands of people I've met over the years, you've had that same frustrating experience: the moment where knowledge and action don't connect. You know better, but you don't do better. You plan, you prepare, but you don't pull the trigger. Then comes the internal beating, the doubt, the guilt, and even shame. You tell yourself you're lazy, uncommitted, or not cut out for success. But that's not the truth. Not even close.

What you're experiencing is something I now refer to as the invisible barrier. It's not a lack of desire, discipline, or direction. It's not about laziness or ignorance. The invisible barrier is a deeper, internal resistance that sits just beneath your conscious awareness. It quietly sabotages your progress while convincing you that you're the one at fault. It's sneaky, persistent, and, if left unchecked, can derail even the most capable and well-intentioned person.

This book discusses how to identify obstacles, address them systematically, and establish a new approach based on honesty, adaptability, and effective mindset strategies. The following chapters

1

discuss why people may hesitate to act even when they know what to do, and outline ways to move from potential to action.

If you're feeling stuck, remember, you're not broken. You've just been struggling with something unseen. Let's bring it into the open and move forward together.

II. Unpacking the Invisible Barrier

The invisible barrier has everything to do with our subconscious beliefs, the deep-seated thoughts and emotional imprints we carry that shape our behavior without us even realizing it. Your subconscious is like a silent operating system, running in the background 24/7, filtering your perceptions, controlling your habits, and steering your decisions. It's not malicious, just programmed. The problem is that many of us are running outdated or faulty code.

You might consciously say, "I want to be successful," but if your subconscious is still holding onto beliefs like, "I don't deserve success," or "Success will cost me my relationships," you'll keep sabotaging yourself. You'll get close to a breakthrough and then pull back. You'll have a productive week, then disappear for a month. It's not a matter of discipline. It's a matter of identity and belief.

Take, for example, the business builder who books a full day of follow-ups. He's blocked out the time, has his list, and even has scripts ready. But as the hour approaches, his stomach tightens. He suddenly feels the urge to clean his desk, check emails, or scroll social media. That's not laziness, it's his invisible barrier whispering, "What if they reject you?" "What if you succeed and can't handle it?"

Or the woman who's on the brink of launching her online course. She's been preparing for months. But instead of publishing it, she tweaks the landing page for the 12th time or re-records videos that were already good enough. Underneath the surface is the belief, "I'm not good enough to lead," or "People will criticize me."

These stories aren't rare; they're everywhere. And they're not because people don't care or don't want it badly enough. It's because the subconscious mind always wins if left unchallenged. Bob Proctor once said, "You can't outperform your self-image." And it's true. If deep down you don't believe you're worthy of the result, your actions will reflect that belief, no matter how much conscious effort you apply.

The good news? That programming can be rewritten. But you can't change what you're unwilling to confront. So, this part of the journey is all about increasing awareness and making the invisible visible. The only way to deal with what's been running your life behind the scenes is to bring it out into the light and examine it with honesty and grace.

We'll explore how to identify these limiting beliefs, how they were formed, and how to begin shifting them. Because the moment you change your beliefs is the moment your results start to shift, too. Not gradually, but immediately. Because once you're no longer fighting yourself, the energy you used to spend in resistance becomes the fuel for forward motion.

III. The Limits of Knowledge

One of the biggest lies we've been sold, especially in the personal development and business world, is that knowledge is power. It sounds good, doesn't it? Neat, simple, and encouraging. But here's the truth: knowledge isn't power. Knowledge is only potential power. It's like a gym membership. You can have it, pay for it, carry the card in your wallet, and never experience a single result. It's what you do with the knowledge that changes your life.

This is a common challenge that many individuals encounter. For decades, I was the most informed, well-read, audiobook-devouring network marketer you could imagine. I could quote chapter and verse from Napoleon Hill's Think and Grow Rich, recite Earl Nightingale's The Strangest Secret, and quote some of Jim Rohn's seminars from beginning to end. I could break down the compensation plan of half a dozen companies in my sleep. And yet, I wasn't seeing the success I thought all that knowledge should have guaranteed me.

Why? Because information without application doesn't equal transformation. Read that again. Information without application doesn't equal transformation.

Napoleon Hill famously wrote, "Action is the real measure of intelligence." That statement hits hard when you think about how much we've all consumed without implementation. Hill dedicated more than twenty years to researching the era's most accomplished individuals, concluding that their success was attributed not to superior intelligence but to their proactive approach and commitment to action. They made decisions quickly. They acted on faith. They moved, even when they didn't have all the answers.

Earl Nightingale, in The Strangest Secret, pointed out that "Success is the progressive realization of a worthy ideal." Not the accumulation of knowledge, not the reading of books or watching YouTube videos. Success is about moving forward, progressing toward a clear goal. You could be sitting with a library full of wisdom, but if you're not translating it into daily action, it remains dormant. It's like planting seeds and never watering them.

Think about how easy it is to fall into the trap of overconsumption. We get a dopamine hit from learning something new. It feels productive. It feels exciting. However, we often proceed to the next video, podcast, or quote without taking the necessary, albeit uncomfortable, actions that truly bring about meaningful change in our lives. We've become conditioned to confuse learning with growing.

The real growth happens when you apply pressure to your comfort zone. When you stop reading about calling prospects and actually pick up the phone. When you stop watching others take action and finally record that video or publish that post. It's not glamorous. It's not always fun. But it works.

In this book, we're going to build a bridge between what you know and what you do. Because knowing isn't enough. We're going to talk about how to apply wisdom. And that starts with challenging this myth that the answer is just one more book, one more mastermind, one more module away. No, the answer is already in you. The next step is yours to take.

IV. Resistance: Identifying Your Inner Blocks

If the invisible barrier is the root, resistance is its visible fruit. Resistance can manifest in various forms, such as procrastination, avoidance, perfectionism, fear, doubt, anxiety, distraction, and busyness. It's what happens when the subconscious mind tries to protect us from perceived danger, even if that "danger" is in reality just discomfort or unfamiliar territory.

Fear frequently presents the most significant obstacle to progress. This may manifest as fear of failure, fear of success, fear of judgment, or fear of rejection. It masquerades as logic. It sounds like, "Maybe I should wait until I'm more prepared," or "What if people think I'm a fraud?" But underneath it all, it's your brain's way of trying to keep you safe by keeping you still.

Then there's the comfort zone, the silent killer of dreams. The comfort zone isn't a physical place; it's a psychological state where familiarity is prioritized over growth. It's the state of mind where your habits, beliefs, and routines feel safe, even if they aren't serving you. Stepping outside of that zone triggers alarms in the mind: "This is risky!" "You've never done this before!" "Play it safe!" And so, we do nothing. We tell ourselves we'll start on Monday, or next month, or once we feel more confident.

Unfortunately, we have it backward. Confidence doesn't come before action. It comes as a result of taking action.

Graham Cooke often says, "Truth isn't just information, it's an encounter." That encounter with truth is what shatters resistance. When you see who you really are, when you understand that your identity is rooted in God, not in fear or failure, you begin to challenge every lie resistance throws at you. You stop negotiating with limiting beliefs and start standing on truth.

Graham also talks about the importance of upgrading your internal narrative. Most resistance is fueled by outdated stories: "I've always been shy." "I'm not good with people." "I've never been a finisher." These stories become self-fulfilling prophecies. But what if your story could change? What if instead of saying, "I've always been this way," you declared, "I'm in the process of becoming someone new"?

Resistance thrives in silence. It wants you to be isolated and ashamed. But the moment you speak it, acknowledge it, and name it, it starts to lose its grip. This is why mentorship, community, and spiritual connection are so important. They provide mirrors, reminders, and reinforcements when resistance comes knocking.

You're not weak for feeling resistance. You're human. But you don't have to bow to it anymore. This section of the journey is about calling out those inner blocks with honesty and compassion. Because once you can identify resistance for what it is, a protective mechanism rooted in fear, you can begin to choose something greater: faith, purpose, and forward motion.

V. The Subconscious Mind: Your Greatest Ally or Adversary?

To understand why we get stuck, and stay stuck, it's critical to look at the subconscious mind. This hidden part of your mind is powerful. It stores your beliefs, your habits, your emotional triggers, and your sense of identity. In fact, neuroscientists estimate that 96% - 98% of our behavior is driven by the subconscious. That means you're operating on autopilot most of the time, running patterns you may not even be aware of.

Bob Proctor built much of his life's work around this idea. He taught that if you want to change your results, you must change your paradigm, your internal system of beliefs and mental habits. If you don't, the subconscious mind will always override your intentions. That's why affirmations, vision boards, and action plans don't work unless they're connected to a deeper shift in belief. You can't outwork your inner programming. Eventually, it catches up to you and pulls you back to where it's safe, familiar, and manageable.

Napoleon Hill echoed this when he wrote, "The subconscious mind will translate into its physical equivalent, by the most direct and practical means available, any order which is given to it in a spirit of belief." That's not just theory, that's how humans are wired. What we believe deeply enough and feed often enough, eventually shows up in our results. Not because of magic, but because of alignment. If you don't believe you're capable or worthy, you'll subconsciously find ways to prove yourself right. You'll hesitate. You'll shrink. You'll unconsciously sabotage opportunities.

On the other hand, when your subconscious becomes your ally, when it's trained to support your faith, your identity, and your calling, you move with ease. You start attracting ideas, people, and opportunities that align with your internal shift. You begin to embody your vision instead of just chasing it. That's the power of reprogramming.

But here's the catch: the subconscious doesn't change through force. It changes through repetition, emotion, and faith. That's why habits matter. That's why journaling matters. That's why visualization, prayer, and meditation matter. Each of these practices reinforces new beliefs. They plant new roots. They begin to tilt the scale so that instead of resistance pulling you back, your inner wiring starts to pull you forward.

Your subconscious mind is always working. The question is: for whom? For your growth or your fear? For your vision or your old story? You get to decide. And it starts by becoming aware of what beliefs you've been carrying, and intentionally choosing which ones get to stay and which ones have to go.

This chapter has laid the foundation for what's really going on behind the scenes when you feel stuck. Now that you can see the invisible barrier, you're already ahead of where you were. The rest of this book is about giving you the tools, strategies, and faith-fueled perspective to push through it and rise.

VI. Personal Revelation: The Power of Mentorship

If there's one thing that completely changed the trajectory of my journey, it was discovering the power of mentorship. And I don't mean casual advice or surface-level coaching. I mean real mentorship. An ongoing guidance from someone who sees what you can't, calls you higher, and walks with you through the messy middle.

For over 40 years, I was in and out of different network marketing companies. I followed every script, studied every recommended book, and listened to every audio program I could get my hands on. I did the work; or so I thought. But the truth is, despite all my effort, I kept hitting the same ceiling. I had the knowledge, I had the desire, but I couldn't break through.

It wasn't until a company event not long ago that the truth hit me like a freight train. I was sitting in a breakout session, surrounded by top leaders who were sharing their stories. They spoke with confidence, clarity, and conviction. And then I noticed a theme: every single one of them mentioned that they had invested in mentorship. This wasn't mentioned as part of a formal training, but I noticed it. Mentorship gave all of them guidance beyond books and audios. They didn't just consume content; they submitted to a process.

In that moment, I realized I had been trying to piece together my breakthrough alone, hoping information would do what only transformation can do. I'd been collecting puzzle pieces without ever inviting someone to help me put them together. That's when everything began to shift.

Mentorship doesn't just teach you new strategies. It helps you see your blind spots. It shows you what you're missing, not just in business, but in mindset, in character, in belief. The right mentor sees beyond what you say and reflects what's actually going on beneath the surface. For me, it clarified what I had been misunderstanding for years.

I thought I had a discipline problem. What I really had was an identity problem. I thought I lacked strategy. What I really lacked was belief. And that shift from trying harder to thinking differently was ignited through mentorship. My mentor didn't give me all the answers. They asked better questions. They challenged my assumptions. They refused to let me stay stuck in my old story.

Since then, I've invested in multiple mentors, some business-oriented, some faith-driven. And I'll tell you right now: if I could go back and change one thing about my entire 40-year journey, it would be this. I would have found a mentor sooner.

You were never meant to figure it all out alone. God uses people to help us grow. Mentorship isn't weakness, it's wisdom. And it may just be the missing key between knowing what to do and finally doing it.

VII. The Role of Faith in Breaking Barriers

At some point, every strategy hits a wall. Every system, every productivity hack, every mindset trick runs out of steam. That's when you realize: success isn't just mechanical. It's spiritual. The battles you fight in business, or life, are often battles of belief. And belief, at its core, is a spiritual matter.

Scripture says, "As a man thinks in his heart, so is he" (Proverbs 23:7). Notice it doesn't say as a man thinks in his mind. It says heart. That's a deeper level. That's where faith lives. It's where doubt lingers, too. And the truth is, many of the obstacles we face aren't out there, they're within us. Fear, unworthiness, shame, doubt, these are spiritual issues as much as they are emotional ones.

The Bible is filled with stories of people who faced invisible barriers, some internal, some external, and broke through them by faith. Moses didn't feel qualified. Gideon saw himself as the weakest of the weak. Peter denied Christ three times. And yet, every one of them stepped into a new story, not because they finally got all their ducks in a row, but because they trusted something (and Someone) greater than themselves.

Faith rewires the narrative. It tells you that your past doesn't define your potential and that the obstacle in front of you isn't bigger than the God within you. Jesus said, "If you have faith the size of a mustard seed, you can say to this mountain, 'Move from here to there,' and it will move"

(Matthew 17:20). That's not poetry. That's a principle. Faith shifts things, internally first, and then externally.

But faith isn't a feeling. It's a choice. It's choosing to act as if what God said is truer than what you see, what you fear, or what you've experienced. It's standing on promise when your reality screams otherwise. It's moving forward when you don't feel ready, because you trust the One who called you.

Here's the thing: spiritual maturity doesn't always look like more knowledge. Sometimes it looks like surrender, like trading control for obedience, or like releasing outcomes and focusing on alignment. When you do that, you stop striving and start flowing. You stop forcing and start following.

The invisible barrier may feel immovable, but it's not eternal. Faith is the tool God gives us to demolish strongholds (2 Corinthians 10:4). That includes every false belief, every limiting pattern, every fear that's been holding you hostage.

So, if you're facing resistance, don't just ask what you need to learn. Ask what you need to believe. Ask where you need to trust. Ask how you can invite God into the battle, not just as a helper, but as the leader.

Faith doesn't eliminate struggle. But it gives you the power to rise in the middle of it. And that's how invisible barriers break, when faith speaks louder than fear.

VIII. Practical Exercises and Reflection

Understanding the invisible barrier is a powerful first step, but transformation happens when you take that awareness and turn it into action. That's what this section is about. You've explored the roots of subconscious resistance, the role of fear, the importance of mentorship, and the power of faith. Now it's time to start identifying those inner blocks and gently dismantling them.

Let's start with a few tools you can use to surface subconscious beliefs:

1. The Belief Audit
Take out a sheet of paper or open a journal. Write down one specific goal you've struggled to achieve. Maybe it's building your business, sticking to a routine, or stepping into a new leadership role. Under that goal, write the first thoughts that come to mind when you imagine succeeding at it. Don't filter yourself. Be brutally honest.

Now ask yourself: What would it mean about me if I succeeded? What would it mean if I failed? What fears pop up? What emotions come with those thoughts? These questions will help you uncover the limiting beliefs that may be blocking you, beliefs like "Success will make me unrelatable," or "If I grow too much, I'll lose my relationships."

2. Thought Replacement Practice
Once you've identified a limiting belief, challenge it. Ask: Where did this belief come from? Is it 100% true? What belief would serve me better? Write out a truth-based replacement, like: "I can grow and still stay connected to the people I love," or "I am worthy of abundance because of who I am, not because of what I achieve."

Then repeat it daily. Speak it aloud in the mirror. Pray over it. Visualize it. Train your subconscious to accept it as the new default.

3. Identity Anchoring
Write out a description of the person you want to become. Not just what they do, but who they are. How do they think? What habits do they have? How do they show up in challenging moments? Then start acting like that version of yourself now, not later. Identity drives behavior, and behavior reinforces identity.

4. Guided Reflection Questions

Use these prompts for deeper clarity:

What area of my life do I feel most stuck in right now?

What story am I telling myself about why I'm stuck?

Whose voice am I listening to most, fear or faith?

What action am I avoiding, and what would happen if I just took it?

What would change if I fully trusted that I'm equipped for this season?

5. Accountability Exercise

Share one insight or breakthrough with a trusted friend, mentor, or journal. There's power in naming your truth out loud. It breaks the secrecy of self-sabotage and invites alignment and action.

The goal here isn't to fix everything overnight. The goal is to begin to create a pattern of reflection and action that disrupts old programming and opens space for breakthrough.

You've come a long way in this chapter. You've faced some hard truths, maybe even uncovered wounds or fears you didn't realize were there. Honor yourself for that. The invisible barrier isn't invisible anymore. And that means it doesn't have power over you as it once did.

The next chapters will continue to give you tools and truths to build on this momentum. But don't rush past this work. Sit with it, reflect, and most importantly, act.

IX. Summary and Next Steps

You've just completed a chapter that digs into the real reason so many of us get stuck, despite having the knowledge, the desire, and the opportunity. The invisible barrier is real. It may be subtle, yet it exerts considerable influence. However, by identifying, analyzing, and addressing it, meaningful progress can begin.

We've explored how subconscious beliefs shape your behavior, often without your awareness. We've looked at how resistance shows up through fear, perfectionism, procrastination, and overthinking. You've learned that information alone doesn't create change, and that action must be fueled by identity and belief. You've seen how your subconscious mind can either support or sabotage your growth depending on the story it's running. And we took a deep dive into the power of mentorship, the necessity of faith, and the importance of doing inner work, not just learning more strategies.

Let me be very clear: just reading this chapter won't change your life. But taking action on what you've just read can. The greatest breakthroughs don't come from knowing more. They come from aligning your actions with your values, your beliefs with truth, and your efforts with your identity in Christ.

So, where do you go from here?

First, don't skip the work. Go back and engage with the exercises at the end of the previous section. Journal through the guided reflections. Identify the limiting beliefs that have been running the show behind the scenes. And start rewriting those scripts. Speak truth to yourself. Declare new possibilities. Choose to believe what God says about you, not just what life has taught you.

Second, commit to being honest. Real transformation doesn't happen when you pretend you've got it all together. It happens when you show up raw and real, willing to admit you're stuck, but not willing to stay that way.

Third, get support. Whether that's mentorship, community, or accountability, don't try to fight the invisible barrier alone. We weren't designed to grow in isolation. Mentors, leaders, and peers play an important role in providing guidance, support, and valuable perspective throughout our personal and professional development.

And finally, prepare your heart for what's next. The chapters ahead are going to challenge you even deeper. You'll learn how to break old patterns, make real decisions, develop discipline, and take inspired action. You'll begin building the kind of life and business that flows from faith, purpose, and inner freedom

Remember: the invisible barrier loses power the moment you choose to confront it. You've done that here. That's huge. That's the beginning of everything.

Let's keep moving forward because the breakthrough you've been praying for isn't somewhere out there. It's on the other side of what you've just begun

Chapter 2: Breaking the Cycle: Letting Go of Old Patterns

I. Introduction

I used to think I was just someone who struggled with consistency. Year after year, I'd set goals, get inspired, build some momentum, and then, without fail, fall right back into the same cycles. I'd skip the uncomfortable calls, delay launching that new project, start strong, then slowly drift back to default mode. I'd beat myself up for it, of course. I told myself I just needed more discipline or motivation. But deep down, I started wondering: why do I keep ending up in the same place?

It wasn't until I began doing some deeper inner work, real mindset and spiritual work, that I realized I wasn't dealing with a lack of discipline at all. I was trapped in old patterns. And those patterns weren't random. They were ingrained, automatic, and deeply familiar. They had formed years ago through repetition, trauma, fear, and even well-meaning teachings. They weren't just behaviors; they were internal scripts written into my subconscious.

Old patterns are those predictable, automatic responses we default to when life gets stressful, when we're challenged, or when we step outside our comfort zone. They're the thoughts that say, "Play it safe," the reactions that choose avoidance over engagement, and the habits that quietly sabotage progress. They're how the past shows up in the present, and how it hijacks your future if you're not careful.

Some patterns are rooted in childhood, things we saw, heard, or experienced that shaped how we learned to survive or seek approval. Others developed through repeated failures, disappointments, or fear of judgment. Over time, they form neural pathways that become our go-to responses, even when we consciously want something different. That's why it can feel like you're fighting yourself. You are. Part of you wants growth, while another part is trying to keep you "safe."

These patterns don't just affect personal growth; they shape how we build relationships, run our businesses, handle money, respond to opportunities, and deal with conflict. They dictate how much success we allow ourselves to experience before we pull back. They create ceilings we can't seem to break.

Old patterns aren't permanent. They can be identified, challenged, and replaced. It takes awareness, intentionality, and often some discomfort, but it's possible. And that's what this chapter is about. It's about recognizing the cycles that keep you stuck, understanding where they came from, and learning how to let them go so you can build new ones that serve who you're becoming.

This chapter is going to be raw and real. Because letting go of old patterns isn't just about mindset hacks, it's about deep internal shifts. It's about grieving what no longer fits and stepping into something better. You may even feel some resistance creep in as you read. That's okay. That's normal. It just means we're getting close to something that matters.

So, let's dive in. Let's expose the patterns that have had too much control for too long and begin writing a new script.

II. Recognizing Old Patterns

How do these old patterns actually form? And more importantly, how can we start to spot them before they sabotage us again?

Patterns are essentially habits of thought, emotion, and behavior. They're grooves in the brain, formed over time through repetition and reinforced by our environment and experiences. Some come from trauma. Some from early successes or failures. Some from beliefs passed down through culture, religion, or family. Eventually, they become automatic. You don't even think about them; they just happen.

Say, for example, you were ridiculed in school for speaking up in class. That moment might've cemented a belief in your subconscious: "Speaking up is dangerous." Fast forward twenty years, and every time you need to present on a team call or record a video, you hesitate. You may not consciously remember the school experience, but the pattern it created still governs your behavior.

Or maybe, like me, you spent years in network marketing feeling excited one minute and paralyzed the next. You'd start strong every Monday, make a few calls, maybe even enroll someone, but by Wednesday, you were ghosting prospects and avoiding follow-ups. Not because you didn't want success, but because an old script had taken over. "I always fall short." "I'm not consistent." "People like me don't win big."

Patterns show up in business when you constantly pivot from one strategy to another, never giving anything time to work. They show up in finances when you make more money, but still end up broke. They show up in relationships when you keep dating the same kind of person or attracting drama. The situations look different, but the core behavior is the same.

Here's a key point: old patterns are familiar, but not necessarily true. They feel safe because they're known, even the dysfunctional ones. But just because something is familiar doesn't mean it's serving you.

Recognizing these patterns starts with observation. Begin paying attention to your default reactions. When you feel triggered, ask: What emotion am I feeling? What story am I telling myself right now? What action do I usually take in this situation? These questions reveal the loop you're running and give you the opportunity to step out of it.

The enemy of growth is autopilot. When you live unconsciously, you live out old patterns by default. But when you start noticing, when you name the behavior, the thought, the emotion, you interrupt the cycle. And that's the beginning of change.

In the next section, we'll explore how to challenge these old patterns and begin rewriting them, so you're no longer a product of your past but a participant in your purpose.

III. Impact of Old Patterns

When we don't confront and break our old patterns, the cost isn't just a missed opportunity; it's a life lived far beneath our potential. These ingrained loops don't just keep us stuck; they shape who we believe we are and what we believe is possible. Over time, they can create a quiet resignation, a sense that "this is just how I am" or "maybe this dream just wasn't meant for me."

That belief is a lie.

One of the most powerful things Jim Rohn ever said was, "Your life does not get better by chance, it gets better by change." He wasn't talking about big, dramatic decisions. He was referring to the small, consistent, intentional shifts that stack up over time, those daily disciplines, those changed habits, those moments where you choose growth instead of comfort.

When you stay in old patterns, your habits don't support your goals. Your thoughts sabotage your momentum. Your emotional reactions drain your energy. Think of how many people set goals at the beginning of the year with fire in their belly, only to burn out by February. Why? Because the pattern of quitting early, the pattern of losing belief, the pattern of not following through, kicks back in. And without something stronger to replace it, the cycle repeats.

Doing What You Know

Old patterns create what Jim Rohn called a "mild disaster." You don't crash all at once. You slowly drift. You settle, you tolerate, and one day, you wake up realizing that years have passed, but not much has changed. The job is the same. The income is the same. The emotional battles are the same. The dreams are quieter.

It's not because you're lazy or undisciplined. It's because the pattern was never addressed at the root.

In my own life, I've seen the cost of letting old patterns run the show. I'd get just enough traction in my business to feel hopeful, then retreat I'd join new opportunities with excitement, then let hesitation and fear talk me out of showing up fully. I convinced myself I was just "processing" or "waiting for the right time," but really, I was stuck in an avoidance loop.

And every time I stayed stuck, I reinforced the belief that I wasn't capable of more.

Breaking this cycle starts with seeing the pattern and then understanding the cost of staying in it. Not just the financial cost. The emotional and spiritual toll is even heavier. Every time you choose fear over faith, comfort over calling, familiarity over freedom, you chip away at your confidence, your energy, and your God-given purpose.

As soon as you name the pattern, you reclaim your power. Awareness doesn't fix everything, but it gives you a door. And when you pair that awareness with action, everything begins to change.

In the next section, we'll explore how to challenge and rewire those patterns at the source, so you're not just managing your behaviors, you're transforming your identity.

IV. The Comfort Zone Trap

One of the main reasons people stay stuck in old patterns is because they've unknowingly built their lives around comfort. Not joy, not fulfillment, just comfort. The familiar, even when it's limiting or painful, feels safer than the unknown. That's the grip of the comfort zone.

Bob Proctor used to say that the comfort zone is where dreams go to die, not because people don't want more, but because they never learned how to get uncomfortable on purpose. Most people associate comfort with success. If it feels easy, if it feels familiar, then it must be right. But the truth is, growth always demands a departure from the known. Real transformation happens at the edges of discomfort.

The comfort zone isn't just about sitting on the couch or putting things off. It's more subtle than that. It's the tendency to say, "I already know this," when faced with new learning. It's the belief that you've tried everything when you've only scratched the surface. It's replaying old conversations in your head rather than making the call that might change everything. It's choosing routine over risk. And it's deadly to your growth.

Comfort often disguises itself as logic. You'll say things like, "It's not the right time," or "Maybe after things settle down," or "I just need to get more organized first." And it sounds reasonable. But underneath it all is fear. Fear of failure. Fear of rejection. Fear of not being enough.

I remember a time in my network marketing journey when I had every tool, every script, every product. But I was still stalling. I realized I wasn't afraid of the process; I was afraid of becoming the version of me who actually succeeded. Because that person had to let go of being liked, being careful, and being comfortable. That person had to risk being misunderstood, outgrowing friends, and facing new expectations. And honestly, part of me wasn't ready for that.

The comfort zone doesn't just hold you in place; it shrinks your vision. You start setting smaller goals to match what feels manageable. You stop dreaming altogether and instead, focus on getting through the day. You confuse contentment with complacency. But deep down, you know. You know you're capable of more.

To break free from the comfort zone, you have to decide that discomfort is no longer your enemy. In fact, it's the doorway to everything you want. Start seeking it out in small ways. Speak up when you'd rather stay silent. Reach out when you feel like being alone. Launch the project even if it's not perfect. Every time you do, you expand your capacity.

As Bob Proctor taught, your subconscious mind doesn't care whether the pattern is helpful or harmful; it just wants to keep you alive and safe. It's your job to reprogram it by choosing differently, consistently, and deliberately. Your comfort zone isn't your home. It's your prison. And the key to breaking out has always been in your hands.

In the next section, we'll dive into practical strategies for challenging and rewriting those limiting patterns, so you can step fully into the life you were created to live.

V. Identifying Your Specific Patterns

You can't change what you don't understand. That's why one of the most important steps in breaking free from old cycles is getting crystal clear on what those cycles actually are. I'm not talking about vague generalizations like "I procrastinate" or "I get distracted." I'm talking about the specific day-to-day behaviors and thought loops that keep pulling you off course.

Jim Rohn often said, "Success is nothing more than a few simple disciplines practiced every day." But the flip side is true too: failure is just a few errors in judgment repeated over time. And the problem is, most of those errors aren't conscious. They're habits, automatic responses, patterns we've rehearsed for years without realizing it.

So, how do you spot them?

Start by paying attention to your friction points. Where do you feel stuck or frustrated the most? For me, it used to happen every time I committed to a 90-day blitz in my network marketing business. I'd map out my calls, set my goals, even get accountability partners. But by week two, I was behind. Then came the excuses: "I've been too busy," "My leads weren't great," "I'll catch up next week."

That was my pattern. Start strong, stall out, rationalize, retreat.

It wasn't about the business model or the tools. It was about me falling into a loop I hadn't taken the time to understand. Once I slowed down and looked at it, I saw what was really going on: the moment things got hard or uncertain, I defaulted to avoidance. And under that avoidance was fear, fear of rejection, fear of wasting time, and fear of not being good enough.

Bob Proctor taught that our behavior is driven by paradigms, deep, often hidden mental programs that shape how we see ourselves and what we believe we're capable of. If you've always believed you're not consistent, your subconscious will find ways to prove that belief true. It'll whisper suggestions that lead to procrastination. It'll downplay your wins and exaggerate your setbacks. And unless you interrupt that voice, it runs the show.

One of the simplest ways to start identifying your patterns is to journal after moments of resistance. Ask yourself: What did I feel? What story did I tell myself? What did I do instead of what I planned to do? This isn't about self-shaming, it's about truth. And truth is what sets you free.

Another clue is repetition. If you notice the same outcomes showing up again and again in your finances, your relationships, or your business, there's likely a pattern underneath. Same burnout. Same arguments. Same income level, no matter how hard you work. These aren't random. They're the results of repeated, often unconscious choices.

Here's the good news: once a pattern is visible, it becomes vulnerable. You can't change what you haven't named. But once you name it, you can start rewriting it. You can replace the avoidance loop with action. You can replace self-doubt with truth. You can replace hesitation with bold moves.

We're not talking about overnight change. We're talking about awareness followed by alignment. See the pattern and own it. And then, step by step, do something different.

In the next section, we'll explore how faith and courage work together to help you challenge what's familiar, face the unknown, and finally move forward with confidence.

VI. Faith and Courage: Key Ingredients for Change

Faith and courage are often talked about as lofty ideals, reserved for the spiritually elite or the outrageously bold. But in my experience, they're not just lofty, they're necessary. Especially when you're trying to change the story you've been living for years. Letting go of old patterns isn't just a mindset shift; it's a spiritual step. It's you declaring, with intention, "I'm no longer available for whom I used to be."

But let's be honest. That decision feels like jumping off a cliff. The comfort zone may be stifling, but at least it's predictable. Faith asks you to walk even when you can't see the whole staircase. Courage demands you move before you feel ready. Most people wait for fear to go away before taking action, but real courage is doing it scared.

There was a time I believed that once I knew enough, I'd act, that once I felt confident, I'd move. But years passed, and the knowing never bridged the gap to doing. It wasn't until I began leaning into faith, believing in what I couldn't yet see, and pairing it with daily, often uncomfortable courage, that things started shifting, not just in my results, but in my identity.

The Bible says, "Faith is the substance of things hoped for, the evidence of things not seen." That's not just poetic. It's practical. When you've spent decades repeating the same patterns, you won't see the results right away. You have to believe before the breakthrough. You have to act as if what you want is already yours, even when your circumstances still look the same.

And that's where courage walks in. Courage is the willingness to go first, before you have proof. It's picking up the phone to follow up with a lead, even though the last five didn't answer. It's showing up on social media to share your message, even when you feel invisible. It's holding the vision of the future you're building, even when no one else sees it yet.

Faith gives you the blueprint. Courage lays the bricks.

When you combine the two, the walls of your old patterns begin to crack. You start saying "yes" to things you used to avoid. You stop waiting for permission or perfection. You become a different version of yourself, one who is led by calling instead of comfort, purpose instead of patterns.

If you've been stuck in old loops, it's not because you lack intelligence or desire. It's because you've been fighting internal battles with external tools. Faith and courage are the inner weapons. And the good news? You already have them. You just have to use them.

In the next section, we'll look at how to practically apply these inner shifts by building new patterns of action that align with your purpose, your potential, and the life you're truly meant to live.

VII. Practical Steps to Interrupt Patterns

Recognizing patterns is half the battle. The other half is breaking them daily, intentionally, and repeatedly. This is where most people get stuck. They think awareness alone creates change. But awareness without action is just observation. It's action that rewires the brain, reshapes behavior, and redirects momentum.

The first step is to introduce friction into the automatic loop. If you always check your phone the moment you wake up, try moving it to another room. If you scroll when anxious, delete the app for a day and replace that urge with a walk or a journal prompt. The goal isn't to become perfect, it's to interrupt the routine long enough to make a better choice.

One of the best tools I use is the "Pattern Interrupt Journal." It's simple. Every time you notice yourself falling into an old pattern, you stop and write it down. What triggered it? How did it make you feel? What did you do instead? Over time, this journal becomes your playbook. It reveals triggers, thought loops, and common excuses. And when you can see them, you can break them.

Another strategy: create pre-loaded decisions. If you know that 3 p.m. is when your energy crashes and you usually grab sugar or scroll Instagram, have a plan ready. Walk around the block. Drink water. Call a mentor. You don't wait to decide in the moment. You decide before the moment arrives.

A third technique is what I call "Micro Wins." These are small, doable actions that reinforce a new pattern. Don't try to run five miles if you haven't walked in a year. Walk for five minutes. Don't try to prospect 100 people—reach out to three. Build confidence through consistency. Your brain rewards completion. Every micro win becomes a vote for the person you're becoming.

Leverage visual cues, too. Sticky notes with truth statements on your mirror. A whiteboard in your office with your new identity written on it. Alarms on your phone that remind you to stay present. These aren't gimmicks, they're pattern interrupters. They keep you awake to your goal in a world designed to keep you asleep.

And finally, speak life. Out loud. Declare your new identity. "I am consistent." "I take bold action." "I follow through." Say it even when it doesn't feel true, especially then. Because every declaration is a seed. And every seed, given time and nourishment, grows.

Pattern interruption is about creating space. Space between trigger and response. Space between old behavior and new choice. And in that space is your power.

VIII. Embracing New, Empowering Patterns

It's one thing to spot an old pattern. It's another to choose a new one, and walk it out every day, especially when the old voices try to pull you back. This is where intention becomes everything. If you don't decide ahead of time who you want to be and how you want to respond, you'll default to who you've always been.

Embracing new, empowering patterns starts with a vision. Who do you want to become? Not just what do you want to accomplish, but what kind of person are you becoming in the process? When you see yourself as an individual who honors commitments, demonstrates reliability, exhibits leadership, and embraces bold compassion, your behavior increasingly aligns with that identity.

That's why I encourage people to write identity-based affirmations. Not "I want to be disciplined," but "I am someone who follows through." Not "I hope I can lead," but "I am a leader who empowers others." These aren't wishful thoughts. They're declarations. They anchor your behavior to a new identity.

Another strategy is creating a "pattern interrupt" ritual. When you feel yourself slipping into the old response, procrastinating, complaining, or retreating, have a go-to move that flips the script. It might be stepping outside for 90 seconds of fresh air and deep breathing. It might be putting on music and moving your body. It might be reading one paragraph from a book that reconnects you to your higher self. The point isn't what you do, it's that you interrupt the old cycle before it gains momentum.

Earl Nightingale said, "You become what you think about." That applies to patterns, too. If you dwell on failure, you'll recreate it. If you think about growth, resilience, and faith, your behavior will follow. So feed your mind on purpose. Surround yourself with books, mentors, messages, and people who reflect the life you're building, not the one you're leaving behind.

Ultimately, empowering patterns aren't just about productivity. They're about identity. You're no longer someone trying to succeed; you're someone who does what successful people do, because it's who you are. And that shift changes everything.

IX. Moving Forward with Clarity and Confidence

Breaking old patterns isn't a one-time event. It's a way of life. If there's one truth that separates the achievers from the dreamers, it's this: those who succeed are not the ones who get it right all the time, they're the ones who keep showing up, even when it's hard. Especially when it's hard.

You've taken a big step by exploring your patterns, where they came from, how they've impacted you, and how to interrupt them. But awareness alone doesn't change your life. Action does. And now you get to walk it out.

Start small. Pick one pattern you've identified and commit to disrupting it. Maybe it's procrastination, or negative self-talk, or shutting down when challenged. Don't try to fix everything at once. Choose one, track it daily, and celebrate the micro wins. When you fall back into it, don't beat yourself up. Interrupt it, reset, and move forward. Progress isn't linear. It's messy, but it's worth it.

Confidence isn't something you wait for. It's something you build. Every time you take a new action, you cast a vote for your future self. And every vote counts. You don't need to feel confident to act; you gain confidence because you acted. Over time, those small decisions to show up, speak up, or follow through will build a rock-solid belief in who you're becoming.

But don't walk this road alone. Reach out to a mentor, a friend, or a support group. Share your intention. Get accountability. When you surround yourself with people who are also committed to growth, your odds of lasting change skyrocket. Iron sharpens iron.

And don't forget your faith. As you take these steps, trust that God is walking with you. When you feel weak, ask for strength. When you feel unsure, ask for wisdom. You were never meant to break the cycle alone. His grace is more than enough for every place where your willpower falls short.

In the chapters ahead, we'll build on this foundation. You'll learn how to make firm, lasting decisions. You'll explore how faith, focus, and discipline align to drive real results. But for now, your job is simple: keep moving. Keep showing up. Keep choosing new patterns that reflect who you really are, not who you used to be.

The cycle is breaking. The fog is lifting. And your next steps, though imperfect, are already building a new future. Stay with it. You're not just changing habits. You're rewriting your story.

Chapter 3: The Power of Decision: Committing to Change

I. Introduction

It's funny how the most powerful moments in life often sneak up on you. For me, it happened on a random Tuesday. There was nothing remarkable about the day, no significant occurrences or dramatic revelations. Instead, it was a calm acknowledgment that I had grown weary of repeating the same patterns. I had been doing the dance of "almost" for far too long; almost consistent, almost successful, almost ready. That day, I sat in my car outside a prospect's house, lead sheet in hand, and stared at the steering wheel. I knew what to do. I'd rehearsed the script, visualized the close, and prayed for courage. But my hand wouldn't reach for the door handle.

And then something in me snapped, or maybe, something finally clicked. I heard my own voice inside say, "Ray, decide. Don't try. Don't see how it goes. Decide."

That was the moment everything began to shift.

This chapter is about that moment. The one where a blurry intention turns into a crystal-clear decision. Because until you decide, nothing really happens. You might dabble. You might hustle. You might even get results. But without a firm, committed decision, you're always negotiating with your goals. You're leaving the back door open just in case it gets hard. And it will get hard.

Napoleon Hill, in Think and Grow Rich, said that indecision is the seed of fear. The more you hesitate, the more fear grows. But when you make a decision, when you commit with finality, you slam the door on fear.

You tell your subconscious mind, "This is who I am now." And your subconscious starts working in harmony with that identity.

Jim Rohn used to say, "Indecision is the thief of opportunity." Not because opportunities disappear, but because we do. We shrink, delay, and second-guess. But when you make a real decision, your energy shifts. You walk differently, speak differently, and show up differently. Decision creates alignment.

The problem is that most people never really decide. They wish, hope, and maybe even plan. But they keep one foot on the brake. They try to hedge their bets. They want guarantees before they commit. And in doing so, they stay stuck in limbo, caught between desire and doubt.

In this chapter, we're going to unpack what a true decision looks like. We'll explore why most people avoid making them, how to recognize when you're still playing it safe, and how to make decisions that lock you into progress, not just for a day, but for a lifetime.

This isn't about hype or motivation. It's about ownership. It's about saying, "This is the life I've chosen, and I'm going to live it fully." Because the truth is, nothing changes until you change. And it all starts with a decision.

Let's dive in.

II. Understanding the Nature of Decision

There's a massive difference between making a choice and making a decision. Choices are easy. They're often casual, low-risk, and made from a place of convenience. "What do I want for dinner?" "Should I make a few calls today or wait until tomorrow?" Choices can be reversed, postponed, or made without consequence.

But a decision, that's something entirely different.

A true decision is final. It's backed by commitment. It doesn't leave room for negotiation or retreat. The word "decision" comes from the Latin root decidere, which means "to cut off." A real decision means you get rid of all other options. Once you choose, you can't go back or change your mind.

Bob Proctor explained that decision-making is not about gathering more information or waiting for the perfect moment. It's about who you decide to be. Most people believe they need more time, more knowledge, or more confidence before they make a move. But Bob would argue that the act of deciding is what causes growth, not the other way around. Decide now and grow into it as you move forward.

Napoleon Hill hammered this idea in Think and Grow Rich. He studied hundreds of the most successful men of his time, and he found one universal trait among them all: decisiveness. Once these men made a decision, they rarely backed out. They weren't reckless, but they didn't waver. They knew the power of a committed mind. Hill warned that procrastination, disguised as indecision, kills dreams faster than failure ever could.

You've probably made decisions in the past that weren't real decisions. Maybe you said you were "going to try harder" or "be more consistent." But the results told a different story. Why? Because there was still a backdoor. You were still entertaining the idea of quitting, of waiting, of easing off when it got uncomfortable.

This is where many people get stuck. They confuse preference with decision. Wanting something is not the same as deciding to have it. A preference says, "It would be nice if…" A decision says, "This is happening, no matter what."

When you step into decision with clarity and firmness, your entire psychology aligns. Your mind stops looking for exit strategies and starts finding solutions. Your body shows up with new energy. Your actions start reflecting your intention, and that's when momentum begins.

In this section, I challenge you to look at the decisions you've been avoiding. What areas of your life or business have been stuck in limbo? What have you been putting off until "the time is right"? Let today be the day you stop choosing and start deciding. Cut off the escape routes. Step fully into your future.

Because once you decide, truly decide, life starts making room for the version of you that's ready to show up.

III. Why Decisions Determine Destiny

Every major turning point in your life can be traced back to a decision. Not a wish, not a vague intention, but a decision. One moment where you drew a line in the sand and said, "No more of the old, I'm stepping into the new." These are the decisions that shape our destiny, not because of the decision alone, but because of the consistency, commitment, and identity that follow.

Jim Rohn used to say, "It's not what happens that determines the quality of your life. It's what you do about what happens." Life throws all kinds of circumstances our way. The key difference between the person who thrives and the one who stays stuck is how they decide to respond. And that response begins with a committed decision.

The decisions you make are like a compass. They set the direction of your life. Even if you're a few degrees off from your intended destination, the act of making a decision gets you moving. You can't steer a parked car. And you can't change your life without first deciding to do so. Movement creates clarity. Action reveals the path. But the engine that starts it all is decision.

Most people underestimate the ripple effect of a single decision. One firm commitment can reshape your health, your relationships, your finances, and your faith. It doesn't happen overnight, but it begins the moment you commit. And once you do, the world begins to reorganize itself around that commitment. Resources show up. People appear. Opportunities surface. Why? Because your new identity is sending a different signal, and life responds to who you're being, not just what you're saying.

This is why indecision is so dangerous. It robs you of clarity. It drains your energy. It keeps you in a cycle of start and stop. You tell yourself you're making progress, but you're really just circling. Jim Rohn called this "mental dawdling." It's when you spend more time thinking about doing something than actually doing it. And over time, this mental loop becomes a lifestyle.

But the opposite is also true. The moment you decide, your energy changes. You're no longer waiting for the right moment; you're creating it. You start taking ownership of your life instead of blaming circumstances. That's when doors open. That's when confidence builds. That's when your life begins to shift in visible, tangible ways.

So, what does this mean for you right now? It means that no matter how long you've been stuck, no matter how many times you've failed, you can choose differently today. You can draw that line in the sand. You can make a decision that says, "This is who I am now. This is what I do. This is where I'm going."

Your destiny isn't written in your circumstances. It's written in your decisions. Choose boldly.

IV. Common Obstacles to Making Decisions

If making powerful decisions were easy, everyone would do it. But the truth is, most people hesitate because they're up against some very real inner obstacles. These barriers can be subtle or loud, but they all lead to the same result: paralysis.

One of the biggest culprits is fear. Fear of failure, fear of judgment, fear of making the wrong choice. Fear convinces us that staying still is safer than moving forward. It whispers that if we wait a little longer, things might get clearer. But clarity doesn't come from waiting. It comes from moving. You learn in motion, not in stillness.

Then there's indecision, which often masquerades as wisdom. We tell ourselves we're being cautious, thoughtful, even responsible. But behind that mask is often just doubt. Indecision feels like a gray area, but it's really just a form of resistance. It's your subconscious trying to protect you from the discomfort of growth.

Procrastination is another subtle enemy. We delay making decisions not because we don't care, but because making a decision means we're on the hook. There's no one else to blame. We stall by telling ourselves we need more time, more research, or more motivation. In reality, we're just avoiding responsibility.

Uncertainty also plays a major role. We want guarantees. We want to know the outcome before we act. But life doesn't work that way. Jim Rohn put it this way: "You cannot change your destination overnight, but you can change your direction overnight." Decisions shift your direction, even when you can't see the entire path.

These obstacles show up in everyday life and business. Think about how many times you've avoided following up with a prospect, launching a project, or investing in yourself because you weren't "ready." You were probably battling one or more of these inner blocks. I've been there more times than I can count.

So how do you overcome them? First, recognize them. Name the fear. Acknowledge the doubt. Call out the procrastination. Then, decide anyway. Courage isn't the absence of fear. It's the choice to move through it. It's deciding that your future matters more than your comfort.

Remember this: indecision costs you more than a wrong decision ever will. A wrong decision at least moves you forward. It gives you feedback. It helps you grow. But indecision? It keeps you stuck. And the longer you stay stuck, the harder it gets to move.

The good news is, once you understand these obstacles, you can face them head-on. You can interrupt the cycle. And in the next section, we'll talk about exactly how to do that: how to break the paralysis and start making decisions that pull you toward the life you're meant to live.

V. The Role of Clarity in Decision Making

Before you can commit to a powerful decision, you need to get clear on what you actually want. Sounds simple, right? But you'd be surprised how many people struggle here. They know what they don't want, such as a stressful job, a failing business, or toxic relationships, but ask them what they do want, and the answer gets vague.

Clarity isn't just about having a goal. It's about understanding the why behind it. What lights you up? What kind of life are you really trying to create? What values matter most to you? When you answer those questions, decision-making becomes easier because you're aligning your choices with your core values.

A powerful technique to gain clarity is the "Perfect Day" exercise. Close your eyes and imagine the ideal day in your ideal life, from the moment you wake up until the moment your head hits the pillow. Where are you?

Who are you with? What are you doing? How do you feel? The more detail you add, the more your subconscious starts to recognize that vision as possible and worth moving toward.

Another useful exercise is the "Five Whys." Start with a surface-level goal like "I want to earn more money." Then ask, "Why do I want that?" Maybe your answer is, "To feel more secure." Ask why again. "Because I've felt unstable most of my life." Keep going until you hit the emotional root. That's your real motivator, and that's what gives power to your decisions.

Sometimes clarity comes from contrast. Reflect on your past experiences: what drained you and what energized you? Which environments made you feel small, and which ones made you feel like you could fly? These clues are road signs pointing to your truest path.

Jim Rohn said, "If you don't design your own life plan, chances are you'll fall into someone else's plan. And guess what they have planned for you? Not much." That hits hard because it's true. If you're unclear, someone else will be glad to fill in the blanks for you.

Once you're clear, decision-making becomes less about figuring things out and more about aligning your actions with your vision. You don't need to debate every opportunity or second-guess every move. You simply ask, "Does this move me closer to the life I want?" If yes, go. If no, let it go.

Clarity fuels confidence. Confidence fuels action. And action fuels momentum. But it all starts with clarity.

So don't rush past this step. Take time to get honest with yourself. Journal. Meditate. Pray. Ask the hard questions. Your future depends on it.

VI. Faith-Based Decision Making

Faith is more than a spiritual comfort; it is a foundational element in the decision-making process. When logic wavers and emotions fluctuate, faith anchors us. It provides a lens through which we interpret risk, uncertainty, and challenge. This section isn't just about religious belief. It's about trusting something bigger than yourself as you step into the unknown. And for those of us grounded in biblical truth, the power of faith-driven decisions can't be overstated.

The Bible is filled with men and women who made life-altering decisions rooted in faith. Abraham left everything familiar simply because God told him to go. He didn't have GPS, a strategic plan, or even a clear destination, just a promise. And yet his faith became the foundation for a legacy that shaped nations. That's the power of a faith-filled decision.

Think of Moses. He didn't feel qualified. In fact, he tried to talk God out of choosing him. "Who am I to go to Pharaoh?" he asked. But when Moses finally decided to obey, miracles followed. The Red Sea parted. A nation was set free. That decision didn't come from confidence in himself; it came from trust in the One who called him.

Jesus Himself modeled the ultimate faith-based decision. In the Garden of Gethsemane, facing unthinkable pain, He said, "Not my will, but Yours be done." That wasn't resignation. That was divine alignment. It was a decision anchored in obedience and eternal purpose, even when everything in the natural screamed to run the other way.

Faith-based decision making requires surrender. It means releasing your need to control every outcome and trusting that God sees a bigger picture. Proverbs 3:5-6 says it clearly: "Trust in the Lord with all your heart and lean not on your own understanding; in all your ways acknowledge Him, and He will make your paths straight." That's not a suggestion, it's a roadmap.

When I look back over my life, the best decisions I ever made were the ones that didn't make sense on paper but were confirmed in prayer. Times when I felt an inner nudge, a spiritual prompting, that said, "Move." It rarely felt comfortable. It almost never felt easy. But it always led to growth, impact, and transformation.

Faith doesn't eliminate fear. But it does overpower it. When your decision is rooted in faith, fear no longer gets to drive the bus. It may still ride along, but it won't dictate the direction.

So if you're standing at a crossroads right now, unsure of which path to take, pause. Breathe. Ask God. And when you feel that peace, that still, small voice nudging you forward, decide. Don't wait for perfect clarity. Trust that the path will become clear as you walk it.

Faith isn't passive. It's active. It doesn't sit back and wait. It moves forward, even when the next step is hidden. Because in faith-driven decisions, you're not walking alone.

Let that truth settle in: You are led, you are guided, and you are equipped. Make your next decision with that confidence.

VII. Building Decisive Habits

Decisiveness is not just a character trait; it's a muscle, one that grows stronger with use. You don't wake up one day as a naturally decisive person. You build it, one choice at a time. And the best part? It's a skill that anyone can develop.

Start with the small things. Every day, you make hundreds of minor decisions: what to eat, what to wear, when to respond to that message. These seemingly insignificant choices are your training ground. Decide quickly. Train yourself to act without second-guessing. This isn't about being reckless, it's about learning to trust your judgment.

Earl Nightingale often emphasized the power of habit and how we become what we repeatedly do. He said, "Don't let the fear of the time it will take to accomplish something stand in the way of your doing it. The time will pass anyway." Developing the habit of decisive action may take effort, but it's time well spent

One way to strengthen this habit is to give yourself time limits. If you're faced with a non-life-altering decision, set a timer for 60 seconds. Make the best choice you can and move forward. This helps break the cycle of analysis paralysis. You'll begin to trust that most decisions don't require overthinking; they just require action.

Another technique is to pre-decide your values and priorities. When you know what matters most to you, decision-making becomes clearer. If health is a core value, you don't need to deliberate over whether to go to the gym or grab fast food. The decision was already made when you chose that value.

Consistency matters, too. Don't just make a strong decision once; build it into your routine. Decide daily to stay aligned with your goals. Review your commitments each morning. Ask, "What decisions do I need to make today to stay on track?" The more often you practice this, the more second nature it becomes.

And finally, learn to reflect without regret. Every decision is feedback. Some will go better than others, but each one teaches you something. Instead of obsessing over whether you made the perfect choice, focus on what you can learn and how you'll grow. That mindset builds resilence, which is essential for long-term success.

Building decisive habits isn't just about getting more done; it's about becoming the kind of person who follows through. Someone who doesn't flinch in the face of uncertainty. Someone who moves forward with confidence, even when the outcome isn't guaranteed.

So start now. Decide to be decisive. And let your actions build the future you've been waiting for. Clarity isn't just about having a goal. It's about understanding the why behind it. What lights you up? What kind of life are you really trying to create? What values matter most to you? When you answer those questions, decision-making becomes easier because you're aligning your choices with your core values.

VIII. Leveraging Mentorship for Stronger Decisions

One of the greatest catalysts for powerful decision-making is mentorship. When you have someone who's walked the road ahead, who can see the pitfalls and help you navigate the twists and turns, your confidence in your decisions grows exponentially. Mentors don't just give advice. They help shape your thinking. They show you what's possible when you commit fully, and they hold you accountable when fear tempts you to retreat.

For decades, I operated solo. I read the books. I listened to the audios. I did the "self-study" grind that's become so common in personal development. But it wasn't until I invested in real mentorship that everything began to click. I was at a network marketing event when it hit me: every single top leader I admired had worked with mentors. They hadn't just relied on willpower or information. They had submitted themselves to a process of guided growth.

That realization changed everything. Suddenly, I understood that my lack of results wasn't because I lacked drive or discipline; it was because I lacked alignment and accountability. A mentor helps bring your blind spots into view. They challenge your limiting beliefs. They call out your excuses with love. And more than anything, they model what a decisive life actually looks like.

There's something about being around decisive people that sharpens your edge. Their clarity is contagious. Their standards pull you higher.

When you see someone else make bold, faith-driven decisions, it becomes harder to justify your hesitation. That's what happened to me. I stopped asking "What if?" and started asking "What's next?"

Mentorship also fast-tracks your learning curve. Instead of spending years figuring things out on your own, you get access to hard-won wisdom. You benefit from someone else's experiences; their mistakes, their breakthroughs, and their momentum. That kind of shortcut isn't cheating. It's smart. Because time is your most valuable resource and mentorship helps you use it wisely.

More importantly, a good mentor won't let you hide. When you're wavering on a decision, they'll remind you who you said you wanted to become. They'll challenge you to live up to your commitments and to get out of your comfort zone. And in those moments when doubt starts to creep back in, they'll speak truth louder than your fears.

If you've never had a mentor, I encourage you to seek one out. Whether it's a coach, a leader in your field, or someone further down the road, don't wait for them to find you. Be intentional, ask, and invest. Honor their time and take their guidance seriously. And if you already have one, lean in. Let them stretch you.

The decisions you make will never outgrow the level of belief and vision you carry. A mentor helps to expand both. And when those two expand, so does your capacity to choose boldly, lead confidently, and live intentionally.

You don't have to figure it all out alone. You weren't meant to. The wisdom, encouragement, and accountability that come from a mentor can be the very thing that unlocks your next level. So, make a decision today, not just to find a mentor, but to become someone who's coachable, committed, and ready to rise.

Mentorship isn't just a support system. It's a growth system. It aligns your decisions with higher standards, bigger vision, and deeper purpose. And in doing so, it reinforces what this chapter has been all about: choosing to live decisively.

Let your next move be bold. Let it be informed. Let it be mentored.

IX. Action Steps for Committing to Change

Decision without action is just a good intention with a fancy name. This section is where you take everything you've been learning and put it into action. Commitment starts the moment you stop overthinking and start executing. So, let's make it practical.

1. Set Clear, Non-Negotiable Decisions

Think about one area of your life that's been floating in uncertainty, something you've been "meaning to do" but haven't fully committed to. Write it down. Now, instead of writing it as a to-do or a goal, reframe it as a decision. For example, instead of "I want to be more consistent in business," write "I am building my business daily, no matter what." The shift in language signals a shift in mindset.

Decisions aren't made in your head. They're made in your habits. So, follow up your decision with one immediate action that aligns with it. Make the call. Book the appointment. Invest in the course. Move the needle today.

2. Declare Your Decision Publicly

This step is scary for most people, but it's powerful. When you say something out loud, especially to someone else, it adds weight. It adds accountability. You're no longer just thinking about it. You're being it. Tell a trusted friend, mentor, or team member what you've decided and what it means for how you'll now operate.

Then ask them to hold you to it. Let them check in with you. Give them permission to challenge you if you drift. That kind of support will strengthen your resolve.

3. Create a Commitment Ritual

Every day, take five minutes to review your decision. Speak it out loud. Visualize yourself living it. Write it down again if needed. You are training your subconscious mind to follow your lead. Repetition is the bridge between thought and behavior. It turns intention into identity.

Your ritual could also include reading a scripture or a quote that reinforces your commitment. For example: "I have set the Lord always before me; because He is at my right hand, I will not be shaken." (Psalm 16:8) Let truth shape your belief, and let belief fuel your behavior.

4. Track Progress and Course Correct

Decisions aren't about perfection. They're about direction. Start measuring your progress, not to judge yourself, but to stay aware. Keep a simple journal or checklist of the actions you're taking. Reflect weekly: What's working? What's not? What decisions need reinforcement?

When you drift (and you will), don't beat yourself up. Realign. Recommit. The path to transformation is rarely a straight line, but as long as you keep choosing to move forward, you're winning.

5. Reflective Questions

To help solidify your commitment, take time to answer these questions in writing:

What decision am I avoiding, and why?

What would change if I fully committed to this decision?

Who can support me in honoring this decision?

What daily habit can I adopt that supports this choice?

How will I respond when resistance shows up?

The goal here is to build emotional and mental clarity around your decision. Clarity fuels confidence. Confidence fuels consistency.

X. Summary and Preparation for Next Steps

We've covered a lot in this chapter, but it all boils down to one simple truth: your life will always reflect your decisions. Not your wishes, not your potential, but your decisions.

We explored the difference between casual choices and committed decisions, and how the latter reshapes your identity and your outcomes. We uncovered the obstacles that keep most people stuck, such as fear, procrastination, and indecision, and offered real strategies to overcome them. We dug into the vital role of clarity and faith in guiding strong decisions, and we looked at how building decisive habits can create momentum that carries you through resistance. Finally, we highlighted the impact of mentorship in sharpening your decision-making edge and accelerating your growth.

But this isn't the end. It's a launching point.

If you've felt paralyzed by indecision in the past, I hope this chapter gave you both clarity and courage. The goal wasn't just to inspire you; it was to activate something in you. The next time you're faced with a fork in the road, I want you to hear these words echoing in your mind: decide. Not someday, not when everything lines up. Do it now!

Your future is not waiting for perfect conditions. It's waiting for your decision.

In the next chapter, we'll explore how to align your decisions with your core values and internal compass. Because once you know how to make a powerful decision, the next question is: how do I stay aligned with it? That's where faith and focus come in.

So, take a moment, right now, to look back at the decisions you've made or avoided, and ask yourself: What do I need to commit to today?

Then do it.

Let this be the day your life begins to change.

Make the decision. And don't look back.

Chapter 4: Faith and Focus: Trusting Your Inner Compass

I. Introduction

There was a time when I believed success came down to doing all the right things. Make the calls. Say the script. Follow the system. And I did it, religiously. But something always felt off, like I was rowing a boat with all my strength, but the current was dragging me somewhere else entirely.

One day, after another disappointing result, I remember sitting in silence, not frustrated but curious. I asked myself a simple question: "What am I not seeing?" It wasn't about tactics. It wasn't about effort. It was deeper than that. I realized I had been ignoring the quiet voice within, the inner compass that was trying to point me toward something more aligned, more purposeful.

That was the beginning of a new chapter in my journey, not just in business, but in how I lived. I started paying attention not just to what was expected, but to what was right for me. I began to trust those nudges, those inner promptings that often didn't make logical sense but felt undeniably true. And the more I listened, the more peace and direction I experienced. That's when I learned: faith and focus are inseparable.

This chapter is about learning to trust your inner compass. Not the external noise. Not what everyone else is doing. But that deep, God-given sense of direction inside of you. We all have it, though most of us have been trained to ignore it in favor of logic, fear, or approval.

Faith isn't just about believing something out there. It's about trusting what's been placed in you. That includes your intuition, your values, and your sense of calling. And focus? That's the act of aligning your actions with that inner conviction, day after day.

When faith and focus work together, your path becomes clearer. You stop chasing everything and start moving intentionally. You don't need to know every step. You just need to trust the next one and take it.

In this chapter, we're going to explore what it means to truly trust your inner compass. We'll look at how faith strengthens focus, why distractions are so dangerous, and how to cultivate the kind of spiritual clarity that leads to decisive, purpose-driven action. We'll pull insights from Scripture, from mentors like Graham Cooke, Bob Proctor, and Jim Rohn, and from personal experience, both mine and others who've walked this road.

Success without alignment isn't success at all. You were never meant to force your way forward in fear. You were designed to move forward in faith, led by a still, small voice, strengthened by a clear focus, and supported by wisdom that comes from above.

It's time to stop spinning your wheels. It's time to stop looking outside for what God has already placed inside. It's time to trust your inner compass and walk boldly in the direction of your calling.

Let's get into it.

II. Defining Your Inner Compass

When we talk about your "inner compass," we're referring to that quiet, consistent voice within you. Some people call it intuition. Others see it as spiritual guidance. Whatever you call it, it's real, and it's one of the most powerful tools you have. It's the signal beneath the noise; the whisper of truth that nudges you forward when everything else feels unclear.

Your inner compass is deeply connected to your values, your faith, and the purpose God placed inside you. It's not just a hunch or a guess. It's rooted in a divine partnership, the Spirit of God working through your thoughts, emotions, and experiences to steer you in the right direction. Graham Cooke often talks about how God loves to communicate in whispers, not shouts. That's how our inner compass operates. It doesn't force. It guides. And it gets stronger the more we trust it.

One of the biggest reasons people struggle with decision-making or direction in life is because they've been taught to ignore their inner compass. We're told to "be logical," "follow the rules," or "do what everyone else is doing." When logic and group opinion overpower intuition, we lose touch with our inner truth.

The Bible is full of references to inner guidance. Proverbs 3:5-6 says, "Trust in the Lord with all your heart and lean not on your own understanding; in all your ways submit to Him, and He will make your paths straight." That's not just a spiritual idea; it's a practical strategy. Trusting in something deeper than your current level of understanding can lead to breakthroughs you never expected.

Jesus Himself said in John 10:27, "My sheep hear My voice, and I know them, and they follow Me." Hearing His voice isn't always about thunder or burning bushes. Often, it's about paying attention to the gentle nudges, the convictions that won't go away, the sense of peace that comes when you finally stop striving and start listening.

As you learn to tune into your inner compass, you'll find that it doesn't just help you make decisions, it helps you focus. It eliminates distractions. It simplifies your path. Instead of chasing every opportunity or spinning your wheels in confusion, you begin to walk with purpose, one step at a time.

The more you align with that inner guidance, the more confident you become, not because you know everything, but because you trust the One who does.

Now let's explore how that trust, or faith, actually sharpens your focus and propels you forward.

III. Why Faith Enhances Focus

Faith is more than belief in something unseen. It's the foundation of trust that allows us to stay steady even when the path ahead isn't fully visible. When you truly trust in something greater than yourself, your mind becomes less cluttered with fear and doubt, and your focus sharpens naturally. That's the connection between faith and focus: trust clears the fog.

Bob Proctor often said that faith is the ability to see the invisible and believe in the incredible. He taught that we're always moving toward what we believe, consciously or unconsciously. So, when your belief is strong, when it's rooted in faith, your actions line up with it. You no longer second-guess every move. You move with confidence because you're anchored in something unshakable.

Napoleon Hill echoed this sentiment in Think and Grow Rich, emphasizing that faith is the starting point of all accumulation of riches and the basis of all miracles. In Hill's view, faith isn't passive. It's the mental attitude that allows you to visualize your goal and pursue it relentlessly. He called faith a state of mind that may be induced by autosuggestion, which is simply repeating to yourself what you desire until your subconscious accepts it as truth. Once your subconscious accepts it, your behavior follows. Focus becomes effortless because you're internally aligned.

When your faith is strong, your attention stays locked on the goal, not the obstacles. Think of Peter walking on water in Matthew 14. As long as his eyes were on Jesus, he walked on the water, but when he looked at the wind and the waves, when his faith gave way to fear, he began to sink. Focus is fragile without faith. But with faith? You can walk through storms and stay steady.

Distractions lose their power when you're deeply anchored. The opinions of others, the temporary setbacks, the moments of confusion, they don't sway you as easily when your foundation is built on faith. That's why faith isn't just a spiritual virtue; it's a practical asset.

This section invites you to examine where your faith is placed and how that's affecting your focus. Are you trusting your fears more than your calling? Are you placing faith in your limitations instead of your possibilities? Because whatever you trust most will lead your focus. And wherever your focus goes, your energy flows.

Faith and focus, working together, create a powerful force that moves you from hesitation to clarity, from scattered effort to purposeful progress. And that's exactly what you need to start living the life you were created for.

Let's now take a look at what tries to pull you away from that focus, and how to overcome it.

IV. Overcoming Distractions and Doubt

Distractions and doubts are subtle, persistent forces that pull us off course. They rarely arrive all at once. Instead, they creep in slowly, moment by moment, stealing our time, attention, and confidence until we look up and wonder how we ended up so far off track.

Distractions can be external, like social media, email, or the never-ending to-do list. But more often, they're internal. Thoughts like, "What if I'm not good enough?" "What will people think?" or "Maybe I should just wait until I'm more prepared." These thoughts might sound reasonable, but they carry a dangerous undercurrent: they erode focus by feeding doubt.

Doubt is one of the most effective tools the enemy uses to derail your destiny. It's not just a feeling; it's a seed that, when watered with fear and inaction, grows into a full-blown narrative that keeps you small. And when doubt joins forces with distraction, it creates a powerful resistance that pulls you away from your inner compass.

Faith is the antidote. Not blind faith, but anchored faith, a trust in God's plan, in your purpose, and in the guidance He's given you.

Let's be real: you will never have a completely distraction-free environment. The world is noisy. Life is messy. But when you learn to center yourself in faith, distractions lose their grip. You stop being pulled in a thousand directions because you've chosen to follow one path, His.

Take the story of Nehemiah. When he was rebuilding the walls of Jerusalem, he faced constant distractions and attacks. People tried to lure him away, discourage him, and intimidate him. But his response was clear: "I am doing a great work, and I cannot come down." (Nehemiah 6:3) That's the power of focused faith. Nehemiah didn't deny the noise around him. He just refused to give it more weight than his calling.

You can do the same.

Start by identifying your top distractions. What tends to pull your attention away from what really matters? It could be the constant ping of notifications or the compulsion to check stats, scroll, or compare. It could be self-doubt disguised as research or planning. Write them down. Name them. Because what you don't name, you can't confront.

Then, ask yourself, what do these distractions cost me? Every moment you spend in distraction is a moment you're not building the vision God placed in your heart. That's not meant to guilt you; it's meant to wake you up.

Now, let's talk about doubt. Doubt thrives in the absence of clarity. That's why keeping your vision front and center is so important. Write your goals down daily. Speak your faith out loud. Surround yourself with people who remind you of what's possible. Use Scripture to anchor your mindset. Romans 10:17 says, "So then faith comes by hearing, and hearing by the word of God." Make faith your daily input, and it will become your default output.

Another practical way to disarm doubt is to take action. Action silences doubt faster than any pep talk. Every step you take, no matter how small, proves to your brain that you're moving forward. And progress, even imperfect progress, builds confidence.

Remember this: doubt often feels loudest right before a breakthrough. It's a sign you're stretching, that you're stepping into new territory. Don't run from that discomfort. Use it as confirmation that you're on the right path.

In summary, overcoming distractions and doubt isn't about achieving perfection. It's about developing awareness, practicing discipline, and choosing faith again and again. Keep your focus aligned with your calling. Trust the One who called you. And when the noise tries to pull you away, do what Nehemiah did: stay on the wall.

You are doing a great work. Don't come down.

V. Developing Trust in Your Intuition

Learning to trust your intuition isn't about becoming mystical or overly emotional. It's about recognizing and honoring the way God often communicates with us, gently, persistently, and quietly. Your intuition is the Holy Spirit's whisper, prompting you to step in a direction that logic may not always understand.

The first step in developing trust in your intuition is to slow down. We often miss divine direction because we're moving too fast, chasing productivity instead of peace. Carve out quiet time in your day, even if it's just five or ten minutes. Get still. Breathe. Ask a simple question, like "What is mine to do today?" Then listen. Don't force an answer. Just wait. You'll be surprised how often clarity comes when you finally give space for it.

Another technique is to start journaling. Write down those hunches, those inner nudges, even if they don't make sense at the time. Over time, you'll notice patterns. You'll begin to see how certain thoughts keep returning or how peace consistently follows a particular idea. That's your inner compass trying to guide you.

You can also strengthen your intuitive awareness by reflecting on past decisions. Think about a time you ignored your intuition and later regretted it. What did that inner warning feel like? How did it try to get your attention? Then consider a time when you followed your gut, even when others doubted you, and it worked out. How did that feel different? This type of reflection builds confidence in your ability to discern God's subtle direction.

Spiritual practices like prayer and meditation also deepen your connection to God's guidance. Don't just pray for answers, pray for awareness. Ask for ears to hear and eyes to see. Trust that God is always speaking. The issue isn't His silence; it's usually our volume.

Here are a few questions to guide your connection to your inner compass:

What recurring thought or idea keeps nudging me?

When do I feel most at peace, even if the next step is unclear?

What voices in my life are helping me tune in to God's voice, and which ones are drowning it out?

Finally, act on your intuition. It builds trust. The more you follow those inner urges and see how they bear fruit, the more you'll learn to trust them next time. Start small. Follow the prompt to call someone. Say yes to the opportunity that excites your spirit. Take the step that scares you but won't leave you alone.

Your inner compass was never meant to be a backup plan. It's your primary navigation system. Trust it, train it, and follow it. And watch how much easier it becomes to stay aligned with your calling.

In the next section, we'll look at biblical stories that show what faith and focus look like when they're fully alive in someone's life.

VI. Biblical Models of Faith and Focus

Throughout Scripture, we find stories of men and women who demonstrated unwavering faith and laser-sharp focus. These weren't people with perfect clarity or flawless track records. They were ordinary individuals who made extraordinary decisions by trusting God's direction, even when it didn't make sense.

Let's begin with Abraham. God asked him to leave his homeland, his family, and everything familiar to go to a place He would show him. Not a destination, but a direction. Abraham didn't get a full itinerary. He got a nudge and a promise. And yet he went. Hebrews 11:8 says, "By faith Abraham obeyed when he was called to go out to a place... and he went out, not knowing where he was going." That's faith and focus in action. Abraham trusted his inner compass, God's voice, and acted on it.

Then there's Moses. He doubted himself, argued with God, and felt completely inadequate for the task. But when he embraced God's calling, he led an entire nation out of slavery. Moses stayed focused not on his own strength, but on God's presence. He even said in Exodus 33:15, "If your presence does not go with us, do not send us up from here." Moses understood that real focus doesn't come from self-confidence but from spiritual alignment.

And let's not forget Peter. He stepped out of the boat and walked on water toward Jesus. It was his focus on Christ that made the impossible possible. But the moment he shifted his attention to the wind and waves, he began to sink. Matthew 14 reminds us that losing focus, even momentarily, can derail us. But it also reminds us that Jesus is always ready to reach out when we call.

These stories are more than ancient history. They are blueprints. They show us that faith isn't about knowing every detail; it's about trusting the One who does. Focus isn't about eliminating distractions perfectly; it's about fixing your eyes on something higher.

When we face decisions, obstacles, or uncertainty, we can draw strength from these biblical examples. Like Abraham, we can take the next step, even when the path is unclear. Like Moses, we can lead from a place of divine presence, not personal power. And like Peter, we can keep our eyes fixed on Jesus, knowing that even if we stumble, grace will meet us there.

Let these stories remind you that you're not walking this journey alone. You have a God who speaks, who guides, and who equips you. Trust Him. Follow Him. And like those who came before you, you'll find that faith and focus are more than just ideas. They are forces that move you forward.

VII. Integrating Faith with Practical Actions

Faith isn't a substitute for action. It's what fuels action. One of the biggest mistakes people make in the personal development world is separating the spiritual from the practical. They pray without planning, or they plan without praying. True power lies in combining the two, living in a way that brings spiritual insight into real, tangible movement.

Faith tells you where to go. Focus helps you get there. But it's your actions that make the journey real. Jim Rohn used to say, "Don't let your learning lead to knowledge. Let your learning lead to action." That principle is just as true spiritually. You can have the strongest convictions in the world, but if they don't show up in your behavior, they'll never transform your life.

So, how do you integrate faith with practical steps? Start by aligning your daily routines with your values. If you believe God is leading you to impact others through your business, make your schedule reflect that. Carve out time for preparation, connection, and execution. Don't just hope for results, work toward them with intention.

Next, develop habits that strengthen your faith while pushing you forward. That could be starting each day with prayer and journaling, followed by a focused work session on your most meaningful project. It might mean replacing idle scrolling with reading Scripture or listening to a faith-based podcast that keeps your mind sharp and your spirit encouraged.

Also, bring faith into your decision-making. Don't just evaluate options based on money or efficiency. Ask: What choice brings me closer to the person I'm called to become? What would obedience look like in this situation? Invite God into your business meetings, your phone calls, and your daily tasks. Let Him be the CEO.

When you do this consistently, your actions become an extension of your faith. You stop second-guessing every move and start stepping forward with confidence, knowing that you're not operating on your own. You're co-laboring with God.

That's where the magic happens. Not in the wishful thinking, but in the gritty disciplined doing, motivated by a deep sense of purpose. Your life begins to move in the direction of your highest calling, one faithful step at a time.

VIII. Sustaining Focus Through Challenges

Faith and focus are easy when things are going smoothly. When the bills are paid, relationships are peaceful, and your plans are working out, it's not hard to stay centered. But the true test of your inner compass is how well it holds up when life throws you off course.

Setbacks are inevitable. Delays, disappointments, detours, these are all part of the journey. What separates those who keep going from those who quit is not talent or luck, but clarity of purpose and the ability to stay focused through the storm.

Earl Nightingale once said, "Don't let the fear of the time it will take to accomplish something stand in the way of your doing it. The time will pass anyway." That perspective is powerful. It reminds us that time is moving whether we're focused or not. The only question is: will you move with purpose, or drift with distraction?

Staying focused during challenges requires a deeper trust, not just in your plan, but in God's plan. It means recognizing that setbacks can serve you. They're not signs to quit. They're often signs to slow down, pay attention, and realign.

When things fall apart, ask: What am I being shown here? What lesson is hidden in this delay? Instead of resisting the storm, lean into it with curiosity. Let it clarify what really matters.

Here's a practice: when you feel distracted or discouraged, take a break and pray for clarity. Write down what you're feeling and then remind yourself of your "why." Go back to the vision that started you on this path in the first place.

Also, simplify. Focus doesn't always mean doing more. Often, it means doing less, with greater intensity and alignment. When you're overwhelmed, it's usually because you're trying to control too much. Step back, focus on one meaningful action, and let the rest unfold in time.

Remember, your inner compass doesn't disappear in hard times. It just gets harder to hear. The noise of fear, doubt, and anxiety can drown it out. That's why quiet practices like meditation, journaling, and solitude are so important. They help you tune back in.

Most importantly, hold onto faith. Even when the next step is unclear, trust that God hasn't left you. Hebrews 11:1 reminds us, "Now faith is confidence in what we hope for and assurance about what we do not see."

When your external world feels unstable, let your faith be your anchor and your focus be your guide. That's how you keep going, not perfectly, but purposefully.

Let's now explore the importance of mentorship and how spiritual guidance can sharpen our focus even further.

IX. Mentorship and Spiritual Guidance

One of the most underestimated forces behind clarity and focus is mentorship. In the context of faith and personal growth, mentorship becomes more than just advice or accountability. It becomes a spiritual lifeline. Having someone who has walked the path, who hears from God, who knows how to quiet the noise and lean into spiritual truth, can radically shift the way you show up in your journey.

For years, I thought mentorship was optional. I'd read the books, listened to all the audios, and attended every event. I was a sponge for information, but I was lacking transformation. The truth hit me at a network marketing event where I discovered that nearly every top earner had invested deeply in mentorship. They weren't just following systems; they were guided by coaches who helped them uncover blind spots, confront limiting beliefs, and stay spiritually grounded.

Spiritual mentorship doesn't just help you stay on task. It helps you discern what tasks even matter. It challenges you to align with what God is saying over what your fears are screaming. It teaches you how to recognize your inner compass and honor it.

I remember a time when I was completely stuck. On paper, everything should have been working. But something inside me felt off. I brought it to a mentor, someone who had both business experience and spiritual maturity. She didn't give me a to-do list. She asked me questions that made me dig deeper. She helped me realize that I had made a decision out of fear, not faith. That conversation changed the trajectory of my business and my mindset.

Mentors can help you hear God more clearly, not because they have all the answers, but because they help you get quiet enough to hear them for yourself. They hold up a mirror, call out the gold in you, and remind you of your calling when you forget.

If you want to grow in focus, seek out voices of wisdom. Don't just chase results, seek alignment. The right mentor won't just point you toward success. They'll help you become the kind of person who can carry it with grace and purpose.

Spiritual guidance, whether through mentorship, prayer, or Scripture, serves as a stabilizing force when your faith wavers and your focus blurs. It grounds you. It lifts you. It realigns you with truth.

As you move forward, be intentional about who you let speak into your life. Surround yourself with people who elevate your thinking, challenge your distractions, and call you higher. Because in the noise of the world, we all need voices that point us back to what matters most.

X. Practical Exercises and Reflection

It's one thing to understand the concepts of faith and focus. It's another thing to put them into daily practice. This section gives you practical tools to apply what you've learned and reinforce your inner guidance with real-world action.

Tool #1: Morning Alignment Routine

Start your day by centering yourself. Spend five minutes in silence or prayer. Ask yourself: "What is most important today?" Let your inner compass guide your priorities. Then write down three actions you can take that align with your purpose and values.

Tool #2: Faith and Focus Journal

Each evening, take 10 minutes to reflect on your day. Answer these questions:

Where did I feel most in alignment today?

Where did I get distracted or lose focus?

What is one thing I'm grateful for?

What insight did I receive from God or my inner compass today?

Doing this consistently trains your brain to recognize patterns, gain clarity, and listen more deeply.

Tool #3: The "One Thing" Exercise

Choose one area in your life or business where you've been feeling stuck. Write down everything you've been doing to try to fix it. Then, ask: "What is one aligned step I can take that comes from a place of faith, not fear?" Take that step before the day ends. Do this weekly.

Tool #4: Distraction Detox

Pick a day to eliminate the top three distractions in your life, whether it's social media, email, unnecessary meetings, or negative people. Use that time for reflection, creativity, or deep work that matters. See what clarity surfaces.

Tool #5: Scripture Meditation

Choose a verse each week that reinforces trust, purpose, or spiritual focus. Write it down. Meditate on it daily. Speak it out loud when doubt creeps in. Let it become a filter for your thoughts and decisions.

Guided Reflection Questions:

What has my inner compass been trying to tell me lately?

What am I doing that feels out of alignment?

What do I need to let go of to move forward in faith?

Who can I seek out for spiritual mentorship or encouragement?

These tools aren't about perfection. They're about presence. They're about building the muscle of spiritual alignment, day by day. Use them, modify them, and make them part of your routine.

Because when your faith is firm and your focus is clear, you stop chasing things that don't matter and start building a life that does.

XI. Chapter Summary and Preview

As we close out this chapter, take a moment to reflect on what you've learned. Faith and focus are not just complementary concepts; they're powerful forces that can reshape your direction and deepen your impact. When they operate together, they create alignment between your purpose, your thoughts, and your actions.

We began by talking about your inner compass; that still, small voice that often gets drowned out by noise, fear, and pressure. But when you slow down and pay attention to that internal guidance, you start to recognize the subtle ways that God leads you. The more you listen, the more clearly you hear.

You've also learned that faith is not just a belief in something unseen, but a trust in what God has already placed within you. Focus is how you honor that trust by taking aligned, intentional steps each day. Distractions will come. Doubts will rise. But your ability to return to your center, to trust that inner compass, will make all the difference.

We explored stories of biblical figures who modeled what it means to follow divine direction despite fear, uncertainty, or opposition. From Abraham to Peter, these examples show that clarity doesn't come before obedience. It often comes after. Faith leads, and focus follows.

The practical tools and exercises offered were not just activities; they are gateways to transformation. By practicing daily alignment, journaling, meditating on Scripture, and seeking mentorship, you're not only reinforcing what you believe but actively living it.

As you move forward, remember that success isn't just about achieving goals. It's about becoming someone who is deeply aligned with purpose, unwavering in faith, and disciplined in focus. That kind of person doesn't just react to life. They shape it.

In the next chapter, we'll take this alignment even deeper. We'll explore how to build momentum in your life through consistent action and how small, faithful steps lead to lasting transformation.

You're no longer wandering. You're on a path. Stay focused and stay faithful. The best is still ahead.

Chapter 5: Becoming Who You're Meant to Be

I. Introduction

I'll never forget the day I caught a glimpse of who I was really meant to be. It didn't happen at a seminar or during some epic life moment; it was quiet and simple. I was sitting alone in my car, having just left a meeting and feeling completely out of alignment. I had said all the right things, wore the right smile, and nodded at the right times. But inside, I felt like a stranger to myself.

Something inside me whispered, "You weren't made to blend in. You were made to show up."

That moment cracked something open in me. Not because it was loud or dramatic, but because it was real. For the first time in a long time, I was willing to ask the deeper question, not "What should I be doing?" but "Who am I becoming?"

Most people never slow down enough to ask that question. We get caught up in doing, producing, and achieving. And somewhere in the noise of goals and obligations, we lose touch with who we truly are. We start to wear identities handed to us by our parents, our culture, or our past failures. We put on masks to be accepted, to fit in, or just to survive. But those masks become heavy. And after a while, they bury the person we were created to be.

This chapter is about peeling back those layers. It's about returning to the core of who you are, not just in the eyes of the world, but in the eyes of God. Becoming who you're meant to be doesn't mean striving to achieve something. It means aligning with the truth that was already planted in you.

Your identity isn't something you create from scratch. It's something you uncover. Something you reclaim. Something you remember. God placed purpose in you before you were ever born. The journey now is to walk that purpose out in real life, in real time, with clarity, courage, and conviction.

Over the next several sections, we're going to explore what it means to live from your true identity, not the one shaped by fear, comparison, or performance, but the one grounded in truth, grace, and calling. You'll discover how to shift the way you see yourself, how to align your daily habits with your core values, and how to show up consistently as the person you were always meant to be.

The world doesn't need a copy of someone else. It needs you, the real you, the called you, the equipped you. And that version of you is already within reach. You don't have to earn it. You just have to embrace it.

Let's begin the journey of becoming who you're meant to be.

II. Understanding Your True Identity

Understanding your true identity is one of the most important steps on your journey to becoming who you're meant to be. At its core, identity is about alignment between who God created you to be and how you're showing up every day. If there's a disconnect between the two, you'll always feel off-center, no matter how much success you appear to have on the surface.

So many people live their lives wearing masks. They perform roles they were never meant to play, often trying to earn love, validation, or a sense of purpose by becoming someone they think they should be. But deep down, they feel exhausted, empty, and unfulfilled. Why? Because they're disconnected from their true identity.

Graham Cooke teaches that identity is not something you have to strive to create. It's something you discover through a relationship with God. He describes it as "finding the you that God already sees." That means your job isn't to invent a new self, it's to unlearn the false identities you've picked up and get reacquainted with the person God always intended you to be.

This isn't just a spiritual idea, it's practical. When you begin to see yourself the way God sees you, capable, called, worthy, and equipped, you start to act differently. You take risks that align with your calling. You say no to things that don't. You stop compromising just to fit in or be accepted. You operate from a place of inner security instead of outward performance.

There's a passage in Ephesians 2:10 that says, "For we are God's masterpiece. He has created us anew in Christ Jesus, so we can do the good things He planned for us long ago." That verse reminds us that our identity isn't just about who we are, it's about what we're here to do. And we can't fulfill our purpose if we're living from a false sense of self.

When you know who you are, everything else begins to fall into place. Your decisions become clearer. Your focus sharpens. You stop needing external approval to feel valuable. You're no longer swayed by the ups and downs of circumstances, because your identity is rooted in something unshakable.

Take time to reflect on the masks you've worn and the stories you've believed about yourself that don't align with God's truth. Then begin the process of trading those lies for truth. Journal what you know to be true about who you are in Christ. Surround yourself with people who call out your authentic self instead of encouraging your performance-based identity.

Becoming who you're meant to be isn't about becoming someone new. It's about finally giving yourself permission to be the person God designed from the beginning. That's where freedom lives. That's where transformation begins.

III. The Gap Between Current Reality and Desired Identity

There's a gap that every person has to navigate at some point in life, the distance between who you are right now and who you know you were created to become. That gap shows up in our habits, our confidence, our thoughts, and especially in our results.

Most of the time, we try to bridge that gap with effort. We grind harder, we set new goals, and we change strategies. But none of that works if we don't first address the real problem, how we see ourselves.

Bob Proctor said, "You can never outperform your self-image." And he's right. Your current reality is a reflection of your current identity. If you believe deep down that you're not good enough, not capable, or not worthy of success, then your actions will always unconsciously align with that belief, even if your intentions say otherwise.

Earl Nightingale described this as the "strangest secret." We become what we think about. If your dominant thoughts are rooted in limitation or lack, those beliefs will shape your behavior. And behavior over time becomes your life.

This is why simply setting goals doesn't work for most people. If your identity hasn't caught up to your goals, you'll sabotage yourself. You'll procrastinate, hesitate, or abandon the mission completely. It's not because you're weak. It's because your subconscious doesn't believe that the goal is consistent with who you are.

To close the gap between your current self and your desired identity, you have to start thinking from the place you want to arrive, not just thinking about it. You have to ask yourself daily, "What would the version of me who already has this result believe, think, and do?" And then begin to embody that now, not later.

This is more than visualization. It's about inner transformation. You're not faking it till you make it. You're aligning your thoughts, emotions, and actions with a new identity, a true identity that's already within you, waiting to be expressed.

When you bridge that internal gap, external changes begin to follow You speak differently. You show up with more confidence. You take bolder actions. And people respond to you differently because they sense the shift.

So don't just chase results. Transform the self that's producing them. Work on the inside first, and the outside will catch up. That's how you become who you're meant to be.

IV. Shifting Your Self-Image

Shifting your self-image is one of the most powerful things you can do to create lasting change. It's not about pretending or putting on a new face. It's about intentionally reshaping the way you see yourself so your beliefs begin to support the kind of life you want to live.

Self-image isn't fixed. It's flexible, but it takes conscious effort to change. Most of us have been walking around with a default image of ourselves, formed by years of past experiences, parental influences, cultural messaging, and internalized criticism. That image becomes the invisible thermostat of our lives. No matter how high we try to rise, we eventually snap back to what we believe we deserve.

Bob Proctor taught that your self-image is like the set point of your personal thermostat. If you want different results, you have to raise that set point. But how do you do that?

First, you begin by creating a clear, compelling image of the person you want to become. Write it down. What does that version of you think, believe, and do? How does that person walk into a room? How do they handle challenges? How do they speak, act, and decide? Be detailed. Don't hold back.

Next, immerse yourself in that image daily. Visualize it, speak it, feel it. Affirm it out loud. Instead of waking up and reacting to life, start your day by reminding yourself of who you are becoming. This creates alignment. And with consistency, it starts to rewire your subconscious.

Another powerful exercise is to confront and rewrite the limiting beliefs tied to your old self-image. What thoughts or phrases have you repeated over the years that have shaped your view of yourself? Maybe things like "I'm not disciplined," or "I'm not a leader." Write those down. Then, one by one, challenge them. Replace each lie with a truth grounded in faith and purpose. "I am developing discipline daily." "I am equipped and called to lead."

Finally, take action. Nothing cements a new identity like acting in alignment with it. When you start making decisions from your upgraded self-image, it sends a signal to your subconscious that this new identity is real. Each step builds momentum.

The journey of shifting your self-image is not about striving for perfection. It's about shedding what no longer serves you and choosing to believe what God says is true about you. It's not overnight, but it is possible. And it's worth it, because the more you walk in the truth of who you really are, the more your life will reflect it.

V. Role Models and Their Influence

Identifying and learning from role models can be a powerful catalyst in your journey of becoming who you're meant to be. Role models provide us with living, breathing examples of what is possible. They reflect back to us qualities that resonate with our deeper calling, and their example can help us unlock aspects of our identity that we didn't fully recognize or believe were available to us.

A great role model isn't someone you try to become a carbon copy of. Instead, they serve as an inspiration, a mirror that helps you see your own potential. Their courage, discipline, or spiritual insight awakens something already within you. The goal isn't imitation, it's activation.

In my own journey, I've looked to mentors and leaders whose lives radiated authenticity. These were people who didn't just talk a good game. They lived with intention. They made decisions from a place of alignment. And they had fruit in their lives that came from walking in integrity with their calling. Watching them reminded me that it was not only okay to be myself, it was essential.

Scripture is filled with powerful role models who embodied transformation. Think about Abraham. Called out of his familiar surroundings, he had to leave behind what was known in order to follow the voice of God. He didn't have a clear roadmap, but he had faith. And that faith shaped his identity as the father of nations.

Or Moses. He doubted himself, wrestled with insecurity, and even tried to convince God that he wasn't the right man for the job. But over time, through obedience and trust, Moses stepped into the leader he was always meant to be.

Then there's Peter. Impulsive, emotional, and even unreliable at times. Yet Jesus saw past all that. He saw Peter's potential, and in the end, Peter became a foundational figure in the early Church. His transformation didn't come from perfection. It came from perseverance and proximity to Jesus.

What all these figures have in common is that they didn't start out as the person they became. Their journeys were marked by growth, resistance, and course correction. But each of them leaned into their process. They listened, followed, and stayed in the game.

In today's world, it's easy to look at people who are living powerfully and assume they've always had it together. But if you dig into their stories, you'll find struggle, surrender, and steady progress. Let that encourage you. You don't need to be perfect to begin. You just need to be willing to grow.

So, take time to identify the role models who light something up in you. Study their stories. Learn from their mistakes and their victories. Let their lives sharpen your own. And above all, remember that your life can serve as a model to someone else. As you step into your authentic self, you give others permission to do the same. That's the power of influence and the gift of becoming.

VI. Faith and the Power of Transformation

The transformation from who we are to who we're meant to be is not simply a matter of motivation or personal discipline. At its core, it's a spiritual journey. Faith is what turns possibility into reality. Faith bridges the gap between potential and fulfillment, between intention and embodiment. It is the power source behind all true change.

Scripture is filled with reminders that transformation is not only possible, it's expected. Romans 12:2 tells us, "Do not conform to the pattern of this world, but be transformed by the renewing of your mind." That verse doesn't just suggest change; it commands it. But notice how the change happens: through the renewing of your mind, not the striving of your will.

Transformation begins with belief. It begins with choosing to believe that what God says about you is truer than what your past says, truer than your circumstances, and truer than the lies you've believed. When faith becomes the lens through which you see yourself, everything begins to shift.

This is where many people get stuck. They want to change. They even try to change. But deep down, they don't believe it's really possible for them. Maybe they've failed before. Maybe they've been told they'll never measure up. Maybe they've internalized shame and fear. But faith overrides all of that. Faith is the courage to believe again.

It's not just about believing in God; it's about believing God. Believing that He meant it when He said you are fearfully and wonderfully made. Believing that He has plans to prosper you, not to harm you. Believing that He who began a good work in you will carry it through to completion.

Transformation isn't behavior modification. It's identity revelation. It's waking up to the truth of who you are in Christ and allowing that truth to inform how you live. As you grow in faith, you begin to walk differently, talk differently, and make decisions from a new place.

This kind of change doesn't always happen overnight. It's often slow, layered, and uncomfortable. But it's also deeply fulfilling. Because it's not about becoming someone you're not; it's about becoming more of who you truly are.

In practical terms, faith-fueled transformation might look like making decisions that reflect your values even when they're inconvenient. It might mean stepping into opportunities that stretch you. It might mean forgiving someone, or yourself, and letting go of old narratives that no longer serve you.

Ultimately, transformation through faith is about surrender. It's about trusting that God is not only willing, but eager to help you become the person He already sees when He looks at you. And as you align your faith with your actions, you'll find yourself stepping into a version of life that once felt out of reach.

You're not here to settle. You're here to grow, to rise, and to reflect God's nature more clearly every day. Faith is the power that makes that growth possible. It's the engine behind your becoming.

VII. Building Habits of Authenticity

Once you've started to shift your self-image and align with your true identity, the next crucial step is to build habits that reinforce that alignment. This is where many people stall. They catch a vision of who they want to become, but they don't anchor it with consistent action. That's why building habits of authenticity is so important. It gives structure to your transformation.

Jim Rohn famously said, "Discipline is the bridge between goals and accomplishment." It's not enough to simply want to be your authentic self. You have to live it out every day. And that requires building patterns of behavior that reflect who you truly are.

Start with your morning. How you begin your day sets the tone for everything that follows. Begin with practices that reconnect you to your identity: prayer, journaling, reading Scripture, or reviewing your personal affirmations. These rituals aren't just spiritual maintenance; they are your alignment tools.

Next, examine your environment. Are you surrounding yourself with people, messages, and experiences that reinforce your authentic identity? Or are you stuck in settings that constantly pull you back into old patterns? If you want to live as the person you're meant to be, you have to intentionally create a life that supports that version of you.

Another key habit is reflection. Set aside time weekly to evaluate your actions. Are they aligned with your core values? Are you showing up in ways that honor your true identity? This isn't about shame or self-criticism; it's about honest assessment. Small, consistent course corrections are what lead to major transformation over time.

And remember, authenticity isn't about being perfect. It's about being consistent. When you fall off track, and you will, return to your identity. Remind yourself of the truth. Reconnect with God. Realign your actions.

Jim Rohn also emphasized the power of personal development. He often said, "Work harder on yourself than you do on your job." Why? Because when you grow, everything around you grows. Your relationships, your business, and your opportunities all expand in proportion to your growth.

So, build your habits accordingly. Choose reading material that sharpens your thinking. Surround yourself with mentors who challenge you. Practice gratitude. Speak life. Take action from your values, not your fears.

These are the habits that shape your identity. And when done consistently, they hardwire authenticity into your life. Over time, being the real you won't feel like something you have to work at. It'll feel like home.

VIII. Overcoming Resistance to Change

Change sounds exciting until you have to live through it. That's when resistance shows up. Not just in the form of external obstacles, but internally, right between your ears and deep in your heart. Resistance is subtle, persistent, and often disguised as logic. It whispers things like, "This is too hard," "What if I fail?" or the classic, "You're not ready."

Resistance is part of the transformation process. It's not a sign that you're failing. It's a sign that you're moving forward.

Any time you begin stepping into a more authentic version of yourself, your old identity will fight to survive. That version of you, the one who learned to play small, avoid risk, and seek approval, doesn't want to die quietly. It will throw up every defense it can to keep you in familiar territory. Why? Because familiarity feels safe, even when it's dysfunctional.

That's why so many people start strong but stop short. They hit resistance and interpret it as a sign to turn back, when in reality, it's the threshold of breakthrough.

One of the first steps to overcoming resistance is simply recognizing it. Resistance can look like procrastination, perfectionism, fatigue, excuses, or even physical discomfort. It's anything that keeps you stuck when you know the path forward. Name it. Own it. When you expose resistance, it loses some of its power.

Spiritual resistance runs even deeper. It's the kind that challenges your identity and tests your faith. It sounds like, "Who do you think you are to live like this? To lead others? To speak truth?" These attacks aren't just mental. They're spiritual. And they require spiritual answers.

Romans 12:2 says, "Do not conform to the pattern of this world, but be transformed by the renewing of your mind." That transformation doesn't happen once. It happens daily. And the renewing of your mind requires replacing old thoughts with truth. Not just positive thinking, but *truth*, the kind of truth that comes from Scripture, from communion with God, from remembering who He says you are.

When resistance shows up, lean in instead of backing off. Pray, journal, and speak out loud what you believe. Call a mentor or accountability partner. Remember past moments when you pushed through and came out stronger. This isn't your first battle, and it won't be your last, but you've already won more than you realize.

Let me share a quick story. A woman was mentored years ago who wanted to launch a ministry, but she kept hitting a wall. Every time she planned a launch date, fear crept in. She told herself she wasn't polished enough, educated enough, or ready. But when she talked through it with her mentor, it became clear the resistance had nothing to do with readiness. It had everything to do with identity. She didn't yet believe she was called. Once she began to speak truth over herself daily, truth from Scripture, from prayer, and from her mentors, she broke through that fear. Today, that ministry is flourishing.

You might be facing the same kind of resistance right now. Not because you're weak, but because you're growing. The enemy of your soul knows your potential and would love nothing more than to keep you comfortable, distracted, and off course. But you weren't made for comfort. You were made for impact. And the only way to fulfill your purpose is to push through the internal friction that tries to hold you back.

Remember that resistance is not your enemy. It's your signal. It tells you that something powerful is trying to emerge. Don't silence it, respond to it. Use it as fuel. Let it sharpen your faith and clarify your mission.

Overcoming resistance isn't about being fearless. It's about being faithful. When you stay committed to becoming who God made you to be, even when it's uncomfortable, you invite grace into your growth. And grace is what turns effort into transformation.

IX. Mentorship in the Journey to Authenticity

If there's one thing I wish I had discovered earlier in my journey, it's this: you can't become the person you're meant to be alone. No matter how driven, talented, or spiritually grounded you are, you need people, specifically mentors, who can see what you can't, challenge what you've settled for, and call out the greatness inside of you.

For years, I operated in isolation, assuming that reading enough books and listening to enough trainings would eventually unlock my breakthrough. And don't get me wrong, those tools were valuable. But they didn't bring transformation. Not until I was willing to humble myself, invest in real mentorship, and let someone walk with me did things begin to shift.

A good mentor doesn't just give you advice. They reflect back the person you're becoming. They listen between the lines and call you out when your words and actions don't align. They don't coddle your comfort zone, they confront it. Not to shame you, but to stretch you.

One of the most transformative conversations I ever had was with a mentor who had built the kind of life and business I was aspiring toward. I came to the conversation frustrated and stuck in a cycle of self-doubt. I explained how I felt unqualified, unsure, and out of place. I'll never forget what she said: "Ray, the reason you feel unqualified is because you're stepping into something you haven't fully owned yet. But that doesn't mean it's not yours. It just means you're in transition."

That single sentence reframed everything for me. She wasn't just coaching me through a moment; she was showing me how to own my next level. And that's the power of mentorship. It gives you language for your transition and tools for your transformation.

Throughout Scripture, we see this pattern repeated. Moses had Jethro. Joshua had Moses. Elisha had Elijah. Timothy had Paul. Even Jesus invested deeply in mentoring His disciples. Authentic transformation happens most powerfully in the context of relationship. Why? Because real growth requires accountability, feedback, encouragement, and sometimes correction, all things that mentors provide when invited into your journey.

Mentorship also protects you from isolation. When you're growing into a new identity, it's easy to second-guess yourself. It's tempting to retreat when resistance shows up or to fall back into old patterns when no one's watching. But a mentor keeps you anchored. They remind you of what you've committed to when your feelings try to talk you out of it.

If you've never had a mentor, start by praying for one. Ask God to bring someone into your life who is walking in alignment with their purpose, who has fruit on the tree, and who is willing to invest in others. Then be willing to invest in that relationship through time, humility, and, when appropriate, financial commitment. Free advice can be helpful, but transformation often requires investment.

And if you already have a mentor, lean in more fully. Don't just ask for answers, ask for perspective. Let them speak into the parts of your life that feel uncomfortable to reveal. Vulnerability is the soil where growth takes root.

Most importantly, remember this: mentorship is not a shortcut; it's a multiplier. It won't do the work for you, but it will accelerate the process if you're willing to be teachable. The path to authenticity isn't paved with independence. It's marked by wise guidance and faithful companionship.

So, as you continue becoming who you're meant to be, ask yourself: Who am I learning from? Who am I letting speak into my life? And am I willing to be coached, stretched, and challenged in service of the person I'm becoming?

Because that version of you, the real you, is worth it.

X. Practical Exercises and Reflection

Transformation isn't just an idea, it's a practice. Becoming who you're meant to be requires more than awareness. It takes action, reflection, and consistency. This section offers you some simple yet powerful exercises to help you bridge the gap between inspiration and embodiment. These are tools you can return to again and again as you grow deeper into your true identity.

1. The Identity Audit

Grab a journal and answer the following questions with total honesty:

What labels have I been carrying that no longer serve me?

What have I been pretending to be in order to be accepted?

Where in my life am I living from fear instead of authenticity?

Now shift gears. Write a new list:

What qualities define the person I know I'm becoming?

How would that version of me think, speak, act, and respond?

What decisions would that version of me stop putting off?

This exercise is meant to bring clarity. You can't shift what you haven't acknowledged. And you can't fully step into the new until you're willing to let go of the old.

2. The True You Statement

Using what you uncovered in your identity audit, craft a short "I am" statement that captures the essence of your authentic self. Not based on who you've been, but who you are becoming. Examples:

"I am a bold, faith-driven leader who inspires others through truth and action."

"I am consistent, focused, and aligned with God's purpose for my life."

"I am no longer defined by fear. I walk in clarity, courage, and conviction."

Write it. Speak it daily. Place it where you'll see it every morning. Let it recalibrate your identity on the days you forget who you are.

3. The Alignment Tracker

For the next 7 days, take five minutes at the end of each day to ask:

Did I act today in alignment with who I'm becoming?

Where did I shrink, avoid, or pretend?

What did I learn, and how can I respond differently tomorrow?

Write your reflections without judgment. The goal isn't perfection. The goal is awareness and alignment. You're rewiring habits and thought patterns that may have been in place for years. Grace is essential.

4. Visualize the Future You

Take 10 minutes in silence. Close your eyes and picture yourself one year from now, fully aligned with your true identity. What do you see? Where are you? What are you doing? Who are you surrounded by? How do you carry yourself? What has changed?

Now write about it in the present tense, as if it's already real. Let your imagination partner with your faith. As Proverbs 23:7 reminds us, "As a man thinketh in his heart, so is he." Visualization is a tool for internalizing what's possible.

5. Anchor in Scripture

Find 1–3 scriptures that speak directly to your identity in Christ and your calling. Some favorites:

"You are a chosen people, a royal priesthood..." (1 Peter 2:9)

"I can do all things through Christ who strengthens me." (Philippians 4:13)

"You did not choose me, but I chose you..." (John 15:16)

Write these verses down. Meditate on them. Declare them out loud until they feel truer than the limiting beliefs you've carried.

These exercises aren't meant to overwhelm you. Start with one. Practice it. Let it become part of your rhythm. Becoming who you're meant to be is a daily walk, not a single leap. And each small step you take is a vote for your true self.

XI. Chapter Summary and Preview

This chapter has taken you deep into the process of becoming who you're truly meant to be, not just in theory, but in practice. At the heart of it all is this truth: your identity is not something you earn, perform, or fabricate. It's something you uncover, embrace, and express. You were created on purpose, with purpose, and for a purpose. The journey is about alignment, not invention.

We began with the idea that most people drift through life wearing masks handed to them by others: family, culture, past wounds, or fear of rejection. Those masks may have served a purpose once, but now they stand in the way of authenticity. The path to transformation begins with removing what's false so you can make room for what's true.

You explored how to rediscover your true identity through spiritual growth and self-reflection. With guidance from thinkers like Graham Cooke, Bob Proctor, and Earl Nightingale, and with insight from Scripture, you learned that your identity is already set by the One who created you. Your role is to recognize it, accept it, and live it out.

We discussed the gap between where you are and who you feel called to be, and how that tension is not a sign of failure, but an invitation to grow. Shifting your self-image takes work, but it's possible. You now have the tools to clarify your ideal self, break free from old identities, and build habits that support the real you.

You looked at the role of faith in transformation and how scripture reinforces your ability to change through God's renewing power. You studied the impact of role models, the wisdom of mentors, and the importance of disciplined, consistent action. You practiced reflection and learned how to identify internal resistance, not as a dead end, but as a doorway to deeper alignment.

Finally, you engaged with hands-on exercises designed to move your transformation from concept to daily practice. Journaling, visualization, affirmations, and daily alignment keep you grounded as you move forward.

Here's a quick recap of the key takeaways:

Identity is uncovered, not created – you're not building a new you, you're stepping into who God already sees.

There is a gap between where you are and who you want to be – closing that gap requires conscious effort, reflection, and faith.

Self-image matters – when you elevate how you see yourself, your actions and results follow.

Habits shape authenticity – the consistent things you do every day either reinforce or resist your true identity.

Faith fuels transformation – through scripture, prayer, and spiritual practice, you gain the strength and clarity to live from truth.

Mentorship accelerates growth – you don't have to figure it out alone. Seek guidance, and you'll gain perspective and courage.

As we move forward, keep one thing in mind: transformation is not a one-time event. It's a lifelong journey of becoming, refining, and aligning. You won't always get it right, and that's okay. What matters most is that you stay connected to who you are, who you're becoming, and why it matters.

In the next chapter, we'll shift from the internal work of identity to the practical reality of living it out. That means confronting fear, self-sabotage, and the internal voices that try to keep you small. It's one thing to believe in your calling. It's another to walk it out boldly, especially when resistance shows up.

But you're ready.

You've begun the journey back to yourself. You've learned to recognize the false, embrace the truth, and step forward with intentionality. Now it's time to reinforce that identity by dealing with the barriers that try to block your progress.

Let's keep going. The best version of you isn't just possible, it's already waiting.

Chapter 6: Overcoming Fear and Self-Sabotage

I. Introduction

I remember sitting in the parking lot of a hotel conference center, just minutes away from a business event that could have changed the trajectory of my life. I was dressed for success. I had my notes, my pitch, even my courage rehearsed. But as I sat there gripping the steering wheel, an invisible wall rose up in front of me. My chest tightened. My thoughts spiraled. What if I mess it up? What if they think I don't belong? What if I succeed and can't sustain it?

That was the moment I came face-to-face with a truth I had spent years avoiding: it wasn't the business or the opportunity that was holding me back. It was me. More specifically, it was the fear I had allowed to run the show. And worse, it was the subtle, sneaky habit of self-sabotage that would show up just when I started gaining momentum.

Fear doesn't always scream. Sometimes it whispers, "Play it safe. ' Sometimes it disguises itself as logic: "Now's not the right time." It can even wear the mask of unworthiness: "Who am I to think I can do this?" And self-sabotage? It's even trickier. It tells you you're being realistic while quietly pulling the rug out from under your own progress.

If you've ever found yourself stuck at the edge of a breakthrough, not because the opportunity wasn't there, but because something inside you pulled back, then you know exactly what I'm talking about. The problem isn't a lack of knowledge. It's not even a lack of talent or opportunity. Most of the time, it's internal resistance rooted in fear. And left unchecked, it evolves into patterns of self-sabotage that quietly and consistently derail your best efforts.

Over the years, I've worked with and observed countless individuals in the world of personal growth and network marketing. Some had incredible drive, others had talent to spare. But the ones who truly made progress weren't the ones who never felt fear. They were the ones who learned how to confront it, process it, and move forward in spite of it. They developed the awareness and discipline to spot self-sabotage and replace it with intention and courage.

Fear and self-sabotage are two of the most destructive forces in personal transformation. They're internal thieves, stealing dreams, delaying progress, and distorting your self-image. But here's the good news: they're not permanent. They're patterns, and patterns can be interrupted, rewired, and replaced.

In this chapter, we're going to look closely at the nature of fear and how it operates, not just as a feeling, but as a learned response that can be unlearned. We'll uncover the roots of self-sabotage, how it shows up in ways you might not expect, and what you can do to break those cycles. We'll draw from timeless wisdom, both psychological and spiritual, to show you how fear gets planted, how it grows, and most importantly, how to uproot it for good.

We'll also examine the critical role faith plays in overcoming fear. I'm not just talking about religious belief, but deep, unshakable trust in yourself, in the God who created you, and in the purpose you've been given. Faith and fear both demand belief in something unseen. You get to choose which one you feed.

This chapter will also offer you practical tools, exercises, habits, and reflections designed to help you identify your specific fear triggers and the ways you may be sabotaging your own progress without even realizing it. You'll learn how to replace fear with faith and hesitation with clarity. And just as importantly, you'll gain the confidence to keep showing up, even when it's uncomfortable.

So, if you're tired of getting in your own way, of dreaming big but falling short, of starting strong but quitting halfway through, then this chapter was written for you. Not to shame you, but to empower you. Because fear and self-sabotage don't have to win. Not this time. Not anymore.

II. Understanding Fear

Fear is one of the most misunderstood and mismanaged forces in our lives. At its core, fear is not inherently bad. It was designed to keep us safe, to alert us to danger, and to help us survive. But for most of us, fear has stopped being a protective mechanism and has become a paralyzing one. It doesn't just keep us from harm, it keeps us from growth.

There are two broad categories of fear: rational and irrational. Rational fear serves a purpose. It keeps you from walking into traffic or touching a hot stove. It's tied to real, immediate threats. But irrational fear is different. It's rooted in our imagination, our past wounds, or our limiting beliefs. It's the fear that tells you you're not good enough. The fear that says, "What if I fail?" or worse, "What if I succeed and I can't handle it?"

Napoleon Hill, in his classic Think and Grow Rich, identified six basic fears that sabotage success: the fear of poverty, criticism, ill health, loss of love, old age, and death. He called these the "ghosts" that haunt our decision-making and limit our potential. These fears don't always shout; they often whisper. And those whispers can be more damaging than we realize.

Bob Proctor built on Hill's insights by emphasizing that fear often shows up as doubt and worry. According to Proctor, doubt and worry are forms of negative visualization. We create vivid mental movies of everything that could go wrong, and then we respond emotionally as if they're already happening. The body reacts to imagined failure the same way it reacts to real danger. And over time, this response becomes a habit.

The most dangerous thing about fear is not the fear itself, but how we react to it. Most people avoid it. They shrink from opportunities, delay decisions, or stay stuck in jobs, relationships, and routines that don't serve them. And then they wonder why they feel stagnant or frustrated.

Understanding fear means recognizing that most of it isn't real, at least not in the way we experience it. The acronym often used is F.E.A.R.: False Evidence Appearing Real. Fear masquerades as wisdom. It pretends to be caution, when really it's control. It poses as logic, but it's actually limitation.

But here's the good news: fear is also a compass. The presence of fear usually points to the edge of your current comfort zone. It shows up right before a breakthrough. The key isn't to eliminate fear, it's to master your relationship with it. You do that by exposing it, challenging it, and moving forward anyway.

The next time you feel fear rise up, ask yourself: Is this fear rational or irrational? Is this protecting me or limiting me? Is this pointing to a real danger, or just an internal resistance to growth? That awareness is the first step toward shifting your response.

Napoleon Hill taught that definiteness of purpose is the antidote to fear. When you know who you are and what you're here to do, fear loses much of its power. Bob Proctor added that replacing fear-based thinking with faith-based thinking is a practice, one that begins with the thoughts you allow to take root. You can't eliminate fear through willpower alone, but you can starve it by feeding your faith.

In the next section, we'll look at how fear teams up with self-sabotage to derail your progress and how to spot the subtle ways it may be operating in your own life. But for now, remember this: fear only wins if you let it. And once you learn to see it for what it is, it starts to shrink in the light of truth.

III. Identifying Self-Sabotage

Self-sabotage is one of the most frustrating experiences in personal growth. You have the desire to change. You know what to do. You may even have the skills and the opportunity. Yet somehow, when it's time to act, you find yourself pulling back, hesitating, or engaging in behavior that undermines your own progress. It's as if there's a hidden script playing in the background, convincing you that success is either unsafe, unearned, or impossible.

Self-sabotage often masquerades as logic or humility, but its real motivation is fear. Fear of failure, fear of success, fear of rejection, fear of responsibility. And the tricky part is that it doesn't always show up as outright refusal to act. Often, it hides behind subtle behaviors and thought patterns that seem harmless at first.

Here are some of the most common signs of self-sabotage:

Procrastination: You delay important tasks or decisions, not because you're lazy, but because deep down, you're afraid of what will happen if you follow through. You may fear doing it wrong, being judged, or even succeeding and having to maintain the outcome.

Perfectionism: You set impossibly high standards for yourself, then avoid starting because you know you can't meet them. This "all-or-nothing" thinking keeps you stuck, spinning your wheels under the illusion of high standards.

Overcommitting: You say yes to everything and everyone, leaving yourself no time or energy for what really matters. This is often a subconscious strategy to avoid focusing on your true goals, where the risk of failure or exposure feels greater.

93

Chronic indecision: You analyze everything, hoping to avoid making the wrong choice. But in doing so, you avoid making any choice. And no progress gets made.

Negative self-talk: You constantly tell yourself that you're not ready, not good enough, or not qualified. These internal scripts shape your reality by influencing what you believe you can or should pursue.

Creating chaos: Sometimes, people unconsciously stir up drama or conflict just as things are beginning to go well. It's a way to pull the plug on momentum and return to a more familiar, if frustrating, baseline.

Let's look at a real-life example. Imagine someone who has always dreamed of starting their own business. They take courses, read books, and even begin planning their launch. But right before they're ready to go live, they convince themselves that the timing isn't right. Maybe they need one more certification, one more tweak to the website, one more month to prepare. A year goes by, and the business hasn't launched. That's self-sabotage masked as preparation.

Another example: someone finally starts seeing progress in their health and fitness journey. They're feeling better, gaining confidence. Then suddenly, they skip a week at the gym, binge on fast food, and say, "I knew I couldn't keep it up." This is classic upper-limit behavior. When things start going right, the subconscious mind kicks in and says, "This isn't who we are," and drags you back to your old normal.

These patterns are frustrating not because we're unaware of them, but because we often are aware but repeat them anyway. That's because self-sabotage is rarely about willpower. It's about subconscious programming. It's the beliefs you've internalized, often from childhood, about what you deserve, what's safe, and what's possible.

To identify self-sabotage, start by becoming an observer of your own behavior. Look for patterns, especially in areas where you feel stuck or keep falling short. Ask yourself:

What was I thinking right before I backed out?

What emotion do I associate with moving forward?

What story am I telling myself about what's possible or what I deserve?

Awareness is the beginning of change. Once you see the pattern, you can begin to challenge it. And that's where the real transformation begins. In the next section, we'll explore where these patterns come from and how to begin uprooting them at their source.

IV. The Roots of Fear and Self-Sabotage

Before we can overcome fear and self-sabotage, we have to understand where they come from. These aren't just bad habits or poor choices. They're rooted in deep psychological and emotional patterns that often developed long before we were aware of them.

Fear typically doesn't emerge out of nowhere. It is often influenced by previous experiences, unaddressed issues, or patterns learned during childhood. As children, we absorb messages about ourselves and the world based on how we're treated, what we hear repeatedly, and what we observe. If you were told you had to be perfect to be loved, you might grow up fearing failure. If you were criticized or rejected for speaking up, you may now fear visibility or confrontation. These early experiences form subconscious beliefs that shape how we see ourselves, what we expect from life, and what we believe we deserve.

Self-sabotage is often a defense mechanism. It's a way of staying safe, emotionally speaking. If success feels unfamiliar or unsafe, the subconscious mind will find ways to pull us back to what's comfortable, even if that "comfort zone" is filled with limitations. Your brain isn't trying to ruin your progress. It's trying to protect you from perceived threats. But the problem is, the threat is rarely real. It's a ghost from the past, still shaping your present.

Graham Cooke talks about how we often live from "orphan mindsets", the internal belief that we are alone, unworthy, or disconnected from love and purpose. These mindsets cause us to operate from fear instead of faith, striving for identity instead of living from it. When you don't know who you are or whose you are, fear takes the driver's seat. You try to control everything, protect yourself from pain, and avoid failure at all costs. And in doing so, you sabotage your ability to grow, to risk, and to fully show up.

Transformation begins when you recognize that these patterns are not permanent. They're not your identity. They're just programming and programming can be rewritten. Graham teaches that God is not interested in fixing the old version of you. He's about renewing your mind and awakening you to the truth of who you already are in Him. When you believe you are loved, chosen, and equipped, fear begins to lose its grip. You no longer have to prove yourself or protect yourself. You simply need to agree with what God already says about you.

Another key root of fear is unresolved emotional pain. Many people carry wounds from betrayal, failure, or loss that they've never fully processed. Those wounds become fear triggers. You might avoid relationships because of past heartbreak or resist leadership because of a time when you were humiliated. These aren't logical decisions, they're emotional reactions. And until those emotions are acknowledged and healed, the fear will continue to run the show.

So, how do you begin to uproot these destructive patterns? It starts with awareness, followed by grace. You can't shame yourself out of fear. But you can lovingly confront it. Ask yourself: Where did this belief start?

What am I trying to protect myself from? Is this belief aligned with truth, or with a past pain?

Then begin the work of reprogramming your mind with truth. This means intentionally focusing on scripture, affirmations, and teachings that reinforce your worth, your calling, and your identity. Speak truth out loud. Declare who you are. Surround yourself with voices that remind you of what's possible through faith.

Healing the roots of fear and self-sabotage isn't always quick, but it is possible. And once you start pulling up those roots, you'll find the soil is ready for something new; faith, confidence, purpose, and power.

V. The Role of Faith in Conquering Fear

Fear thrives in uncertainty, but faith thrives in truth. One of the most powerful tools you have to overcome fear is your faith, not just belief in yourself, but belief in something greater than yourself. Fear says, "What if I fail?" Faith says, "Even if I fail, God is still with me." And that changes everything.

Throughout scripture, we're told again and again not to be afraid. In fact, "Do not fear" is one of the most repeated commands in the Bible. Not because fear is a sin, but because God knew it would be one of the most persistent enemies we'd face. And He gave us the antidote: faith.

One of the clearest biblical principles for overcoming fear is found in 2 Timothy 1:7, which says, "For God has not given us a spirit of fear, but of power, love, and a sound mind." That verse alone redefines the conversation. If fear doesn't come from God, we don't have to entertain it. What we have been given is power (the ability to act), love (the assurance of being seen and valued), and a sound mind (the clarity to think and choose wisely). That's a strong foundation to stand on when fear shows up.

Faith is not denial. It doesn't pretend problems don't exist. It simply places greater trust in God's truth than in the circumstances. David didn't pretend Goliath wasn't real, he just believed God was bigger. When you anchor your faith in the promises of God, fear begins to shrink in comparison. It may still whisper, but it no longer has the final word.

Consider Joshua, who was tasked with leading an entire nation into a land filled with giants and fortified cities. He was stepping into shoes once filled by Moses, and the pressure was enormous. Yet God's instruction to him was simple and direct: "Be strong and courageous. Do not be afraid; do not be discouraged, for the Lord your God will be with you wherever you go" (Joshua 1:9). Joshua's courage didn't come from self-confidence. It came from God-confidence. The same can be true for you.

Another powerful story is that of Esther. A young woman thrust into the role of queen, faced with the life-threatening decision of whether to risk her life to save her people. Fear was real. But when her uncle Mordecai reminded her that she may have been placed in her position "for such a time as this," she chose faith. She acted, and her courage changed the course of history.

What about Peter? Yes, he sank when he took his eyes off Jesus, but don't miss the fact that he got out of the boat in the first place. Eleven other disciples stayed seated, paralyzed by fear. Peter walked on water because, for a moment, his faith was stronger than his fear.

Faith isn't just a belief. It's a choice, a posture, and a lens through which we see the world. When you decide to view your challenges through the lens of faith, your questions change. Instead of asking, "What if I fail?" you start asking, "What is God trying to teach me through this?" Instead of saying, "I can't handle this," you say, "I can do all things through Christ who strengthens me."

Faith doesn't eliminate fear completely. But it gives you the strength to act anyway. It helps you push through discomfort, make bold decisions, and stay grounded in the truth of who God says you are.

If you're facing fear today, whether it's fear of rejection, failure, success, or the unknown, let your faith lead. Speak God's promises over your situation. Pray with expectation. Surround yourself with people who speak life and remind you of the truth. And remember, courage isn't the absence of fear. It's moving forward in spite of it, with your eyes fixed on the One who goes before you.

VI. Techniques to Overcome Fear

Fear may be a universal emotion, but it doesn't have to be a permanent obstacle. You can learn to manage fear, move through it, and even transform it into fuel for progress. The key lies in developing practical strategies, methods that don't just make fear disappear, but give you the power to act in spite of it.

One of the most effective first steps in managing fear is naming it. Sounds simple, but many people avoid this. Fear thrives in ambiguity. The moment you define it, whether it's fear of failure, rejection, criticism, or the unknown, you begin to take away its power. Write it down. Say it out loud. Face it. You can't conquer what you won't confront.

Next, examine the story behind the fear. Often, fear is rooted in a false narrative we've been rehearsing subconsciously. "If I fail, people will laugh at me." "If I try again and it doesn't work, I'll prove I'm not good enough." These inner scripts are rarely accurate, and they're almost always exaggerated. When you bring those thoughts into the light, you can begin to challenge and reframe them.

Jim Rohn taught that personal empowerment begins with awareness and responsibility. He often said, "You cannot change your destination overnight, but you can change your direction." That applies directly to fear. You don't have to become fearless overnight, but you can change how you respond to fear starting right now. You don't have to wait until you feel brave to take action. Often, courage shows up after you move, not before.

Visualization is another powerful technique. Close your eyes and picture yourself succeeding at the very thing you're afraid of. See the conversation going well. See yourself stepping onto that stage, launching that product, having that hard conversation, and walking away stronger. Your brain doesn't fully differentiate between imagined and real experiences. The more vividly and repeatedly you visualize success, the more your brain builds neural pathways that support confidence.

Another method is progressive action. Instead of trying to leap over your biggest fear in one giant step, break it down. Take a smaller action today that moves you in the right direction. Afraid of public speaking? Start by sharing a short message on social media. Dreading a big sales pitch? Practice your script with a friend. Build momentum in small, manageable steps. Progress creates confidence.

Journaling is also a helpful tool. Write out your fears. Then write what's true. Write what God says about you. Write about how you've overcome challenges before. Let your own words become a record of faith, not fear.

Don't underestimate the power of movement and physiology either. Fear often creates physical tension. So, change your state. Go for a walk, exercise, or just breathe deeply. Stand tall, smile, even if you don't feel like it. These small physical changes can disrupt the fear loop in your brain and bring clarity.

And finally, speak life. Your words shape your experience. Stop repeating your fears as if they're facts. Start declaring your faith, your power, and your truth. Say things like, "I am equipped for this," "I've handled tough things before, and I'll handle this too," or "Fear doesn't get to decide for me today." Speak it until you believe it.

Jim Rohn frequently emphasized that success is not something you pursue; it's something you attract by the person you become. Overcoming fear isn't about chasing confidence, it's about building it from the inside out. When you take responsibility for your emotions and choose to act anyway, you're not just avoiding fear. You're transforming into someone stronger, wiser, and more resilient.

Fear may not disappear entirely. But it will stop running your life. And the more you apply these techniques, the easier it becomes to rise above fear, not by force, but by faith and action combined.

VII. Interrupting Self-Sabotaging Patterns

Self-sabotage is a silent thief. It doesn't often scream at you, it whispers. It convinces you to procrastinate, to shrink back, to play small. And unless you become intentional about spotting it, self-sabotage can slowly erode your momentum, your confidence, and your results.

The first step in breaking these patterns is awareness. You have to recognize when you're operating in sabotage mode. That begins by identifying your most common triggers. Is it perfectionism? The fear of being judged? An internal voice that says, "Why even bother?" For some, sabotage looks like overcommitting and then bailing. For others, it's waiting for the "perfect" time, which never comes. The patterns are often predictable, but only once you start tracking them.

Start by looking at your past. Think of moments when you backed out of something that mattered to you. What were the thoughts going through your head? What emotions were you feeling? What circumstances were present? Write these down. This becomes your sabotage map.

One of the most effective ways to disrupt self-sabotage is pattern interruption. This is a conscious act of doing something unexpected when the old habit tries to resurface. For example, if your go-to pattern when you're stressed is to scroll social media and numb out, the next time you feel the urge, take a walk instead. Or call a friend who encourages you. The key is to change your state quickly before the behavior locks in.

Another tool is replacement. It's not enough to simply stop a negative behavior; you must replace it with something constructive. If you typically avoid difficult conversations out of fear, replace avoidance with preparation. Practice the conversation. Write out your talking points. Speak it out loud. Do something that builds your confidence instead of allowing fear to take the wheel.

Set up micro-commitments to outsmart sabotage. If you've been self-sabotaging by never completing your goals, break your goals into such small steps that your brain has no reason to resist. Instead of "write a book," start with "write 100 words." Instead of "launch my business," start with "create one social post today." Small wins build momentum and chip away at the lie that says you can't follow through.

Journaling exercises are especially helpful in bringing sabotage patterns to the surface. Here are a few prompts you can use:

"Where in my life do I consistently feel stuck?"

"What emotions do I avoid feeling, and how do I avoid them?"

"When I get close to success, what tends to go wrong, and why?"

"What fear might be hiding behind this behavior?"

Once you've answered these, you're not just guessing anymore. You're seeing the pattern clearly. And what you can see, you can change.

It's also powerful to give your sabotage a name. That may sound strange, but naming your inner critic or self-sabotaging persona (e.g., "Doubtful Dave" or "Procrastination Patty") helps create separation between you and the pattern. The next time that voice shows up, you can say, "Nice try, Dave, but I'm doing it anyway." It gives you the upper hand.

Lastly, don't underestimate the power of accountability. When someone else knows your patterns, your goals, and your desired behaviors, they can call you out when they see sabotage creeping in. A mentor, coach, or trusted friend can provide the perspective you sometimes miss when you're stuck in your own head.

Self-sabotage thrives in silence and secrecy. But when you bring it into the light, examine it, and create simple yet powerful responses, you take back control. These patterns may have served a purpose once, usually protection, but they no longer serve the person you're becoming.

The path to freedom is not about being perfect. It's about being aware, intentional, and consistent. Every time you interrupt a sabotage pattern and replace it with something better, you're choosing progress over paralysis and building the life you were meant to live.

VIII. Mentorship and Accountability

When it comes to overcoming fear and self-sabotage, mentorship isn't optional; it's essential. You can only go so far on your own. Left to your own patterns, beliefs, and blind spots, you'll often repeat the same cycles, even with the best intentions. That's why having a mentor, someone who's walked the road ahead and can speak truth into your life, can be a game-changer.

Mentors offer something that's nearly impossible to give yourself: perspective. They can see when fear is disguising itself as logic. They can spot when you're procrastinating in the name of "planning." And they can help you name the real issue, something that often feels just out of reach when you're caught in your own head.

I remember one conversation with a mentor that changed everything for me. I had been circling the same goal for months. Every time I'd get close to taking action, I'd pull back. I told myself I needed more clarity, more time, or more money. But he wasn't buying it. He looked me straight in the eye and said, "You're not waiting on clarity. You're waiting for fear to go away. And it won't. You'll have to move with it."

That one line exposed the pattern I'd been running on a loop. It broke the illusion that I could think or plan my way out of fear. Mentorship has a way of cutting through the noise and calling you higher. Not with judgment, but with conviction. The kind that reminds you of who you are and what you're capable of.

Mentors also model what's possible. When you see someone who's faced their own fear and come out the other side, it gives you permission to believe the same is possible for you. Their journey becomes a roadmap. Their growth becomes proof. And their presence becomes a steady hand when yours feels shaky.

But mentorship alone isn't enough. You also need accountability; someone who will hold you to your word when your emotions start negotiating. Because let's be honest, when fear and self-sabotage kick in, your brain gets creative. It'll come up with excuses that sound noble and reasonable. "I need to pray about it more." "It's not the right time." "Maybe I'm not called to this after all." Accountability helps you test those excuses against your commitments.

Real accountability isn't about shame or pressure. It's about alignment. It's about having someone who knows what you said you wanted and won't let you settle for less. This could be a mentor, a coach, or even a peer who's walking a similar path. What matters is that they have your permission to challenge you and that you're humble enough to listen.

One of the most powerful ways to use mentorship and accountability together is through regular check-ins. Whether it's a weekly call or a quick message, knowing someone is going to ask you, "Did you follow through on what you said?" makes a huge difference. It shifts your actions from optional to essential.

Another benefit of mentorship is emotional grounding. Fear distorts reality. It magnifies the risk and minimizes your capability. But mentors speak to your identity, not just your performance. They remind you that your value isn't in your results, it's in who you are. That truth is often what you need most when fear is loud and failure feels imminent.

If you don't currently have a mentor, start looking. Pray about it. Be intentional. And when you find someone whose life, values, and results resonate with you, reach out. You don't need a formal agreement to start learning from someone. Listen to their content, read their books, apply their teachings, and show up ready.

Remember, the journey to overcoming fear and self-sabotage isn't meant to be walked alone. You need others. Not just cheerleaders, but truth-tellers. People who won't let you quit when it gets uncomfortable. People who see who you're becoming and call that version of you forward.

You were never meant to do this by yourself. And with the right mentor and accountability in place, you won't have to.

IX. Building Courage and Confidence

Courage and confidence aren't traits you're born with; they're muscles you build. And like any muscle, they require consistent, intentional exercise. The good news? You don't have to wait for a crisis or a huge opportunity to start building them. In fact, it's in the quiet, everyday choices that courage and confidence are forged.

Let's start with courage. Contrary to what many believe, courage isn't the absence of fear; it's action in spite of it. It's deciding to move forward even when your stomach's in knots and your mind is filled with "what ifs." Earl Nightingale once said, "Don't let the fear of the time it will take to accomplish something stand in the way of your doing it. The time will pass anyway." His words are a reminder that fear will always have a voice, but it doesn't get to be the final authority.

To build courage, start by taking small risks daily. Speak up in a meeting, post the video, say yes to the opportunity even when you feel underqualified. These aren't just tasks, they're training sessions. Every time you choose courage over comfort, you rewire your brain to expect growth instead of retreat. Over time, what once triggered fear will feel like a natural next step.

Now let's talk about confidence. Confidence grows when you keep promises to yourself. It's not about being the best in the room; it's about being aligned with your values and your vision. Earl Nightingale emphasized this point when he said, "We become what we think about." Confidence isn't a mystery. It's the byproduct of focused, intentional thinking followed by bold, consistent action.

Here are some daily practices to help you cultivate both:

1. Start with Morning Intentions: Begin your day with purpose. Review your goals, affirm your identity, and set a clear intention for how you want to show up. A strong start grounds you in clarity and gives you a psychological edge over fear.

2. Take: Aligned Action Daily: It doesn't have to be huge, but it has to be aligned. Do something each day that reflects the person you're becoming. It could be making a phone call, saying no to a distraction, or writing that page you've been avoiding. Action builds momentum, and momentum builds confidence.

3. Reflect on Your Wins: At the end of each day, take five minutes to review what you did well. Celebrate the moments you chose courage over comfort. This isn't about inflating your ego; it's about reinforcing the belief that you are capable and growing.

4. Reframe Fear as Fuel: Instead of trying to eliminate fear, reframe it. Fear often shows up at the edge of growth. That's a good sign. Use it as a cue that you're stretching, expanding, and doing something that matters.

5. Learn from the Lows: There will be setbacks. You'll miss the mark. That's part of the process. Confidence isn't built by never falling; it's built by getting back up. Each time you recover from failure or embarrassment, you grow stronger.

6. Speak Life: Be mindful of the language you use about yourself. Confidence is shaped by what you say repeatedly. Replace self-criticism with self-encouragement. Speak to yourself like you would a trusted friend or mentor.

Nightingale also taught that "success is the progressive realization of a worthy goal." That means courage and confidence aren't reserved for the finish line; they're developed in the process of showing up, day after day, in pursuit of what matters. The more progress you see, the more confidence you'll feel. And the more confident you become, the easier it is to take courageous action.

Remember this: you were created with strength, resilience, and the ability to rise. Fear may knock, but you don't have to answer. Every step forward, every act of obedience, and every decision to trust rather than shrink back is shaping you into someone unshakable.

Courage and confidence aren't reserved for the elite. They're available to anyone willing to take action in the face of fear, and that includes you.

X. Practical Exercises and Reflection

Knowledge without application changes nothing. That's why this section is dedicated to helping you do something with what you've just read. Breaking the grip of fear and self-sabotage isn't about a single decision; it's about a series of small, consistent actions that align with who you're becoming. These exercises are designed to help you build that consistency and get beneath the surface of your patterns so real change can begin.

Exercise 1: Identify the Fear

Start by naming your fear. Be specific. Most people say things like "I'm afraid of failure" or "I'm afraid of rejection," but that's just the surface. What's underneath?

Prompt:

What is a fear that keeps showing up for you when you try to move forward?

What do you believe will happen if that fear comes true?

Where did that belief come from?

Write without filtering. Let the real story come out. Often, just seeing it on paper robs it of some of its power.

Exercise 2: Track the Sabotage

For seven days, pay attention to when and how you self-sabotage. This may show up as procrastination, perfectionism, negative self-talk, or "playing small." Write down the time, situation, and thoughts that accompanied the behavior.

Prompt:

What triggers your self-sabotaging habits?

What are you trying to avoid when you engage in them?

Patterns only lose power when you can recognize them before they take over. Awareness is the first step toward mastery.

Exercise 3: The Fear Reframe

Once you've identified your fear and sabotage triggers, reframe them. This means telling yourself a new story, one based on truth, not panic or assumption.

Prompt:

What is a more empowering way to view the fear you've been holding?

What evidence do you have that contradicts the fear?

What does God say about this area in your life?

Write a statement that reflects this new truth and review it daily until it begins to replace the old fear-based narrative.

Exercise 4: Courage Reps

Every day for the next 10 days, do one thing that stretches you, something that challenges your comfort zone but aligns with your growth. It can be small. The goal is momentum, not perfection.

Examples:

Post a video sharing your message

Call someone you've been avoiding

Apply for an opportunity that feels "too big"

Speak the truth kindly in a situation where you usually stay silent

Prompt:

What's one courageous action you can take today that your future self will thank you for?

Track your actions and journal how you felt before and after. You'll likely discover that the fear was more bark than bite.

Reflection Questions

To wrap up this chapter, spend time with these questions. Write your answers honestly, without judgment.

What fears have I allowed to drive my decisions?

What self-sabotaging habits have held me back from living fully?

What would it look like if I responded with courage instead of fear?

How might my life change if I replaced hesitation with boldness?

What spiritual truths can I cling to when fear starts whispering again?

Bonus Practice: Visualization

Close your eyes and imagine a version of yourself who has broken through fear and left self-sabotage behind. See yourself taking bold steps, speaking with confidence, and living in alignment with your calling.

Spend five minutes each morning visualizing that version of you. This isn't wishful thinking, it's programming your subconscious to accept a new normal.

Remember, this chapter isn't about becoming fearless. It's about becoming faith-full. Fear will knock, self-doubt will linger, but now, you have tools. You have truth. And more importantly, you have a God who didn't give you a spirit of fear but of power, love, and a sound mind.

Let this be the chapter where you stop letting fear lead and start stepping fully into who you were born to be.

XI. Chapter Summary and Preview

Fear and self-sabotage are two of the most deceptive and destructive forces we face in personal growth. They wear many masks: procrastination, perfectionism, anxiety, and self-doubt, and they thrive in silence. But this chapter has revealed a critical truth: once fear is exposed and sabotage is recognized, both begin to lose their grip.

We started with the reality that fear is part of the human experience. It's not a sign of weakness; it's a signal. Sometimes it warns us of real danger. More often, though, it highlights the edge of our comfort zone. And it's in that space, just outside the familiar, where growth lives. By understanding the difference between rational and irrational fear, you've begun to reclaim your power. You've learned that fear doesn't have the final say unless you give it permission.

From there, we explored the sneaky nature of self-sabotage. It's not always loud or dramatic. Sometimes it shows up as that quiet voice saying, "Maybe tomorrow." Sometimes it's an invisible ceiling you keep hitting in your income, relationships, or progress, without realizing you're the one reinforcing it. The good news? Every pattern you've built, you can interrupt. And with awareness, intentionality, and faith, you can replace it with a new one.

We dug deep into the roots of fear and sabotage. We looked at the emotional and psychological drivers that fuel these patterns, often rooted in early experiences, wounds, or beliefs that no longer serve us. Then we layered in the transformative power of faith. We reflected on stories of biblical figures who faced enormous fear but moved forward anyway, trusting in something greater than themselves.

You also picked up practical techniques: exercises to name and reframe your fears, strategies to spot sabotage before it starts, and habits that anchor courage into your daily life. With mentorship and accountability, those tools become even more powerful. You don't have to walk this road alone. In fact, you're not meant to.

This isn't about flipping a switch and never feeling fear again. It's about recognizing that courage isn't the absence of fear, it's the decision to move forward in spite of it. It's about trusting that God has equipped you with everything you need to overcome, to heal, and to grow. When fear rises, you now have a choice. When sabotage whispers, you can respond with strength instead of surrender.

As you look ahead, carry these truths with you:

You are not your fear.

You are not your past patterns.

You are not stuck unless you choose to stay stuck.

You are capable, chosen, and equipped.

The next chapter will build on this momentum. You'll move from simply overcoming fear to cultivating a life of intentional courage, resilience, and action. You'll learn how to lead yourself with purpose even when the path is unclear. Because on the other side of fear is not just freedom, it's destiny.

Let this chapter be a turning point. Let it be the place where you stepped playing small and started leaning into who you were created to be. Keep going. Keep choosing courage over comfort. Keep rising when the old patterns try to pull you back.

You're not who you used to be. You're becoming someone stronger, wiser, and more grounded in truth. And the journey ahead will reflect that.

Are you ready for what's next?

Chapter 7: Discipline: The Bridge to Your Dreams

I. Introduction

I can still remember the time in my life when discipline shifted from being a word I avoided to a principle I embraced. It wasn't because I suddenly became more mature or woke up one day with supernatural willpower. It happened in the middle of one of the hardest financial times I'd ever faced. I was hustling multiple gigs, building a business on fumes, and trying to stay grounded in a world that felt like it was pulling me in every direction.

One morning, after another night of "I'll do it tomorrow," I found myself sitting at my kitchen table before sunrise. Bills were stacked to the left, my planner was open in front of me, and my journal stared back at me like it knew I wasn't doing what I said I'd do. I had goals, plans, and dreams. But I wasn't showing up for them, at least not consistently.

That's when the truth hit me. It wasn't a lack of desire that was holding me back. It was a lack of discipline.

And that realization changed everything.

Discipline, for many people, feels like punishment. We resist it because it sounds restrictive or rigid. But real discipline isn't about self-denial or perfection. It's about alignment. It's about choosing the long-term vision over short-term comfort. It's the bridge between knowing what to do and actually doing it.

You can read every book, attend every seminar, and set every intention imaginable, but if you don't develop the discipline to follow through, nothing changes. Motivation might get you started, but discipline keeps you going. And that's where transformation lives.

Jim Rohn once said, "Discipline is the foundation upon which all success is built. Lack of discipline inevitably leads to failure." That might sound harsh, but it's the truth. Discipline is the difference between people who talk about what they want and those who actually create it.

When you look at anyone who's achieved anything remarkable, whether in business, health, relationships, or spiritual growth, you'll find discipline at the core. It's the ability to maintain focus and perseverance when emotions fluctuate, outcomes are not instantly apparent, and distractions are prevalent.

In this chapter, we're going to unpack what real discipline looks like. We'll strip away the myths and replace them with truth. You'll learn why discipline matters more than talent, how it fuels consistency, and how it builds the internal strength necessary to overcome challenges and setbacks.

You'll also discover that discipline isn't just about willpower. It's about systems, routines, and creating an environment that sets you up to win. And it's about connecting your daily actions to a purpose that's bigger than you.

Discipline is the practical side of faith. It's saying, "I believe in what God has placed in me, and I'm willing to show up daily to bring it to life." It's not glamorous. It's not always exciting. But it's powerful and it works.

If you've struggled with consistency in the past, this chapter is going to help you break through. If you've found yourself starting strong but fading when life gets messy, you're going to learn how to stay anchored. And if you've ever believed the lie that discipline just "isn't your strength," we're going to rewrite that story together.

Because the truth is, discipline can be learned. It can be trained and strengthened. And when it is, it becomes one of the most freeing forces in your life. Discipline doesn't box you in, it builds the bridge to your dreams.

Let's walk across it together.

II. Defining True Discipline

For most people, the word "discipline" triggers a knee-jerk reaction. It brings up images of restriction, punishment, or being forced to do things you don't want to do. Maybe you think of a strict coach, a rigid parent, or a school rule you hated. No wonder so many people avoid it. But discipline, in its truest form, isn't about control; it's about freedom.

Let's reframe it. Discipline is doing what needs to be done, even when you don't feel like doing it. It's about honoring your commitments long after the feeling you had when you made them has faded. It's the quiet, consistent follow-through that turns potential into results.

Jim Rohn explained it best when he said, "Discipline is the foundation for achieving any worthwhile goal." He didn't mean forcing your way through life. He meant choosing structure over chaos, purpose over impulse, and clarity over confusion. Discipline is the muscle that lets you stick to your plan when everything in you wants to take the easy way out.

One of the biggest misconceptions is that discipline kills creativity or spontaneity. But the opposite is actually true. When you have structure in place, you create room for your best work to emerge. Your mind isn't cluttered with decisions like, "Should I do this today?" because the decision's already been made. You've committed. That clarity is powerful.

Bob Proctor often emphasized that discipline is about alignment with your purpose. He believed that your ability to discipline yourself is directly tied to how clearly you can see your vision. In other words, the stronger your why, the easier it becomes to stay the course. Discipline isn't just about habit, it's about vision alignment.

If you're unclear about where you're headed, discipline will always feel like a chore. But if you're lit up with purpose and anchored in a meaningful goal, discipline becomes the most empowering thing in your toolbox. It turns dreams into plans and plans into action.

Discipline is a decision. It's not something some people are born with and others aren't. It's not a personality trait. It's a choice. A choice you make over and over again, especially on the days when you'd rather not.

It's choosing the gym over the couch, the journal over the scroll, or the call over the excuse. It's choosing what you want most over what you want now.

When you really understand what discipline is, you stop fighting it. You stop thinking of it as deprivation and start seeing it as empowerment. Every disciplined action is a vote for the future you want to create.

And here's another shift in thinking: discipline isn't about perfection. It's about consistency. You're going to fall off. You're going to miss a day. But disciplined people don't let that derail them. They get back up, re-align with their purpose, and take the next step.

True discipline is also personal. It's not about doing what works for someone else. It's about finding your rhythm, your schedule, and your way of staying focused and on track. What works for a high-level executive might not work for a single parent building a side hustle. And that's okay. What matters is that you develop a system you'll actually stick with.

One of the most freeing insights I ever heard came from Bob Proctor. He said, "You're not disciplined because you're weak, you're undisciplined because you've never trained yourself to be otherwise."

That's empowering. It means you're not broken. You're just untrained. And training starts today.

So, take a moment to let go of every negative association you've ever had with the word "discipline." Replace it with a new one: freedom. Because that's what it really offers. The freedom to live on your terms. The freedom to become who you're meant to be. The freedom to show up with integrity, clarity, and power.

That's the true nature of discipline. And it's available to you right now.

III. Why Discipline Matters

If there's one trait that consistently separates the successful from the stuck, it's discipline. Not talent, not luck, not even passion. Discipline is what carries you when motivation fades. It's the bridge between the life you dream about and the life you actually build.

Discipline matters because success isn't about one big decision; it's about thousands of small ones, made consistently, day after day. Anyone can have a great idea. Anyone can get fired up at a seminar or post a motivational quote online. But very few people are willing to show up day after day, especially when it's inconvenient, uncomfortable, or downright boring. And that's what separates dreamers from doers.

Look at any area of life, business, relationships, health, faith, and you'll find this truth: results come from repeated, intentional action. You don't get fit from one workout. You don't build a thriving business with one post. You don't deepen your faith with one prayer. It's the disciplined follow-through that creates the breakthrough.

Think about an Olympic athlete. Talent may open the door, but it's discipline that keeps them training at 5 a.m., day after day, when nobody's watching. Think about a successful entrepreneur. It's not just vision that gets them where they are; it's the discipline to make the calls, track the numbers, and keep moving forward after setbacks. It's doing the work when it's not fun, when it's not flashy, and when no one's clapping.

Now let's bring it closer to home. Have you ever started something with excitement, only to abandon it when the initial rush wore off? Maybe it was a diet, a business plan, a new routine, or a personal goal. The missing ingredient likely wasn't knowledge or passion. It was discipline.

One of the biggest misconceptions is that discipline is restrictive, that it limits your freedom. But the opposite is true. Lack of discipline leads to chaos, stress, and regret. Discipline gives you control over your life. It helps you say no to distractions so you can say yes to your purpose. It's not punishment. It's protection. It guards your time, your energy, and your calling.

Practical example? Let's say you want to grow your business. You don't need a fancy funnel or perfect branding right out of the gate. You need the discipline to reach out to people daily, to follow up, to post content even when engagement is low, and to keep showing up, trusting that your consistency will compound.

Or maybe you're working on your health. You may not need a new supplement or a crash diet, but you do need the discipline to drink water, move your body, get enough rest, and make better food choices, even when no one's watching.

And in your spiritual life? It's not about having some deep, mystical moment every day. It's about showing up, opening the Word, praying, listening, and trusting. It's the quiet discipline of seeking God when it's not exciting, when it's inconvenient, and when you're tired or distracted. That's where the real transformation happens.

The truth is, discipline is the secret behind everything that works. It's the thread that ties success stories together. And the good news? It's a skill you can build. You don't have to be naturally disciplined. You just have to decide that who you're becoming is worth the effort.

Jim Rohn said, "Success is nothing more than a few simple disciplines practiced every day." Not occasionally. Not when you feel like it. Every day. And the beauty of that is, it takes the pressure off perfection. You don't have to be amazing all at once. You just have to be consistent.

So why does discipline matter? Because your future depends on it. Your freedom depends on it. And the life you really want is waiting on the other side of it.

You don't need to be perfect. You just need to be disciplined.

IV. Identifying Barriers to Discipline

Before you can master discipline, you've got to be honest about what's getting in the way. And let's be real, there's no shortage of barriers. If discipline was easy, everyone would be crushing their goals. But most people aren't. Not because they lack desire, but because they haven't learned to identify and overcome the things that quietly sabotage their consistency.

One of the biggest culprits? **Procrastination.** It shows up in a thousand different disguises, "I'll start tomorrow," "I need to do more research," or the classic "I just don't feel ready yet." But procrastination isn't about laziness. It's usually rooted in fear. Fear of failure, fear of success, or fear of judgment. So instead of moving forward, we stall out, delay, or wait for perfect conditions that never come.

Another barrier is **distraction.** We live in the noisiest time in history. Notifications, social media, and endless entertainment. It's all designed to steal your focus. You can have the best intentions to sit down and work on your business, read your Bible, or prep healthy meals, but one scroll turns into twenty minutes. One notification leads to a rabbit hole. Before you know it, the day's gone, and your priorities are buried under digital clutter.

Then there's **inconsistency.** This one's tricky because it often feels like you're doing the right things, but not long enough to see results. You start strong, then life happens. You get busy, distracted, discouraged. You skip a day. Then two. Then the whole thing unravels. And instead of regrouping, you beat yourself up and call it failure. But inconsistency isn't a character flaw. It's a sign you haven't yet built systems that support your goals.

So, how do you deal with these barriers?

First, get honest about your patterns. Journal them if you have to. When do you procrastinate most? What triggers your distractions? What usually derails your momentum? Awareness is the first step to breaking the cycle. You can't change what you're not willing to face.

Second, shrink the task. A lot of procrastination comes from feeling overwhelmed. So, simplify. Instead of saying, "I need to finish my entire funnel," say, "I'll write one email today." Instead of "I have to change my whole diet," say, "I'll prep one healthy meal." Small wins create momentum, momentum builds confidence, and confidence builds discipline.

Third, manage your environment. If your phone is stealing your focus, turn off notifications. Set app limits. Use airplane mode or do not disturb during your focused work time. Create a workspace that encourages your brain to engage. Don't rely on willpower alone; set yourself up to win.

Fourth, create a rhythm, not a rule. Rigid rules often lead to rebellion. But rhythms allow for grace and structure. Maybe you miss a morning routine one day. No problem, just reset. Don't throw it all out. A disciplined life doesn't mean a perfect life. It means you keep coming back to center. You keep choosing alignment.

Fifth, anchor your actions to your identity. You're not just building discipline for discipline's sake. You're becoming someone. You're stepping into the version of you that God already sees. Remind yourself daily, "I'm a disciplined person because I'm committed to my purpose. I do hard things. I follow through. I show up." Your actions follow your identity, not the other way around.

Discipline is never about pushing harder. It's about aligning better. When you identify and address what's really blocking you, whether it's fear, distraction, or inconsistency, you regain your power. You start to build a life that runs on intention, not impulse.

And here's the kicker: you don't need to remove every barrier before you get started. You just need to notice them, call them out, and make a different choice, one small action at a time.

V. Developing a Disciplined Mindset

Discipline isn't just about doing the right things. At its core, it's about how you think. Long before discipline shows up in your calendar or your habits, it takes root in your mindset. If your thinking is scattered, fearful, or excuse-driven, no habit will hold. But if your thinking is clear, focused, and anchored in purpose, discipline becomes your default, not your struggle.

One of the most powerful shifts you can make is to see discipline not as a restriction, but as a **freedom tool**. Most people think discipline means saying "no" to everything fun or enjoyable. But discipline doesn't steal your freedom, it gives it. Because when you're disciplined, you're not ruled by impulse. You're not jerked around by distractions or moods. You're in charge. You're free to choose what matters over what's easy. That's real freedom.

Napoleon Hill taught this principle with laser clarity. In Think and Grow Rich, he wrote, "Discipline comes through self-control. This means that one must control all negative qualities." He understood that mental discipline is about mastering your thoughts, not letting them master you. That takes work, but it's work that multiplies your results.

Let's talk about a few key mindset attitudes that fuel discipline:

1. Ownership. Disciplined people take full ownership of their lives with no blaming or excuses. If something's not working, they look inward before pointing outward. They've trained themselves to ask, "What can I do differently?" That mindset creates personal power. You stop waiting for circumstances to change and start showing up as the change-maker.

2. Long-term thinking. A disciplined mind isn't obsessed with instant gratification. It's playing the long game. You recognize that every shortcut has a cost, and every small action compounds over time. You learn to delay what you want now for what you want most. That's maturity and strength.

3. Emotional maturity. Discipline doesn't mean you feel like doing the right thing all the time; it means you do it even when you don't feel like it. You train your emotions to follow your commitments, not the other way around. Napoleon Hill called this "definiteness of decision." Once you've decided, your feelings don't get a vote. That's not being robotic, that's being grounded.

Now let's get practical. How do you actually train your mind to become more disciplined?

A. Use autosuggestion. Hill talked about the power of repeating your goals and affirmations daily, out loud, with emotion. Why? Because repetition rewires your beliefs. Say things like, "I am a disciplined person. I follow through, keep my word, and honor my purpose." Your subconscious mind starts to believe it, and when it does, your actions follow.

B. Practice visualization. Spend time daily seeing yourself living with full discipline. Picture yourself getting up early, making the tough calls, pushing through resistance. Imagine how it feels to succeed because you stayed the course. Your brain begins to normalize that identity, and soon, it becomes real.

C. Stay close to purpose. When discipline starts to slip, return to why you're doing it. Discipline without purpose becomes legalism. But discipline fueled by vision is powerful. Ask yourself, "What's at stake if I don't stay consistent?" Sometimes the fire needs to be relit by remembering what you're building and who you're becoming.

D. Monitor your inputs. Your thoughts are shaped by what you consume. Protect your mental diet. Read books that challenge you. Watch content that inspires discipline. Cut out voices that normalize mediocrity. Your environment isn't neutral; it's either pulling you up or dragging you down.

A disciplined mindset isn't something you're born with. It's something you build, one decision, one thought, one refusal to quit at a time.

You don't have to be perfect. You just have to be persistent. Because every time you choose to think like the disciplined version of yourself, that version grows stronger. And before long, discipline won't just be something you do, it'll be who you are.

VI. Faith and Discipline

Discipline doesn't just show up in productivity books or goal-setting seminars. It's deeply spiritual. In fact, Scripture is packed with wisdom about the connection between faith and discipline. While the world may see discipline as a willpower issue, the Bible teaches that it's a fruit of the Spirit, something cultivated in partnership with God, not something we muscle through alone.

Galatians 5:22–23 lists self-control (which is another word for discipline) as one of the fruits of the Spirit. That means discipline is the natural byproduct of a life that's surrendered to God. It grows out of relationship, not religion. You don't earn it, you yield to it. You let the Spirit work in you and through you, shaping your thoughts, your habits, and your responses.

Hebrews 12:11 takes it further: "No discipline seems pleasant at the time, but painful. Later on, however, it produces a harvest of righteousness and peace for those who have been trained by it." There's a powerful promise in that verse. If you're willing to be trained by discipline, if you're willing to go through the discomfort, it leads to something greater: righteousness, peace, and long-term fruit. God isn't interested in quick wins. He's shaping you for something eternal.

Look at the lives of the men and women God used most powerfully. They were people of deep, tested, unwavering discipline.

Moses spent forty years in the desert, first as a fugitive, then as a shepherd, and finally as a leader of a stubborn, complaining people. That kind of endurance doesn't happen without discipline. God gave him instructions, and he followed them down to the detail, even when the people rebelled. That's spiritual discipline: obeying God even when it's not popular, convenient, or immediately rewarding.

Daniel is another powerful example. When he was taken into Babylonian captivity, he could have easily compromised his values. Instead, Daniel "resolved not to defile himself" (Daniel 1:8). He disciplined his appetite, his time, and his prayer life. Even under threat of death, he kept praying three times a day. That level of consistency, even under pressure, made him stand out to kings and preserved his life through miracles. Daniel didn't just have faith, he had disciplined faith.

Paul the Apostle might be one of the clearest pictures of how faith and discipline work together. In 1 Corinthians 9:27, Paul writes, "I discipline my body like an athlete, training it to do what it should. Otherwise, I fear that after preaching to others I myself might be disqualified." Paul didn't coast on his calling. He brought his whole life under submission to his mission. He understood that gifting without discipline can disqualify you, but discipline anchored in faith will take you the distance.

The good news is you don't need to be a spiritual superstar to walk in discipline. You just need to be committed. Start where you are. If you're inconsistent in prayer, build the habit one day at a time. If you struggle with follow-through, ask God to strengthen you. Discipline doesn't have to be perfect to be powerful; it just has to be consistent and Spirit-led.

One of the most practical things you can do is to invite God into your routines. Ask Him to lead your schedule, your habits, and your plans. Then follow through with what He shows you, even when you don't feel like it. That's obedience. That's discipline. And every time you choose obedience over ease, you're building spiritual muscle.

Faith and discipline are not separate forces. They're partners. Faith gives your discipline purpose, and discipline gives your faith traction. Without discipline, faith stays in your head. But when you add discipline, faith becomes movement, action, and transformation.

So don't shy away from the hard work of discipline. Embrace it. Let it train you, stretch you, and grow you. Not for perfection's sake, but for the sake of the calling God's placed on your life. Because the dreams He's given you aren't just going to fall into your lap. They'll be built, step by disciplined step, with Him.

VII. Practical Methods for Cultivating Discipline

Discipline isn't something you're born with, it's something you build. Like a muscle, it grows stronger through consistent use. And the more you develop it, the more reliable it becomes, even when motivation is nowhere to be found. The good news is you don't have to overhaul your entire life overnight. Discipline is built through small, intentional choices that compound over time.

Let's start with your **daily routine**. One of the most powerful things you can do is structure your mornings. Mornings set the tone. They either anchor you or scatter you. A solid morning routine doesn't have to be complicated. It could be as simple as waking up at a consistent time, spending the first 15 minutes in prayer or reflection, reviewing your goals, and tackling your most important task first, before the distractions of the day pile up.

The goal here isn't perfection. It's consistency. If you only stick with your routine when you feel like it, it's not discipline, it's preference. True discipline kicks in especially when the feelings don't.

Earl Nightingale put it this way: "Success is the progressive realization of a worthy goal." He taught that discipline is the vehicle that moves us progressively toward that goal. It's not a flash of inspiration; it's the daily grind, the unseen moments, the private decisions, and the inconvenient choices made over and over again until they become automatic.

One method that works well is **habit stacking**. This means linking a new habit to something you already do. For example, if you drink coffee every morning, use that time to review your affirmations or journal your intentions for the day. If you brush your teeth at night, use that time to reflect on one win and one area you could improve. When you attach new habits to existing ones, they become easier to stick with and less likely to be forgotten.

Another powerful tool is **time-blocking**. This is simply the act of assigning specific times to specific tasks. Don't just write a to-do list, schedule it. Give your focus a destination. Without structure, your day will fill up with distractions, and discipline won't stand a chance. Time-blocking forces you to prioritize and creates guardrails for your energy.

Let's also talk about **environmental cues**. Your environment should support the disciplined version of you. That may mean removing distractions, setting up visual reminders, or changing where you work, pray, or reflect. If your phone is your biggest distraction, set limits or leave it in another room during focused work time. If you're serious about your goals, you have to design your environment to make discipline easier and resistance harder.

It's also vital to **track your progress**. Discipline grows when you see results. Whether it's checking off boxes on a calendar, using an app, or journaling your consistency, find a way to measure the steps you're taking. Earl Nightingale reminded us, "We become what we think about most of the time." Tracking helps you keep what matters most in front of your mind.

And when setbacks come, and they will, don't beat yourself up. Instead, use them as checkpoints. Ask yourself: "What threw me off? What can I do differently tomorrow?" Discipline isn't about being perfect. It's about recommitting every time you fall off track.

People who succeed don't have more willpower than you. They've just trained themselves to show up, whether they feel like it or not. They've built habits that do the heavy lifting when motivation runs dry. They've stopped relying on emotional highs and started trusting systems and structure.

So, if you want to cultivate discipline, don't wait for motivation. Start with structure, stack small wins, set clear priorities, limit distractions, and track your progress. And above all, stay anchored to your why.

Because when discipline becomes a lifestyle, success stops being a possibility and starts becoming inevitable.

VIII. Role of Mentorship in Enhancing Discipline

If there's one secret weapon that can fast-track your growth, sharpen your discipline, and keep you focused when life gets noisy, it's mentorship. Discipline can be forged in solitude, but it's strengthened in community. A mentor provides what no planner, podcast, or productivity app can: real-time accountability, wisdom rooted in experience, and a living example of what's possible.

Mentors don't just inspire, they challenge. They help you see the blind spots you'd otherwise ignore. They don't let you settle for half-hearted effort or hide behind excuses. A good mentor will tell you the truth when you need to hear it, not just when it's convenient or flattering. And that's exactly what makes their influence so powerful when you're working to build consistent discipline.

I remember a time in my life when I was spinning my wheels. I had goals, a vision, and a long to-do list, but I was making very little actual progress. I was great at planning and dreaming, but poor at execution. That's when a mentor of mine stepped in. She didn't criticize or condemn. She just asked one powerful question: "What did you commit to last week, and did you follow through?" When I hesitated to answer, she didn't let me off the hook. She pressed further, not to shame me, but to help me see the gap between what I said I wanted and what I was actually doing.

That one conversation woke me up. And it didn't stop there. Week after week, she held me to my word. If I made a commitment, she expected results. If I didn't follow through, she asked why, and made me face the choices I was making. Through her guidance, I started to show up differently. I didn't just want to avoid disappointing her, I wanted to live up to the version of me she believed in.

That's the power of mentorship. A mentor helps you live with intention. They help you shift from being someone who talks about what they'll do to someone who does what they said they would. They hold the line when your emotions waver. And most importantly, they remind you who you're becoming, especially when you forget.

Jim Rohn once said, "You are the average of the five people you spend the most time with." If that's true, and it is, then choosing the right mentors is one of the most disciplined decisions you can make. Because the people you follow shape your standards. If your inner circle cuts corners, procrastinates, or lacks follow-through, that will eventually rub off on you. But if your mentor models integrity, excellence, and consistency, you'll start raising your game without even realizing it.

Sometimes we think of mentors as unreachable icons, but they don't have to be industry legends or best-selling authors. A mentor can be someone a few steps ahead of you, someone living out the kind of discipline and focus you want to cultivate. They don't need to be perfect, they just need to be walking in the direction you're headed.

So, how do you find a mentor like that? Start by looking for fruit. Don't just listen to what people say, watch how they live. Do they follow through on commitments? Do they stay consistent even when it's inconvenient? Do they operate from values and purpose rather than emotion or pressure? Those are the kinds of people who can sharpen your discipline.

Once you find that person, approach with humility and clarity. Share your admiration and ask if they can offer guidance. And if they say yes, honor their time. Show up prepared. Do what you say you'll do. That's how you make the most of a mentoring relationship, and that's how you build a life grounded in discipline.

Discipline doesn't thrive in isolation. It's cultivated through challenge, accountability, and consistent encouragement. And there's no better source of that than a mentor who believes in your potential and won't let you waste it.

IX. Overcoming Setbacks with Discipline

Every worthwhile pursuit comes with setbacks. Discipline is easy when life is smooth, when your energy is high, and the path is clear. But what about when things go sideways? What happens when the progress stalls, the doubts creep in, and nothing seems to be working? That's where true discipline is tested and strengthened.

Setbacks are not signs that you're off track. More often than not, they're part of the process. They reveal where your commitment lies and whether your actions are rooted in emotion or conviction. When you operate on emotion, you'll quit as soon as it gets uncomfortable. But when your discipline is driven by values, you keep going, even when the motivation fades.

One of the most important lessons I've learned is that discipline isn't about being perfect. It's about being committed. That means showing up when you don't feel like it. It means keeping your word when circumstances shift. And it means choosing progress over excuses, again and again.

Graham Cooke often talks about spiritual resilience, this deep, unwavering steadiness that comes from knowing who you are in God. He teaches that when setbacks come, you don't react from panic or fear; you respond from identity. That mindset shifts everything. You stop seeing challenges as threats and start seeing them as opportunities for refinement. As he puts it, "You don't fight from a place of defeat, you fight from victory."

That doesn't mean setbacks won't sting. They do. They test your resolve. They expose your weak points. But they also invite growth. When handled with discipline, setbacks become the very pressure that forges strength. They clarify what you truly want and what you're willing to go through to get there.

Let me be real with you, there have been times when I wanted to give up. Times when I questioned the dream, the path, and even myself. But every single time I chose to stay consistent, to honor the process instead of abandoning it, I grew. The breakthrough didn't always come instantly, but the person I became through the discipline of showing up? That version of me was stronger, wiser, and more prepared for what came next.

Discipline doesn't mean pushing through blindly. Sometimes, it means pausing to rest, reflect, and recalibrate. That, too, is part of resilience. But you rest with purpose, not as an escape. You don't abandon the mission, you regroup so you can return stronger.

When you hit a wall, lean on structure. Go back to your routines. Rely on the habits you've built. This is why those daily disciplines matter so much, because when your emotions are all over the place, habits give you stability. They remind you that your identity isn't tied to your current results. It's tied to your consistency.

Surround yourself with people who won't let you spiral. This is where mentorship and community are crucial. When you're tempted to pull back or disappear, they remind you of your why. They speak truth when your inner voice is clouded with fear or frustration.

And here's something you need to know: every leader, every high achiever, every person of purpose has faced setbacks. It's not the absence of struggle that defines them; it's how they respond. They don't let a bad day turn into a bad week. They don't let failure write the final chapter. They stay grounded. They stay disciplined.

So, when the storms come, and they will, stand firm. Revisit your vision. Reconnect with God. Reaffirm your values. Then take the next step, no matter how small.

That's what discipline looks like in hard times. It's not glamorous, and it's not always Instagram-worthy. But it's real. It's where growth happens. And if you stay faithful through the storm, you'll come out on the other side with more than just results, you'll come out refined.

Because discipline isn't just what gets you started. It's what carries you through.

X. Practical Exercises and Reflection

Discipline isn't something you master once and never revisit. It's a muscle, one that grows stronger through consistent, intentional use. And like any muscle, it needs structure, tension, and repetition to develop. This section is all about giving you practical ways to strengthen that discipline muscle day by day, step by step.

Let's start with simple, high impact exercises you can implement immediately.

Exercise 1: The Daily Non-Negotiables

Choose three small, meaningful actions you will complete every single day; no exceptions. These should align with your values and goals. For example:

- Read 10 pages of a personal development or spiritual book
- Write down your top 3 priorities for the day
- Spend 10 minutes in quiet reflection or prayer

These aren't meant to be grand gestures. They're meant to build consistency. When you follow through on small things, your confidence grows, and your ability to handle bigger challenges increases.

Exercise 2: The Discipline Audit

At the end of each week, take 15–20 minutes to conduct a personal discipline audit. Ask yourself:

- Where was I consistent this week?
- Where did I make excuses?
- What triggered me to fall off track?
- What small shift can I make to strengthen my follow-through next week?

Honest reflection creates self-awareness, and self-awareness fuels change. You can't correct what you won't confront. This weekly audit keeps you from drifting and gives you a chance to make real-time adjustments.

Exercise 3: The "One-Thing" Method

Each morning, ask yourself: What is the one thing I could do today that would make the biggest impact on my goals? Then discipline yourself to do it first, before distractions, before emails, before the chaos of the day takes over.

It's easy to get busy. But discipline isn't about doing more. It's about doing what matters most. This one practice can transform your productivity and restore your focus.

Exercise 4: Commitment Contract

Write out a 30-day commitment contract with yourself. Define exactly what you will do, when you will do it, and why it matters. Sign and date it. Post it somewhere you'll see every day.

This isn't just symbolic. It's psychological. When you put your intentions in writing, you raise the level of seriousness. And when you see it daily, you reinforce your commitment and identity.

Now, let's go deeper with a few reflection prompts. These aren't just "feel-good" questions. They're designed to challenge you, to expose patterns, and to anchor you in truth.

Reflective Questions:

1. **What does discipline mean to me personally?**
   Is it punishment? Restriction? Or is it freedom, structure, and alignment? How has my view of discipline helped or hindered my growth?

2. **What area of my life needs the most discipline right now?**
   Be specific; your finances, health, spiritual life, relationships, or time management. Where am I avoiding responsibility? Where is inconsistency costing me?

3. **What excuses do I tend to use most often?**
   "I'm too busy," "I'm tired," "I'll do it tomorrow." List them all.
   Then write down a truth that counters each excuse.

4. **Who do I become when I follow through on my commitments?**
   Describe the version of yourself that shows up when you're
   locked in and disciplined. How does it feel? What's different?
   How do others respond to you?

5. **What would change in my life if I stayed disciplined for the next 90 days?**
   Dream big but stay grounded. Visualize the momentum. Write
   out how you would feel, what you would achieve, and what
   internal shifts might take place.

Discipline isn't about restriction. It's about alignment. It's choosing your
future over your feelings. And these exercises aren't just tasks to check
off, they're tools to help you live from the person you know you're
meant to be.

Stay consistent, stay accountable, and stay honest.

Because discipline doesn't just build results, it builds character. And your
character is the foundation your dreams are built on.

XI. Chapter Summary and Preparation for Next Steps

Discipline is often misunderstood. It's not a harsh taskmaster, nor is it a
trait reserved for a select few who were just "born with it." As we've
explored in this chapter, discipline is a bridge; one that connects where
you are right now to where you truly want to be. It's not just about
routines and responsibilities. It's about honoring your vision, keeping
your promises to yourself, and choosing purpose over preference.

We began this chapter with a personal story to illustrate what happens when discipline kicks in, not as a forced grind, but as a powerful ally in creating lasting change. That kind of transformation doesn't happen by accident. It's born from daily choices, from leaning into structure when it would be easier to coast, and from holding yourself to a higher standard because you know there's more in you.

We defined what discipline really is, and just as importantly, what it's not. It's not punishment. It's not perfectionism. It's the consistent application of what matters most. Jim Rohn and Bob Proctor helped us see that discipline is the key that unlocks the life we desire. It's how we build character, create momentum, and close the gap between intentions and results.

We explored the reasons why discipline matters. It's not a nice-to-have; it's the foundation of personal leadership. We looked at practical examples, from health to business to spiritual growth, where consistent discipline created exponential impact.

We got honest about the barriers: procrastination, distractions, and inconsistency. Everyone deals with them. What separates those who grow from those who stay stuck is how they respond to those barriers. Discipline means facing those resistance points with courage and strategy.

We walked through the mindset needed to sustain discipline. Drawing from Napoleon Hill's teachings, we identified the importance of clarity, decision, and repetition. The disciplined mind doesn't rely on emotion to act; it relies on commitment and vision.

We then turned our focus to faith. Discipline isn't just a secular strategy; it's a deeply spiritual principle. The Bible repeatedly honors discipline as a reflection of character, obedience, and preparation. From Joseph to

Paul, we saw how discipline shaped the lives of those who walked with God and carried great purpose.

You were given practical methods to cultivate discipline: daily routines, environment shifts, mindset training, and advice from Earl Nightingale on mastering the mundane. The key isn't to try harder, it's to build better systems. Your results don't lie, they're telling you what your habits are producing.

We also talked about mentorship, how critical it is to surround yourself with people who embody the discipline you want to live out. You don't need more information. You need inspiration, accountability, and modeling. Real growth happens when someone walks with you and calls you higher.

And finally, we addressed the reality of setbacks. Discipline doesn't make you immune to struggle, it makes you resilient in the face of it. Graham Cooke reminded us that persistence isn't just about trying harder; it's about holding onto your identity when circumstances try to shake it.

So, what now?

Here's your challenge: don't just admire the idea of discipline, live it. Pick one area of your life where inconsistency has been costing you: your health, your time, your walk with God, your business, and commit to a 30-day focus. Start small, start steady, but start now.

Use the exercises and reflections from this chapter to guide your progress. Return to them often. As you build these habits into your daily life, you'll notice something powerful: your confidence will rise. Not because life is easier, but because you are stronger.

Discipline won't always feel exciting. But it will always be worth it. It's how you move from hoping for change to creating it. From dreaming about your potential to stepping into it.

You've crossed another important threshold in this journey. And the road ahead is full of opportunities, not just to do more, but to become more.

So, carry this discipline forward. Let it shape the next chapter of your life with intention, strength, and purpose.

The bridge to your dreams is built. Now walk it, one disciplined step at a time.

Chapter 8: Managing Your Mind: Mastering Emotional Control

I. Introduction

I remember a day that should've been a major win. We had just wrapped up a big event, something I had poured my heart and soul into for weeks. The numbers were solid. The energy in the room was great. People were engaged, taking notes, and even lining up to talk afterward. From the outside, everything looked like a success.

But the moment I got back to my car, I completely lost it. My chest tightened. My mind raced. I sat there, overwhelmed by a sudden wave of anxiety and doubt. All I could think was, "Did I mess something up?" "Did I come across as fake?" "What if no one actually got value from what I shared?"

There was no real trigger. Just a flood of emotion that didn't match reality. I wasn't reacting to facts, I was reacting to old patterns, old fears, and old stories I hadn't fully dealt with. And in that moment, it became clear: mastering your emotions is not optional if you want to live at your highest potential.

We talk a lot about strategy, planning, and execution in business and personal growth. The ability to manage your emotions consistently may be the single most important skill you ever develop. Why? Because your emotions determine your energy. And your energy determines your decisions, your pace, your follow-through, and your relationships.

If you don't manage your mind, your emotions will manage you. They'll hijack your focus, derail your confidence, and keep you stuck in reactive mode, especially in high-pressure situations. And if you're trying to build a life of purpose, impact, or legacy, you simply can't afford to let emotional chaos run the show.

Emotional mastery doesn't mean pretending you don't feel things. It's not about hiding your feelings or pretending to be okay when you're struggling inside. It means developing the maturity and self-awareness to recognize what's happening, pause, and choose your response, rather than being ruled by your reactions.

I've learned that the more responsibility you carry, the more crucial emotional control becomes. Whether you're leading a business, a team, a family, or your own personal comeback story, you're going to face resistance. You're going to feel frustration, discouragement, jealousy, doubt, and disappointment. That's part of the human experience. But you don't have to live from those emotions. You can acknowledge them, learn from them, and keep moving in alignment with who you're becoming, not who you used to be.

This chapter is about learning how to take your power back. It's about developing the inner tools that help you stay grounded, clear-headed, and purpose-driven, even when life throws curveballs. You'll learn how to identify your emotional triggers, shift your internal dialogue, and build patterns that support emotional resilience.

We'll pull wisdom from legends like Jim Rohn, Earl Nightingale, Bob Proctor, and Graham Cooke. But more than that, we'll make it practical. Because you don't need more theory, you need tools that work in the heat of the moment, when emotions are high and clarity is low.

Whether you're facing fear before a big decision, battling shame from a past failure, or simply trying to stay focused when distractions and drama are calling your name, emotional mastery is the key to staying on track. It's not just about being in control, it's about being free.

You were made to lead. You were made to rise. But first, you have to master the battlefield between your ears.

Let's dive in.

II. Understanding Emotional Triggers

Emotional triggers are internal switches, small moments or situations that evoke a strong emotional response, often disproportionate to the event itself. They're typically rooted in past experiences, deeply held beliefs, or unresolved pain. And while they may seem sudden or irrational on the surface, emotional triggers are usually predictable patterns we've developed over time.

To understand how emotional triggers shape behavior, think of them as emotional "landmines." When someone steps on one, perhaps unintentionally, they don't cause the explosion; they simply activate something that was already buried inside you. Maybe it's a tone of voice that reminds you of a parent who always criticized you. Or it's a colleague who gets praised for something you did better but never got recognized for. Suddenly, you're not just annoyed, you're spiraling. That's a trigger in action.

In business and personal development, these moments are everywhere. A team member who challenges your authority might not be attacking you, but your immediate defensiveness could suggest a deeper fear of inadequacy. Or maybe a prospect ghosts you after a great conversation, and you go from confident to questioning your worth in minutes. These emotional spikes aren't logical, they're habitual. And unless they're identified, they'll keep running the show.

Here's the tricky part: most people don't realize they're being triggered. They just think they're "having a bad day," or "that person made me mad." But in reality, what's happening is internal. The external situation is just the spark.

For example, I once had a heated exchange with a teammate who missed a deadline. On the surface, my frustration looked justified. But after cooling off and doing some honest reflection, I realized what was really driving my reaction was an old belief that "if I don't control everything, it will all fall apart." That belief wasn't about my teammate, it was about my own fear of things slipping through the cracks and being blamed for failure. Once I recognized that, I was able to have a calm, constructive conversation instead of reacting from anxiety.

Emotional triggers aren't inherently bad. They're signals, opportunities to grow. Every time you get emotionally hijacked, there's a deeper belief or unresolved issue trying to get your attention. And when you pause and examine it, you regain control.

This level of awareness takes practice. Start by tracking your reactions. When you feel your emotions spike, whether it's anger, fear, jealousy, or anxiety, pause and ask:

- What just happened?
- What story am I telling myself about this moment?
- Where have I felt this way before?

The goal isn't to suppress emotion, but to understand its source. From that place of clarity, you can respond with intention instead of reaction.

In business, this kind of emotional intelligence is a superpower. It allows you to stay grounded during tough conversations, make rational decisions under pressure, and lead from a place of strength rather than insecurity. In your personal life, it helps you communicate with grace, deepen relationships, and avoid unnecessary conflict.

Understanding your emotional triggers is the first step toward mastering them. And once you start recognizing those patterns, you can begin to rewrite the scripts that have held you back for years.

Because you don't have to be at the mercy of your emotions. You can be the author of them.

III. Why Emotional Control Matters

One of the most powerful distinctions you'll ever make in your personal growth journey is the difference between reacting and responding. At first glance, they may seem similar, but the outcomes couldn't be more different. A reaction is automatic, impulsive, and usually based on fear or ego. A response, on the other hand, is intentional, measured, and grounded in clarity and purpose.

When you're reactive, your emotions control you. You lash out in anger, retreat in fear, or make poor decisions in the heat of the moment. The consequences often create damage, lost opportunities, broken trust, and regret. But when you practice emotional control, you slow down, assess the situation, and respond from a place of strength and purpose. You lead your emotions instead of being led by them.

Jim Rohn once said, "It's not what happens that determines your life's future. It's what you do about what happens." That simple truth is the foundation of emotional mastery. Life is going to throw curveballs. People will disappoint you. Plans will fall through. But those events don't define you. How you choose to respond does.

Emotional control is what separates those who live reactively from those who lead intentionally. It's what allows a leader to stay calm under pressure, a parent to teach rather than yell, a business owner to recover from setbacks with grace instead of panic. And it's what helps you make better decisions, not just when things are easy, but especially when things get tough.

Earl Nightingale spoke frequently about the role of thought in shaping emotion and behavior. He believed that we become what we think about, and our emotions follow the dominant thoughts we dwell on. If your inner world is filled with negativity, resentment, or fear, your emotional state will reflect that. But if you cultivate a mindset of gratitude, faith, and purpose, your emotional life becomes a source of power and stability.

There's also a compounding effect. When you consistently practice emotional control, you build trust; with yourself and with others. People see you as stable, dependable, and wise. You stop second-guessing your every move and start showing up with conviction. That kind of emotional maturity opens doors that pure talent or ambition never could.

Let's be clear: emotional control isn't about suppressing or denying your feelings. It's about mastering the space between stimulus and response. It's recognizing that while you can't always control what happens, you can control how you interpret it and what you do next.

Think about a business situation where a partner bails last minute, or a deal falls through. The reactive person panics, blames, or gives up. The intentional person pauses, breathes, assesses the facts, and takes the next wise step. That one choice, to respond instead of react, can mean the difference between spiraling or soaring.

In your personal life, it's no different. Emotional control can transform your relationships. Instead of lashing out when you feel hurt, you communicate with honesty and empathy. Instead of shutting down, you stay engaged. Instead of escalating conflict, you become a calming presence.

Practicing emotional control doesn't mean you'll never feel triggered or upset. It means you don't live in that state. You acknowledge the emotion, process it, and then move forward with intention.

This level of control is built through daily practice. Mindfulness, reflection, journaling, and prayer. These are not fluffy routines. They are your training ground for emotional mastery.

The truth is, emotional control is not just a soft skill. It's a superpower. It affects every area of your life: your leadership, your relationships, your performance, and your peace. When you learn to respond with wisdom instead of reacting from impulse, you gain a kind of freedom most people never experience.

And that freedom? It's where true power lives.

IV. Identifying Your Emotional Patterns

One of the most powerful steps you can take toward emotional mastery is to begin noticing your own patterns, those recurring emotional reactions that show up in familiar situations and quietly sabotage your progress. They're subtle at first, often disguised as "normal" responses. But over time, they become emotional loops, repeating the same story and yielding the same results.

Maybe you've noticed that every time you start to gain momentum in your business, you feel overwhelmed and pull back. Or perhaps, when someone questions your ideas, you shut down or get defensive. These are not random occurrences. They are emotional patterns, ingrained responses formed by past experiences, fears, and internal beliefs.

The challenge with emotional patterns is that they often operate just beneath the surface. We don't always see them until they've already steered us off course. That's why awareness is key. You can't shift what you don't first recognize.

Start by reflecting on moments where your emotions overpowered your clarity. What triggered you? Was it criticism, uncertainty, failure, or comparison? Now look deeper: what belief was hiding behind that emotional reaction? Was it "I'm not good enough," "I always mess things up," or "They're better than me"? These beliefs act like emotional landmines, and when they get stepped on, your body reacts even before your mind can catch up.

One of the most effective tools for uncovering these patterns is journaling. Set aside 10 minutes each evening and write down the emotional highs and lows of your day. Ask yourself:

- When did I feel out of alignment today?
- What triggered that emotion?
- What did I believe in that moment?
- How did I respond?
- What could I have done differently?

Over time, you'll begin to see patterns, emotions that repeat, triggers that are consistent, and behaviors that show up like clockwork. That awareness gives you power. Because once you see a pattern, you can interrupt it. You're no longer reacting blindly. You're choosing consciously.

Another helpful practice is emotion tracking. Use a simple log or an app to track your emotional state throughout the day. At regular intervals, perhaps morning, mid-day, and evening, pause and identify what you're feeling. Give it a name. Frustrated? Anxious? Peaceful? Energized? Don't judge the emotion, just name it. Then jot down what's happening around you and what thoughts are running through your mind.

This simple act of tracking does two things. First, it creates space between you and your emotions, making it easier to respond instead of react. Second, it reveals trends over time. You may realize that specific tasks, conversations, or environments consistently lead to stress or discouragement. With that clarity, you can begin making small adjustments, changing how you prepare for those moments, how you recover from them, or how you reframe them.

Bob Proctor often said, "If you can hold it in your head, you can hold it in your hand." That applies to emotions, too. If you can identify and reframe the thought that's fueling the feeling, you can change your emotional experience.

Emotional patterns are not fixed. They're learned, which means they can be unlearned. And when you begin replacing old patterns with new ones, patterns of patience, resilience, faith, and confidence, you not only feel better, you perform better, lead better, and live better.

This isn't about becoming emotionally perfect. It's about becoming emotionally aware. Because awareness leads to choice, and choice leads to change. The more you learn to observe your emotions without judgment, the more you'll be able to transform them into fuel for growth rather than anchors of fear.

Your emotions don't have to run the show. But they can show you where the work is, and that's where true progress begins.

V. Faith and Emotional Stability

One of the most overlooked sources of emotional strength is faith; faith in God, in His plan for your life, and in the promises He's already made. Faith isn't just a belief; it's a stabilizing force. When emotions rise and chaos swirls, faith becomes the anchor that keeps you grounded.

Scripture repeatedly reminds us that emotional stability is not only possible, it's expected of those who walk closely with God. Philippians 4:6–7 says, "Do not be anxious about anything, but in everything, by

149

prayer and petition, with thanksgiving, present your requests to God. And the peace of God, which transcends all understanding, will guard your hearts and your minds in Christ Jesus." That's a powerful promise, not just that peace is available, but that it can guard your heart and mind. That's emotional protection rooted in spiritual truth.

Faith teaches us patience, especially when life doesn't move at our pace. Isaiah 40:31 says, "But those who wait on the Lord shall renew their strength; they shall mount up with wings like eagles." Waiting isn't easy. It tests your emotions and challenges your confidence. But that waiting, when done in faith, produces strength and clarity that rushing never will.

Consider the emotional maturity of biblical figures like Joseph. Betrayed by his brothers, sold into slavery, and wrongfully imprisoned, he had every reason to live in bitterness, anger, and fear. But Joseph held fast to his vision and trusted God's timing. He remained emotionally steady even when circumstances made no sense. That consistency positioned him for leadership and eventually allowed him to forgive those who had harmed him.

Then there's David, the man after God's own heart. His psalms are filled with raw emotion, joy, grief, fear, courage, but he always circled back to trust. In Psalm 42:11 he wrote, "Why, my soul, are you downcast? Why so disturbed within me? Put your hope in God, for I will yet praise Him." David didn't deny his emotions. He brought them to God, processed them in faith, and then chose to rise above them.

Emotional maturity isn't about suppression. It's about submission, submitting your emotions to God, not your circumstances. When fear hits, faith says, "I trust You anyway." When anger flares, faith whispers, "Lord, help me respond in love." When uncertainty clouds your path, faith holds the line: "He who began a good work in me will carry it to completion."

Faith also teaches us to rely on the Holy Spirit, who produces in us the fruit of emotional stability. Galatians 5:22–23 says, "But the fruit of the Spirit is love, joy, peace, patience, kindness, goodness, faithfulness, gentleness, and self-control." These aren't traits we have to manufacture. They grow naturally when we stay rooted in God's presence.

You don't need to be emotionally perfect to walk in peace, but you do need to be spiritually connected. The more time you spend in the Word, in prayer, in honest dialogue with God, the more equipped you'll be to handle emotional storms with wisdom and grace.

Even Jesus modeled emotional mastery. In the Garden of Gethsemane, He felt deep sorrow and anguish. He wept, He prayed, He asked for another way. But then He said, "Not My will, but Yours be done." That's emotional surrender. That's divine strength in the face of overwhelming pressure.

Faith doesn't numb your emotions, it transforms them. It takes fear and replaces it with trust. It takes anger and replaces it with grace. It takes impatience and replaces it with perspective. And over time, those changes don't just influence how you feel, they change who you become.

You become steady, not shaken. Peaceful, not panicked. Grounded, not grasping. And in a world full of emotional instability, that kind of faith-based strength becomes a beacon for others.

VI. The Role of Thoughts in Shaping Emotions

Your emotions don't just appear out of thin air. They are directly influenced by your thoughts. What you dwell on internally eventually shows up externally, on your face, in your tone, in your actions, and in your energy. This is why mastering your mind begins with managing your thoughts.

Bob Proctor taught this principle with absolute clarity: thoughts are the primary cause of feelings. In his teachings, he often explained that everything begins with a thought, and that thought creates a vibration, an emotional response. That emotional response then influences behavior. If you want to change how you feel or act, you must first address the thought that triggered the emotion in the first place.

Here's a simple but powerful way to visualize it: Thought $\rightarrow$ Feeling $\rightarrow$ Action $\rightarrow$ Result. If you want a different result in your life, you must go back and examine the thoughts that are producing the feelings and actions that are leading you to your current reality.

This awareness is empowering because it puts the responsibility, and the power, back in your hands. You're not at the mercy of your emotions. You're the thinker. You can change the thought, and in doing so, you can change the emotional climate within you.

Let's say you're feeling anxious about an upcoming conversation with a team member or business partner. That anxiety didn't generate itself. It came from a string of thoughts, maybe you started imagining the worst-case scenario, or replaying a past conflict. Your nervous system responded to those thoughts as if they were real, and now you're in fight-or-flight mode. But what happens if you shift your thinking?

What if you tell yourself, "I've prepared. I've grown. This conversation will bring clarity, not conflict"? That new thought produces a new feeling, perhaps calm or confidence. And from that emotional state, your actions will look and sound completely different.

Bob Proctor emphasized the power of repetition and focus in reshaping your mental patterns. The more often you think a thought, the more it embeds itself into your subconscious mind. This is why affirmations, visualizations, and declarations are so effective; they're not just about positive thinking. They are tools for programming new belief systems.

Here are a few techniques you can start using to shift your thought patterns and gain greater emotional control:

1. **Thought Awareness Journaling**
    Spend a few minutes each day writing down the thoughts that dominate your mind. Especially when you're feeling off emotionally, ask yourself, "What am I thinking right now?" This helps you identify recurring patterns that are fueling negative emotions.

2. **Pattern Interrupts**
    When you catch yourself spiraling into negative thinking, interrupt the pattern immediately. Stand up, say something out loud, snap your fingers, or take a brisk walk. Break the cycle physically, then redirect your thoughts intentionally.

3. **Affirmation and Meditation Practice**
    Choose affirmations that speak directly to the areas you struggle with emotionally. For example, if you often feel overwhelmed, affirm, "I am grounded. I handle challenges with peace and clarity." Meditate on these truths until they begin to feel real.

4. **Scripture Reframing**
    Use biblical truth to reframe your thoughts. If fear arises, meditate on 2 Timothy 1:7 "For God has not given us a spirit of fear, but of power and of love and of a sound mind." Replace the thought of "I can't handle this" with "God is with me and equips me for every challenge."

5. **Visualization**
    See yourself responding with grace and composure in situations that normally trigger you. The mind doesn't distinguish between

what's vividly imagined and what's real. Visualization rehearses your future emotional responses.

You don't need to be a victim of emotional highs and lows. By mastering your thought life, you're taking control at the source. And as Bob Proctor would say, when you change your thinking, everything else follows. Your feelings stabilize, your actions align, and your outcomes begin to reflect the new mindset you've built, one thought at a time.

VII. Responding Instead of Reacting

One of the clearest indicators of emotional mastery is your ability to respond rather than react. The difference might sound subtle, but it's massive in how it shapes your relationships, decisions, and leadership. A reaction is immediate, impulsive, and emotionally charged. A response is thoughtful, intentional, and grounded in self-awareness.

Reactions come from your conditioning. They're often rooted in past experiences, fears, or emotional wounds. When something triggers you, whether it's a harsh comment, a setback, or unexpected pressure, your nervous system wants to defend or control the situation. You lash out, shut down, or make a decision you later regret.

Responses, on the other hand, come from a place of maturity and alignment. When you respond, you pause. You reflect. You assess what's happening internally before you take action externally. This gives you power. It keeps you from being emotionally hijacked by the moment.

Jim Rohn once said, "It's not what happens that determines your life's future. It's what you do about what happens." That's the heart of emotional responsibility. Life will throw you curveballs. People will let you down. Circumstances will test you. The question is not whether those things will happen. The question is, how will you respond?

One of the most effective tools for shifting from reaction to response is the emotional pause. This is the practice of creating space between stimulus and action. When you feel that surge of emotion, instead of acting immediately, stop. Breathe. Name the emotion. Ask yourself, "What is this really about?" and "What would my highest self do in this moment?"

You can even use a short script to guide yourself through these moments. Here's one example:

Pause. Breathe. What am I feeling? What's triggering this feeling? What outcome do I want here? What response aligns with who I'm becoming?

Practicing this simple inner dialogue can prevent you from sending that heated text, saying something you can't take back, or making a decision from fear rather than faith.

Another helpful technique is reframing. When something upsets you, ask, "How else can I see this?" or "What might God be trying to teach me here?" Shifting your perspective helps you regain emotional balance and see the bigger picture.

Jesus modeled this kind of emotional mastery beautifully. When He was falsely accused, mocked, and ultimately crucified, He didn't react with rage or revenge. He responded with purpose, clarity, and grace. He said, "Father, forgive them, for they do not know what they are doing" (Luke 23:34). That's not passivity, that's power under control. That's the ultimate example of response over reaction.

If you want to build this skill into your life, start small. Notice when you're triggered during minor frustrations: traffic, emails, interruptions. Practice the emotional pause. Use the script. Journal afterward about what you felt and how you handled it. Over time, you'll become less reactive and more grounded. And the people around you will notice.

Emotional growth isn't about becoming numb or detached. It's about becoming wise. It's about being able to feel fully without being controlled by those feelings. You're not bottling emotions up, you're stewarding them.

The goal is to lead yourself well, especially in moments when it would be easier to lose control. Because how you handle those moments determines the trust people place in you, the peace you carry within you, and the growth that flows through you.

The more you train yourself to respond rather than react, the more authority you'll have, not just over your circumstances, but over yourself. And that kind of self-mastery is what creates lasting impact.

VIII. Managing Emotions Under Pressure

Pressure has a way of revealing who we are. When the stakes are high and the stress is real, our emotional foundation is tested. In these moments, we're either governed by fear and overwhelm, or grounded by clarity and calm. The ability to manage emotions under pressure is not just a nice-to-have; it's essential for anyone serious about growth, leadership, or long-term success.

Stress doesn't just show up in life's dramatic moments. It often creeps in during decision deadlines, financial uncertainty, leadership responsibility, or when juggling family, business, and personal growth. The pressure to perform, to not fail, to meet expectations, both external and internal, can trigger old emotional patterns if you haven't done the work to stay grounded.

When things get intense, the untrained mind defaults to chaos. Thoughts race and worst-case scenarios flood in. You might feel paralyzed or reactive. But this is exactly when your emotional mastery matters most.

Anyone can stay calm when life is calm. But emotional maturity shows up when storms roll in.

Graham Cooke often teaches that peace is not the absence of pressure but the presence of identity. When you know who you are, and Whose you are, you can face any situation with calm authority. You stop being tossed by every wave of emotion and instead learn to ride the storm from a place of rootedness.

Cooke uses the analogy of Jesus asleep in the boat during the storm (Mark 4:35–41). While the disciples panicked, Jesus rested. Why? Because He was secure in His identity, His authority, and His purpose. He knew the storm didn't have the final say. He carried peace within, and that peace became power over the storm. That's a picture of true emotional control under pressure.

So, how do you get there?

The first key is **preparation**. Emotional stability is built in advance, not in the heat of the moment. Daily disciplines like prayer, meditation, gratitude, and affirmations reinforce your internal anchors. These practices may seem simple, but they create spiritual muscle memory so that when the pressure hits, you're not scrambling for grounding, you're already standing on it.

Next, **breathe and center**. In high-stress situations, your breath becomes shallow and your thoughts race. Simply pausing to take deep, intentional breaths helps activate your parasympathetic nervous system and restore clarity. Combine breathwork with a centering question like, "What matters most right now?" or "Who do I want to be in this moment?" These reset your focus and identity.

Another practice is to **slow down your reactions**. Pressure makes people speed up. But the wise thing to do is to slow down, mentally.

emotionally, and verbally. Delay your decisions, take a walk, or pray. Consult someone you trust. Let your emotions catch up to your spirit. Don't act from panic, act from principle.

Also, **lean on identity-based thinking**. Remind yourself: "I am calm." "I am capable." "I was made for this." Speak truth over the noise of fear. This isn't about pretending you don't feel pressure. It's about choosing what voice you'll listen to under pressure, the voice of fear or the voice of faith.

Finally, **expect pressure** as part of growth. Don't be surprised by it. Instead, prepare for it. Accept it as a training ground, not a sign of failure. When you embrace pressure as a teacher, not an enemy, you rise above it with grace.

Leadership, influence, and personal transformation don't happen easily. They're forged in pressure. But pressure doesn't have to crush you. With the right mindset and practice, it can strengthen you, refine you, and reveal your truest self.

Remember, storms don't expose your weakness. They expose your foundation. So, build it strong. Anchor it in truth. And when pressure comes, you won't just survive it, you'll shine through it.

IX. Mentorship and Emotional Resilience

If emotional resilience is the ability to bounce back stronger from adversity, then mentorship is the trampoline. Wise counsel has the power to accelerate your emotional growth and ground you when life threatens to unravel your composure. No one builds lasting emotional control in isolation. We all need people who see clearly when we can't, who believe in us when we doubt ourselves, and who remind us who we are when the pressure gets heavy.

There's something powerful about having a mentor who's been where you are and walked through their own emotional valleys. They don't just offer theory, they speak from experience. And because they've weathered storms and stayed standing, they're able to help you navigate your own storms without falling apart. That's the beauty of mentorship: it compresses time. You get the benefit of someone else's hard-earned wisdom, so you don't have to learn everything the hard way.

I remember a time when I was spinning emotionally. I had just experienced a major setback in my business, and self-doubt was eating me alive. I wasn't just disappointed, I was angry, embarrassed, and questioning whether I was cut out for leadership at all. I called my mentor, hoping for a quick pep talk. What I got instead was a hard truth: "You're letting your emotions drive the car. And they're taking you off a cliff. Get back in the driver's seat."

It wasn't said harshly. In fact, it was spoken with so much clarity and compassion that I couldn't even be offended. That moment snapped me out of my spiral. It reminded me that emotional leadership doesn't mean never feeling doubt or frustration; it means not giving those emotions control of your decisions.

Good mentors don't rescue you from your emotions. They help you own them. They teach you to name what you're feeling, understand where it's coming from, and choose how to respond. That's the essence of emotional maturity: the ability to feel fully without being ruled by your feelings.

Another mentor once told me, "Don't trust your emotions to tell the whole truth, but do trust them to tell you something needs attention." That changed how I viewed emotional triggers. Instead of resisting or repressing them, I started to examine them. What story was I believing? What fear was being poked? What expectation had I set that wasn't met?

Over time, I noticed patterns. I saw how I reacted harshly when I felt disrespected, or how I shut down when I feared disappointing others. And each time I brought those patterns into mentorship conversations, my awareness grew, and so did my control. That's the fruit of wise counsel. It acts like a mirror, helping you see what's going on inside so you can shift what's happening outside.

In the Bible, we see examples of mentorship playing a pivotal role in emotional development. Think of Moses and Joshua. Moses mentored Joshua through moments of fear, doubt, and leadership pressure. By the time Joshua took over, he had not just learned Moses' strategies, he had developed emotional resilience by watching how Moses handled conflict, fatigue, and rejection. He was prepared not just practically, but emotionally.

The same is true for you. If you want to grow in emotional control, find someone who models it. Pay attention to how they respond under stress, how they speak when angry, and how they reset after disappointment. Ask questions, invite feedback, and let them challenge you. The more you lean into those relationships, the more resilient you become.

And if you're further along on your own journey, consider mentoring someone else. There's something deeply grounding about helping others grow. It reinforces what you've learned and calls you to a higher level of consistency.

At the end of the day, mentorship isn't about perfection, it's about progress. It's about doing life with people who help you return to center faster, stay grounded longer, and grow deeper than you could on your own. When emotional storms come, and they will, you'll have the support, wisdom, and resilience to weather them well.

X. Practical Exercises and Reflection

Emotional mastery is not a one-time achievement, it's a lifelong discipline. It grows through repetition, reflection, and honest self-assessment. This section offers practical exercises to help you increase emotional awareness, regulate your responses, and deepen your internal stability. These tools aren't just for moments of crisis; they're for cultivating strength every single day.

1. The Emotional Awareness Journal

Start by keeping a simple daily log. At the end of each day, reflect on key emotional moments. Use the following prompts:

- What triggered a strong emotional response today?
- What emotion did I feel most intensely (anger, fear, joy, guilt, etc.)?
- How did I react in that moment?
- In hindsight, how could I have responded more intentionally?
- What belief or thought fueled that emotion?

This exercise will increase your awareness of emotional patterns. Over time, you'll start to spot recurring triggers and uncover the stories driving your responses. This insight is the first step to emotional mastery.

2. Emotional Pause Practice

The next time you feel emotionally overwhelmed, practice pausing before reacting. Count slowly to ten. Take three deep breaths. Then ask yourself:

- What am I feeling?
- What is the real issue here?
- What outcome do I want from this moment?

- How can I respond in alignment with who I want to be?

This brief pause gives your higher reasoning mind a chance to engage before your emotional instincts take over. The more you practice this, the more natural it becomes.

3. The Thought Audit

Thoughts fuel emotions. To change how you feel, you often need to change how you think. Once a week, take time to audit the dominant thoughts you've had. Ask:

- What thoughts dominated my week?
- Were they empowering or limiting?
- What thoughts triggered positive emotions?
- Which ones stirred anxiety, fear, or frustration?
- What truth-based thought can I replace a limiting belief with?

This audit, inspired by Bob Proctor's work, helps you retrain your internal dialogue, which directly affects how you feel and act.

4. Scripture for Emotional Grounding

Choose a few Bible verses that speak directly to emotional strength. For example:

- "Be still and know that I am God." – Psalm 46:10
- "Do not be anxious about anything..." – Philippians 4:6-7
- "For God gave us a spirit not of fear but of power and love and self-control." – 2 Timothy 1:7

Write these verses on cards or keep them on your phone. When emotions run high, read them aloud. Let these truths recalibrate your perspective and bring you back to center.

5. The Weekly Reflection

Set aside 30 minutes at the end of each week to reflect on your emotional growth. Ask yourself:

- Where did I handle emotions well this week?
- Where did I struggle to maintain control?
- What emotional win am I proud of?
- What challenge do I want to handle better next time?
- What is one action I can take this week to grow in emotional mastery?

Use these reflections to adjust your focus. Progress happens when you're both honest and intentional.

6. Identify Your Emotional Anchors

Think of five things that reliably restore peace or clarity when you feel emotionally off. These could be:

- Prayer or worship music
- Going for a walk or exercising
- Talking with a mentor or trusted friend
- Revisiting a favorite book or sermon
- Spending time in nature

Keep this list handy. In moments of stress, go to one of these anchors. They don't eliminate emotions, but they help stabilize you so you can respond wisely.

Emotional control isn't about becoming numb or stoic. It's about becoming responsive instead of reactive. It's about choosing how you show up, even when emotions surge. These exercises will help you build that strength, day by day, decision by decision. Keep practicing, reflecting, and growing. Emotional maturity is within reach, and it's one of the greatest gifts you can give to yourself and everyone you influence.

XI. Chapter Summary and Preview

As we close this chapter on emotional control, let's pause to recognize just how far you've come in understanding and managing your internal world. Emotional mastery isn't about denying how you feel; it's about recognizing your emotions, understanding their origin, and choosing to respond in ways that align with your purpose and identity. In a world driven by reaction, learning to respond with intention sets you apart.

We began by unpacking the idea of emotional triggers, those moments or situations that ignite strong emotional responses. By identifying your triggers, you gained insight into how seemingly small events can spark a cascade of thoughts and feelings. We walked through real-world examples in both personal and business contexts to show that this isn't just theory, it's practical, daily work that brings clarity and peace when applied consistently.

From there, we explored the difference between reactive and intentional behavior. Emotional control is not about suppression; it's about elevation. You don't shove emotions down or pretend they don't exist. Instead, you rise above the initial wave and choose your next move. As Jim Rohn said, "Don't let your emotions control you. Control your emotions." That's what separates people who drift from those who lead with purpose.

We examined how emotional patterns form and how to track them over time. These patterns often operate in the background, but once exposed, they can be redirected. By keeping a journal, reflecting weekly, and doing thought audits, you now have tools to assess how you're doing and course-correct when needed.

We also looked at the spiritual side of emotional strength. Biblical principles taught us about patience, peace, and inner resilience. Figures like Jesus, David, and Paul showed us what it looks like to navigate turmoil without being consumed by it. Their lives were not free from hardship, but they demonstrated how to stay anchored through every storm.

Then we moved into the mechanics of emotional transformation; shifting thoughts to shift emotions, responding instead of reacting, and staying grounded under pressure. Bob Proctor's wisdom reminded us that feelings are secondary. They're created by our dominant thoughts. Change your thinking, and your emotional life will begin to stabilize and empower rather than sabotage.

You also learned how to tap into practical tools like pause techniques, scripting intentional responses, and using emotional anchors. Whether it's prayer, walking, journaling, or a scripture you turn to, these tools are now part of your emotional toolbox.

Mentorship came into play, too, because emotional resilience doesn't grow in isolation. Having a wise, grounded voice to walk alongside you can cut years off your learning curve. Personal stories showed how mentors offered not just insight but presence in emotionally difficult times, reminding you that you're not alone in your journey.

Finally, we wrapped up with exercises designed to take these concepts from theory to transformation. It's not enough to read about emotional mastery, you must live it. Reflect, act, and adjust. That's where real growth lives.

Looking Ahead

Now that you've learned how to manage your emotions, it's time to move forward with bold, intentional action. Chapter 9 will guide you through the process of taking inspired action, not just doing more, but doing what truly matters.

It's one thing to have clarity and emotional control. It's another to step into your life with direction, courage, and momentum. In the next chapter, you'll learn how to turn the internal shifts you've made into visible change in your world. You'll explore the difference between busy work and meaningful action, how to overcome hesitation, and how to develop habits that move you toward your God-given purpose.

Because ultimately, emotional control is the foundation, but action is the bridge. It's how we turn inner alignment into outer impact. You were never meant to stay stuck in emotional cycles. You were created to rise, move, and create. And now, you're ready to take that next step.

So, take a deep breath. A new chapter of growth, momentum, and purpose begins now.

Chapter 9: Inspired Action: Moving Beyond Intentions

I. Introduction

I remember a time in my life when I was obsessed with planning. I had notebooks full of ideas, goals, vision boards, affirmations, everything. I was reading all the right books, listening to the top personal development leaders, and even attending conferences. On paper, it looked like I was headed for a breakthrough. But the truth was, I was stuck. I was mistaking preparation for progress. I had the intention to change my life, but very little actually changed.

One particular moment stands out. I had committed to launching a new project that I was genuinely excited about. I had told people about it. I had even set a deadline. But the day came and went, and nothing happened. Why? Because I never moved from planning into execution. I was waiting to feel ready. I kept tweaking things, overanalyzing, second-guessing, and convincing myself that more preparation was necessary. In hindsight, I wasn't being strategic, I was hiding behind the illusion of progress. I was comfortable in motion but resistant to action.

That experience taught me a vital lesson: **intentions don't change your life, actions do.**

There's a massive difference between having good intentions and taking inspired action. Intentions are rooted in thought. They feel good. They give you the illusion of movement. You can set them, talk about them, and even feel proud of them. But without action, they're powerless. They don't build businesses, restore relationships, or develop character. Intentions are the spark, but they aren't the fire.

Inspired action, on the other hand, comes from a deeper place. It's not just about effort, it's about alignment. It's when your decisions are fueled by conviction, clarity, and a sense of divine timing. Inspired action often feels risky. It doesn't always come with guarantees. But it's bold. It's faith in motion. And it's what bridges the gap between who you are and who you're becoming.

The reason so many people stay stuck is because they confuse thinking about a thing with doing the thing. They feel emotionally rewarded just by setting the intention, and so they stop there. But real transformation only happens when you put feet to your faith. When you stop waiting to feel ready and start showing up anyway.

Taking inspired action doesn't mean you'll have it all figured out. In fact, you probably won't. But it does mean you've made a decision to stop circling the mountain and start climbing it. It means you're done rehearsing the reasons why it's not the right time, and instead you're asking, "What's the next step I can take with what I already know?"

This chapter is going to challenge you to move. Not from pressure, fear, or comparison, but from purpose. You'll learn the difference between forced hustle and spirit-led momentum. You'll recognize the traps of overthinking and hesitation, and more importantly, how to break through them. You'll see how faith, clarity, and commitment work together to produce action that isn't just productive, but transformational.

So, if you've been stuck in planning mode, if you've been sitting on dreams that you know are meant to be lived out, this is your chapter. It's time to shift from "I want to" to "I'm doing it." Not perfectly. Not all at once. But with intention, integrity, and inspired action.

Let's move.

II. The Trap of Good Intentions

Good intentions are sneaky. They feel noble. They sound admirable. They give you the impression that you're on the right track. And in some ways, they are a necessary starting point. But left unchallenged, good intentions can become a trap that keeps you stuck in inaction, all while convincing you that you're making progress.

Here's the hard truth: goals and plans alone don't change your life. You can have the most detailed vision board in the world, the smartest SMART goals, and the clearest five-year plan, but none of it matters if it isn't backed by action. You might impress others with your aspirations, but dreams without movement eventually turn into regret.

Jim Rohn said it plainly: "What's easy to do is also easy not to do." That quote hits like a punch to the gut when you're being honest with yourself. The truth is, the gap between knowing and doing is where most people lose. They read the books. They take the courses. They attend the seminars. But they don't apply. They don't follow through. Why? Because it's easier to consume than it is to commit. It's easier to plan than to push past resistance.

Intentions are safe. They don't require risk. You can dream big and still stay in your comfort zone. But action, especially inspired action, requires courage. It demands clarity, faith, and a willingness to be uncomfortable. This is why many people stay stuck in the trap of good intentions. It gives them just enough momentum to feel productive, without ever having to face the resistance that real action stirs up.

Let's be honest. How many times have you told yourself:

- "I'll start Monday."
- "I just need to get more organized first."
- "Once I finish this book, I'll be ready."

- "I just need a little more time."

These are well-dressed excuses. They hide in the language of preparation, but they delay execution. Jim Rohn also said, "If you don't make a plan for your own life, chances are you'll fall into someone else's plan. And guess what they have planned for you? Not much."

Intentions without follow-through don't just waste time. They erode confidence. Every time you say you're going to do something and then don't, you train your subconscious mind not to believe you. Over time, your self-trust deteriorates. You stop expecting yourself to follow through. And once that happens, you become a slave to hesitation.

The remedy? Action. Imperfect, messy, sometimes awkward action. That's where growth lives. That's where momentum is built. Every time you act in spite of fear or uncertainty, you close the gap between who you are and who you're becoming.

But here's the nuance: we're not talking about frantic busyness or hustle for the sake of movement. We're talking about aligned action, steps that are in sync with your calling, your purpose, and your values. Inspired action feels different. It's not always comfortable, but it's always true. It's the kind of action that requires trust, not just in your ability, but in the bigger picture.

So, if you find yourself caught in the trap of good intentions, take a breath. Then take inventory. What have you been meaning to do that you haven't done? What idea have you been nurturing in secret but haven't brought to life? What decision have you been avoiding because you're afraid to fail?

Start there. And then move, not because you're perfectly ready, but because the cost of waiting is too high.

Good intentions won't take you to your dream. Only action will.

III. Defining Inspired Action

At some point on your journey, you'll be faced with two options: to hustle your way through with brute force and sheer willpower, or to move forward from a place of clarity, alignment, and conviction. The difference between those two paths is massive. One drains you. The other energizes you. One leaves you burned out. The other leaves you fulfilled. That's the difference between forced effort and inspired action.

Inspired action isn't just about doing more. It's about doing what matters, what aligns with your purpose, your values, and the deeper calling inside you. It's not random motion; it's targeted movement with meaning behind it. It's not reactionary; it's intentional. Inspired action flows from the inside out.

But let's be clear: inspired action doesn't always feel easy. Sometimes, the nudge from within calls you to do something bold or uncomfortable. You might feel fear, hesitation, or uncertainty. But underneath all that, there's a knowing. A sense that this is your next right step. That knowing is what separates inspired action from impulsive action or forced effort.

Forced effort is usually driven by pressure, external expectations, self-imposed deadlines, or a need to prove something. It often leads to burnout because the energy behind it is rooted in fear, anxiety, or scarcity. You're pushing, striving, grinding, but there's no peace in it. No rhythm. Just noise.

Inspired action, on the other hand, carries momentum. It comes with a sense of divine timing. It often feels like doors open as you move, not always easily, but purposefully. There's grace in it. And that grace doesn't mean there's no effort; it means your effort is met with flow. It's as if

171

your steps are guided, and things begin to line up in ways you couldn't have orchestrated on your own.

When you take inspired action, you're responding to something greater than emotion. You're answering a call, not just checking a box. You're moving because something within you has aligned, your faith, your purpose, your belief, and now your action becomes a reflection of that alignment.

This doesn't mean you wait around doing nothing until you "feel inspired." That's a trap, too. Waiting for motivation can turn into procrastination. The key is learning to quiet the noise and listen for that deeper prompting, the one that comes from your inner compass, your relationship with God, and your clarity of purpose.

Graham Cooke talks about moving from identity. He teaches that when you know who you are, what you do becomes obvious. That's the heart of inspired action. It doesn't come from striving to become someone. It comes from knowing who you already are and acting in alignment with that truth.

So, how do you recognize inspired action? Here are a few signs:

- It aligns with your values and purpose, even if it challenges your comfort zone.
- It brings a sense of peace, even in the presence of fear.
- It creates momentum, not just movement.
- It feels like a partnership, with God, with your true self, with being in the moment.

And perhaps most importantly, inspired action leaves a residue of fulfillment. Even if the results aren't immediate, you know you moved in truth. That's powerful.

So instead of asking, "What should I do next?" try asking, "What step feels aligned with who I'm becoming?" or "What is God prompting me to do that I've been ignoring?" Let those questions guide your movement.

Because real transformation doesn't come from scattered effort. It comes from taking the right steps at the right time, led by the right spirit.

That's inspired action. And it changes everything.

IV. How Inspiration Works

Inspiration isn't just a random emotional high or a fleeting moment of motivation. It's the ignition point for meaningful movement. It's the spark that makes action feel not only possible but necessary. True inspiration reaches beyond hype and taps into the deep well of emotional and spiritual fuel that drives you forward with purpose.

To understand how inspiration works, you have to start by recognizing its source. It doesn't come from scrolling social media or getting hyped up by temporary external stimulation. Those things can create excitement, but excitement fades fast. Real inspiration is internal. It rises from your core, from your identity, your values, your relationship with God, and your vision for the life you know you were created to live.

Emotionally, inspiration stirs something within you. It's the moment when your heart connects with a possibility and you feel compelled to move. Maybe you hear a story that mirrors your own, or you see someone doing what you've only dared to dream about. Suddenly, you remember that your own dream is still alive. Inspiration reawakens desire. It reminds you that you're made for more, and that taking action isn't just optional, it's essential.

Spiritually, inspiration is even more powerful. It's a prompting, a divine nudge, a whisper from God saying, "This is the way. Walk in it." It's not always loud or obvious. Sometimes it comes as a quiet knowing. Other times it's a surge of clarity that cuts through the noise and brings deep peace. Either way, inspiration tied to divine prompting carries weight. It doesn't just excite you, it anchors you.

Graham Cooke often speaks about living from identity rather than striving for approval or chasing success. He teaches that when you truly understand who you are in God's eyes, fully loved, fully accepted, fully equipped, you begin to live and move from a place of rest and confidence. That's when inspiration becomes powerful. Because it's no longer about proving yourself or keeping up with others. It's about expressing who you already are.

Cooke's perspective invites us to shift from asking, "What should I do?" to "What am I being invited into?" This reframes action as a response, not a requirement. It makes space for partnership with God. Instead of forcing outcomes, you start listening for divine guidance. You begin to act not from pressure but from prompting.

That doesn't mean inspired action is always comfortable. Often, it leads you into unfamiliar or challenging territory. But the difference is this: inspired action feels purposeful even when it's difficult. There's a sense of "I was made for this," or "I'm being led here for a reason," even if you don't fully understand the outcome.

Inspiration also thrives in clarity. When your vision is muddled, it's hard to feel inspired. That's why it's important to regularly revisit your values, your goals, and your identity. Journaling, prayer, meditation, and time in Scripture all help to clear the mental clutter and tune your spirit to what matters most. When you're aligned internally, inspiration flows more freely. You're more sensitive to the nudges, the ideas, the moments of confirmation.

Another key to sustaining inspiration is movement. Inspiration isn't something you wait for; it's something you respond to. And sometimes, it shows up after you start moving. You take one small step, and suddenly the next one becomes clearer. You make a decision, and new energy kicks in. This is why inspired action can't be separated from faith. You won't always see the full picture before you begin. But when you move with a spirit of trust, the path unfolds.

In the end, inspiration is about alignment, your heart, your spirit, and your actions all pointing in the same direction. When you live from identity and tune into divine prompting, inspiration becomes your fuel. And that fuel leads to real, lasting transformation.

V. Aligning with Your Purpose

If you've ever found yourself working hard but feeling like you're going in circles, it's probably because your actions weren't fully aligned with your purpose. Inspired action is powerful, but it's only sustainable when it flows from clarity; clarity about who you are, why you're here, and what truly matters to you.

Clarity of vision strengthens follow-through. When your vision is fuzzy, so is your commitment. You hesitate, second-guess yourself, and waste energy bouncing between ideas. But when you have a crystal-clear vision, distractions lose their power. You begin to say no more confidently, to pivot more decisively, and to pursue your goals with greater intensity.

Purpose is more than just a passion or a career; it's the deeper "why" that fuels your decisions. It's rooted in your identity and tied to your calling. Bob Proctor often emphasized that success isn't about doing more, it's about doing the right things. And the right things come from aligning your daily actions with your deepest desires and God-given purpose.

Proctor taught that we are always acting out of the image we hold of ourselves and the results we expect. If you see yourself as scattered, inconsistent, or unworthy, your actions will reflect that. But if you begin to see yourself as someone with a mission, someone with value to offer, someone guided by purpose, your actions take on a new weight. You no longer chase every opportunity, you choose only those aligned with your purpose.

That's the difference between movement and momentum. Movement is activity. Momentum is progress with purpose. And it only happens when you stop taking action just to stay busy and start taking action that's aligned with your calling.

When you act in alignment with your desires, you engage your whole being, mind, heart, and spirit. There's integrity in your motion. You're not just doing what you think you "should" do. You're doing what resonates deeply with the truth of who you are. That internal harmony creates power. You no longer need external motivation to push you. You're pulled forward by something greater.

This is why vision matters so much. When your vision is clear and compelling, it acts like a magnet. It draws the right ideas, people, and opportunities into your life. But more importantly, it draws you forward. It gives you a reason to get up early, stay focused, and keep going when things get hard. Without vision, even the best plans can stall. With it, even small steps feel meaningful.

Take time to get clear on your purpose. Revisit your core values. Ask yourself: "What would I do if fear wasn't holding me back? What lights me up? Where do I feel most alive and useful?" These aren't just feel-good questions. They're clues. They point you to the path that's uniquely yours.

When your purpose is clear, you stop wasting time on things that don't matter. You let go of people-pleasing. You move from obligation to conviction. You realize that not every good opportunity is your opportunity. And that frees up your energy for what really counts.

It's also important to bring your purpose into your daily routine. Alignment isn't just about big decisions; it's about small, consistent choices. The emails you send, the conversations you have, the way you show up when no one's watching, these are the moments where purpose is either honored or ignored. Make them count.

Bob Proctor used to say, "Decide what you want. Write it down. Make a plan. And then act like the person who already has it." That's alignment. When your thoughts, beliefs, and behaviors are all moving in the same direction, you become unstoppable.

So, ask yourself: "Are my actions today aligned with my purpose?" "Am I moving toward what truly matters to me, or am I just keeping busy?" Inspired action that's aligned with purpose doesn't drain you; it energizes you. It doesn't feel forced, it feels guided.

When you live from that place, your impact multiplies. Your confidence grows. And most importantly, you begin to walk in the fullness of who you were created to be.

VI. Removing Mental Roadblocks

If you've ever had a powerful idea or a clear goal and still found yourself stuck, you're not alone. It's one of the most frustrating experiences: knowing what you should do, even want to do, and yet, nothing happens. That invisible resistance doesn't usually come from a lack of desire. It comes from mental roadblocks. And until those blocks are identified and dismantled, no amount of motivation will consistently move you forward.

The most common mindset blocks that stall inspired action are hesitation, perfectionism, and procrastination. They wear different disguises, self-doubt, fear of failure, overplanning, waiting for the "right time", but they all lead to the same result: delay and disappointment.

Hesitation usually comes from fear. Fear of judgment, fear of making the wrong move, fear of success (yes, that's real), or fear of being seen. It shows up as overthinking, analyzing every possible outcome before taking a single step. Clarity doesn't come before action, it comes through action. The antidote to hesitation is movement. Even small steps create momentum, and momentum builds confidence.

Perfectionism is a sneaky trap. It masquerades as high standards, but really, it's a form of self-protection. If you never release the project, never launch the idea, never make the call, then you can't fail, or so it seems. But in trying to avoid failure, perfectionism ensures you never succeed either. Bob Proctor once said, "Amateurs wait for inspiration. Professionals do it with a headache." That means you move forward even when conditions aren't perfect. Progress over perfection, every time.

Procrastination often gets mislabeled as laziness, but it's rarely about that. It's usually about uncertainty or fear of discomfort. The brain is wired to avoid pain, so when a task feels overwhelming, we distract ourselves with easier things, like scrolling, organizing, or planning endlessly. The solution? Break it down. Turn the big, scary task into the next small, manageable step. Don't aim to write the book, just commit to writing for 20 minutes. Don't try to build the whole funnel, just finish one page. Micro-commitments bypass the brain's resistance and create quick wins.

Another powerful strategy for removing mental blocks is to challenge the story you're telling yourself. Most blocks are built from limiting beliefs: "I'm not ready," "I'm not qualified," "I'm too late." But beliefs are not facts. They're just thoughts you've repeated enough times that they feel true. Start questioning them. Ask, "Is this really true? What evidence do I have? What would I do if I believed the opposite?" The moment you start to poke holes in the lie, the fear starts to lose its grip.

Also, pay attention to your language. Words shape reality. If you constantly say things like "I should," "I hope," "I'll try," you're giving yourself an escape hatch. Swap those for "I choose," "I will," and "I'm committed." Speak like the person you're becoming, not the one you're trying to grow out of.

One more tool: visualize the cost of inaction. We often only think about what could go wrong if we take action, but what about what we lose if we don't? Opportunities fade, confidence erodes, and regret builds. Let that picture motivate you to act now, not later.

Remember, mental roadblocks are part of the process. Everyone has them. The difference between those who succeed and those who stay stuck is not the absence of blocks, it's the willingness to face and dismantle them. You don't need to eliminate every fear before you act. You just need to be more committed to your purpose than to your comfort.

So, pause right now and ask: What's one thing I've been avoiding? What's the block behind it? And what's the next step I can take, not the perfect one, just the next one?

Inspired action isn't about pushing through with brute force. It's about learning to remove the mental noise so that your God-given clarity and energy can rise to the surface. When you break through those blocks, you don't just take more action, you take the right action. The kind that moves your life forward with power, peace, and purpose.

VII. Faith as a Catalyst for Movement

One of the biggest traps we fall into is waiting until everything is perfectly aligned before we take the first step. We think we need to have the full plan, every detail mapped out, the right timing, and the right conditions. But inspired action doesn't work like that. In fact, the most powerful moves we make in life are rarely made with certainty. They're made with **faith**.

Faith is what bridges the gap between what you see and what you know. It's what allows you to move forward even when you don't yet have all the answers. In Hebrews 11:1, Scripture defines faith as "the substance of things hoped for, the evidence of things not seen." That means faith isn't passive, it's a substance, a force. It's the foundation for action.

If you study the heroes of the Bible, you'll find that none of them waited until the path was clear to step out. They moved before the way opened, not after. Think of Abraham. He left everything familiar behind: his home, his land, his family legacy, not because he had a roadmap, but because God said, "Go." That one act of obedience changed the trajectory of history.

Or Moses, standing at the edge of the Red Sea with Pharaoh's army chasing behind. There was no visible escape route. Yet Moses didn't panic; he acted in faith. He raised his staff, trusting that God would make a way. And the sea parted.

Then there's Peter. When Jesus called him to step out of the boat and walk on water, the invitation didn't come with a safety net. Peter had to move while the waves were still crashing around him. His action was inspired, not by logic or certainty, but by faith in the One who called him.

In every one of these stories, faith wasn't just belief. It was belief in motion. That's the heart of inspired action. It's movement born out of spiritual conviction, not external confirmation.

Faith doesn't remove all fear. It simply gives you something greater to trust in than the fear. When you're anchored in your calling, your purpose, your relationship with God, you can move, even when you feel nervous, unsure, or unqualified. Because faith says, "I don't have to see the whole staircase. I just need to take the next step."

I've experienced this firsthand many times. I remember a time when I felt strongly led to invest in a new opportunity that aligned deeply with my values and mission. Logically, the numbers didn't add up. The timing felt off. And yet, I couldn't shake the pull in my spirit. I prayed. I journaled. I asked for clarity. And the message I got was simple: "Move anyway."

It wasn't easy. I battled doubt and resistance every step of the way. But taking that step, before I felt ready, opened doors I couldn't have imagined. New relationships formed. New income streams appeared. And more importantly, a deeper level of trust was built between me and God. I learned that inspired action isn't about certainty. It's about obedience.

Faith-driven action may not make sense to those around you. It may even feel risky. But when God places a vision in your heart, He's already factored in your weakness, your doubts, and your limitations. What He's looking for isn't your perfection, it's your participation.

So, if you're standing at a crossroads, unsure whether to move forward, ask yourself: Am I waiting for proof, or am I willing to act on faith?

The truth is, you rarely get the confirmation before the step. The confirmation comes because of the step.

Faith is the ignition switch for inspired action. It takes your intention and turns it into movement. It doesn't demand clarity, it creates it. And when you move by faith, even the smallest step can lead to miracles you never saw coming.

VIII. Building a Habit of Inspired Execution

It's one thing to be inspired once in a while. It's another to consistently live from that place and take meaningful, aligned action every day. Inspiration might start the fire, but it's habit that keeps it burning. That's where the real transformation happens, not in the occasional high-energy moments, but in the discipline of showing up and executing, even when you don't feel like it.

Inspired execution isn't just about doing more; it's about doing the right things with the right energy, consistently. To build that kind of momentum, you've got to structure your environment and your routine to support inspired action instead of draining it.

Let's start with your environment. Your physical and mental space either fuels your growth or fights it. Is your workspace filled with distractions, clutter, or constant reminders of unfinished tasks? Is your digital space packed with notifications and noise? If your environment is chaotic, your mind will follow. But when your space reflects clarity, purpose, and intention, you're more likely to step into focused, inspired action.

Create an environment that reminds you daily of your calling. Post your vision statement where you can see it. Keep affirmations and scriptures in visible places. Surround yourself with visuals that stir up passion and urgency. These subtle cues help re-center your mind and align your energy toward execution.

Next comes your routine. The most successful people I know don't wait for motivation. They create systems that make execution automatic. They design daily disciplines that ground them, no matter how they feel. That's the key to inspired execution. You don't wait for the inspiration to show up. You put yourself in a position to receive it through discipline and consistency.

Start your morning with intention. Before diving into tasks or distractions, check in with your inner compass. Pray, journal, meditate, and reflect on your goals. Review your "why." These rituals are more than spiritual hygiene; they're the spark that ignites action from the inside out.

Then, set a simple daily target. Don't overwhelm yourself with a long list of to-dos. Instead, identify one or two high-leverage actions that are aligned with your calling. Ask: What one step today would move me forward in the direction of my vision? Then do that thing. No excuses. No overthinking. Just take the step.

This creates a cycle of momentum. As you take action, you feel more empowered. That empowerment creates more clarity. And that clarity leads to more inspired action. It's a loop that builds on itself, and eventually, it becomes a lifestyle.

Don't underestimate the power of small wins. They compound over time. A single outreach, a 15-minute brainstorming session, one video recorded, one decision made; these are not just tasks. They are statements of identity. Every time you execute, you reinforce the truth: I am someone who follows through.

Over time, this builds something powerful, **self-trust**. You start to believe in your ability to act. And once you trust yourself, your confidence soars. You stop questioning whether you're "ready." You stop waiting for the perfect time. You simply move, again and again, with faith and consistency.

Also, be intentional about who you let influence your execution habits. Surround yourself with action-takers, not excuse-makers. Connect with people who stretch you, challenge you, and hold you accountable. If you're always the most driven person in the room, you're in the wrong room.

Finally, give yourself grace. You won't hit the mark every day. Life will throw curveballs. You'll miss targets. But don't let one off day turn into a full derailment. Inspired execution is not about perfection, it's about persistence. Just return to the path. Reconnect with your "why." Take the next step.

Make action a lifestyle, not an event. When you build the habit of inspired execution, you stop needing a motivational kick to get going. You just move, day after day, in alignment with who you are and what you're here to do. And that's where your life begins to change.

IX. Leveraging Mentorship for Clarity and Momentum

Inspired action doesn't happen in isolation. While your inner compass plays a vital role in guiding your steps, mentors help you fine-tune the signal and shorten the distance between thought and execution. They don't just inspire you, they help activate you. Mentorship, when embraced with humility and hunger, becomes one of the most powerful accelerators of progress.

We all have blind spots. We can't see what we can't see. Sometimes, we're too close to our own limiting beliefs, fears, or patterns to recognize how they're slowing us down. A good mentor sees what you're missing, not to criticize you, but to call you higher.

Mentors bring clarity. They help distill your scattered thoughts into focused action. When you're overwhelmed by choices or stuck in analysis paralysis, a mentor doesn't give you more information; they help you make decisions. They ask better questions. They draw out your deeper "why." They challenge your excuses and hold up a mirror to your potential.

I remember a time when I was stuck in planning mode. I had a big vision, but I was overthinking every move. I wanted every piece of the puzzle in place before I took the first step. That's when a mentor looked me dead in the eye and said, "You're not confused. You're scared. Stop hiding behind preparation and start moving your feet." It hit me like a lightning bolt. In that moment, I realized I wasn't lacking clarity; I was avoiding commitment. That push jolted me into action, and it changed the trajectory of my business and personal life.

Mentorship also brings momentum. When you're surrounded by someone who's already walked the road you're traveling, you don't have to guess what's coming next. You can borrow their experience. You can learn from their mistakes and model their mindset. That kind of shortcut is priceless. Instead of wasting years trying to figure it out, you get to move faster and more confidently.

The best mentors don't just give advice, they ask questions that make you think differently. They're not trying to give you their answers. They're trying to help you uncover your own. That's how they help you become, not just act. Because true mentorship isn't about dependency. It's about empowerment.

And mentorship isn't always formal. Sometimes it's a coach you hire. Sometimes it's a leader you study from afar. Sometimes it's a seasoned friend who listens without judgment and then tells you the hard truth anyway. It could even be a spiritual mentor who helps you see things through the lens of faith instead of fear.

What matters is that you seek mentorship with intention. Don't wait until you're desperate. Pursue it now, while you're growing, stretching, and navigating the messy middle. Ask questions. Be coachable. Take feedback seriously. And most importantly, take action on what you're given. Nothing frustrates a mentor more than a capable person who sits on golden advice but never moves.

If you want to take bold steps in your life or business, surround yourself with people who already live with boldness. Let their faith build yours. Let their clarity sharpen yours. Let their movement pull you out of hesitation.

When you leverage mentorship effectively, you'll find that your inspired ideas turn into strategic plans. Your energy gets channeled, your doubts shrink, and your confidence grows. You no longer feel like you're walking alone in the fog. You're walking a path that's been lit by the wisdom of others, and that's one of the smartest moves you can make.

Never underestimate the value of a mentor. Their insight can unlock your next breakthrough. Their belief in you can ignite a level of action you didn't think you had. And their example can remind you what's possible, especially on the days you forget.

X. Practical Exercises and Reflection

It's one thing to understand inspired action intellectually. It's another to evaluate your life and see whether you're actually taking it. This section is about bridging that gap between what you intend to do and what you're actually doing. The goal is not to shame yourself into action but to shine a light on where alignment is missing, and what steps will bring you closer to who you're called to be.

Exercise 1: The Action Audit

Start by reviewing the last seven days of your life. Not what you planned, but what you actually did.

1. Make a simple two-column list:
- In column one, write down your major intentions or goals for the week (e.g., make 10 follow-up calls, start the new marketing project, wake up early to pray and journal).
- In column two, list the actions you took.

Now look for alignment. Did your actions reflect your intentions? If not, what got in the way? Was it procrastination, fear, distraction, or something else?

This audit helps you get real. It lets you see the pattern, not just of behavior, but of belief. Because if you're consistently avoiding certain actions, there's often a limiting belief attached to them. Awareness is the first step toward change.

Exercise 2: The Clarity Compass

Inspired action is all about alignment. So, let's help you identify your next inspired move.

Write down your current top three goals, personal, spiritual, or professional. Under each one, answer the following:

- Why is this important to me?
- What would taking aligned action toward this goal look like this week?
- What's one thing I could do today that feels exciting and purposeful, even if it's a little uncomfortable?

This isn't about finding a "perfect" strategy. It's about tapping into momentum. The actions that feel most inspired are usually the ones that stretch you just enough to move forward without triggering paralysis.

Exercise 3: The Resistance Journal

Every time you feel stuck or hesitant to take action, pause and write it down. Label the resistance. Is it fear of failure? Fear of judgment? Fear of success?

Then ask yourself:

- What would I do right now if I trusted the outcome was already handled?
- What truth from Scripture or your personal belief system could replace the fear?

For example, if fear says, "I don't know enough to start," you might counter it with, "I'm equipped for every good work, and the path will unfold as I move." This is where inspiration meets faith. You don't have to see the whole staircase, you just take the next step.

Reflection Questions

As you sit with these exercises, ask yourself:

- What's one pattern I see repeating that's keeping me stuck in intention instead of action?
- What environments or relationships pull me into procrastination or perfectionism?
- Where in my life have I already taken inspired action, and what did it teach me about myself?
- What does it look like to live one week fully aligned with the person I'm becoming?

These questions are designed to bring your focus inward, because action driven from identity is more sustainable than action driven from pressure or performance.

Inspired action doesn't always look big. Sometimes it's the phone call you've been putting off. Sometimes it's blocking out time to create. Sometimes it's walking away from something that no longer fits who you're becoming. The point is to move, not randomly, but deliberately, with your heart and spirit aligned.

As you move through this journey, return to these exercises anytime you feel the gap widening between knowing and doing. They will serve as checkpoints on your path, reminding you that momentum comes from movement, not perfection. And often, the most powerful steps are the smallest ones taken in faith.

XI. Chapter Summary and Preview

As we close out this chapter on inspired action, it's important to pause and take stock of what we've uncovered. If you've made it this far, then you've probably started to recognize just how often good intentions pose as progress. We set goals, we dream big, we write plans; and yet, we stall. Not because we don't care, and not because we don't know what to do. We stall because we haven't yet bridged the gap between thought and movement. That's where inspired action lives. Not in theory, but in motion.

In this chapter, we peeled back the layers of that gap. We looked at how good intentions, while necessary, can become a trap if not followed by real, consistent steps. Jim Rohn reminded us that the difference between where we are and where we want to be is not knowledge, but disciplined execution. Knowing what to do is not enough. Doing it, over time and with purpose, is what changes everything.

We explored what inspired action really means, not just doing anything for the sake of movement, but taking aligned, purposeful steps that reflect who you are and where you're headed. Inspired action isn't forced or frantic. It's not driven by fear, comparison, or urgency. It's a response to clarity, conviction, and faith. It feels energizing, not exhausting. And even when it feels uncomfortable, there's a deep sense that you're moving in the right direction.

We broke down how inspiration works, how it flows not from hype, but from identity. Graham Cooke's insights showed us that when we live from our true self and listen for divine prompting, our actions become naturally aligned. You don't have to chase momentum. You create it by becoming more and more rooted in who you are and what you're here to do.

Bob Proctor's teachings helped us understand the power of alignment. When your thoughts, feelings, and actions all pull in the same direction, resistance fades and results follow. Clarity of purpose fuels the discipline to act. And faith, as we saw in both biblical principles and personal reflection, becomes the catalyst that moves us forward, especially when the path isn't fully visible.

We also faced the mental roadblocks: hesitation, perfectionism, and procrastination. These are not flaws to feel ashamed about; they're simply signals. They show us where our mindset needs renewing. And when we respond to those signals with courage and intention, we reclaim our power.

The exercises in this chapter were designed to help you turn this awareness into progress. By evaluating your own patterns, reflecting on your alignment, and taking small yet intentional steps, you're no longer just planning a better future. You're stepping into it.

This chapter is a turning point. Up until now, we've explored identity, mindset, discipline, and now, movement. But what's next? Sustaining this journey over the long haul.

That's where **Chapter 10** comes in. It's one thing to act, it's another to keep acting, to build momentum, and to keep going when life gets loud, discouraging, or confusing. The truth is, no one sustains inspired action in isolation. We weren't created to do life or growth alone. We need structure. We need community. We need support systems that reinforce who we're becoming and why it matters.

In Chapter 10, we'll dive into how to create and maintain that kind of support. We'll look at the value of accountability, the power of aligned relationships, and the practical systems that help you stay grounded, focused, and resilient.

So, if this chapter helped you get moving, the next will help you keep moving, with strength, with consistency, and with a tribe of support behind you.

You're not alone in this. Let's keep going.

Chapter 10: Building a Supportive Environment

I. Introduction

There was a time in my life when I believed I had to do everything on my own. It wasn't pride, at least not in the traditional sense. It was more like self-protection, forged by disappointment. I had been let down by people I trusted. I had opened up only to be misunderstood. So, I did what a lot of people do; I put my head down, pulled back emotionally, and tried to outwork my way to success in silence. No accountability, no community, just me, my goals, and the grind.

At first, it felt empowering. I didn't have to explain myself. I didn't have to deal with other people's opinions or judgment. But over time, the weight of going it alone began to show up in subtle ways. I started second-guessing my decisions. My motivation wavered. Progress slowed. And perhaps most importantly, I lost the joy I used to feel when I was connected with others on a shared journey.

Then came a turning point. I attended a mastermind retreat almost by accident. I didn't go looking for community, but that's exactly what I found. I was surrounded by people who were not only pursuing growth in their lives and businesses, but who genuinely wanted to see others win too. They weren't competing. They were lifting each other up. Challenging each other. Celebrating progress, no matter how small. For the first time in a long time, I realized something important: I had been starving for connection without even knowing it.

That weekend changed everything. I walked away with renewed focus, yes, but more than that, I walked away feeling seen. And that's when it hit me: growth doesn't happen in isolation. At least, not the kind that's sustainable or fulfilling. True transformation happens in community, in environments that call out your best, even when you can't see it for yourself.

Your environment isn't just about where you live or work. It's about the people you surround yourself with, the voices you allow into your mind, the habits you repeat, and the culture you create around your goals. You can have the best intentions in the world, but if you're constantly surrounded by negativity, drama, or spiritual disconnection, you'll end up fighting a current you were never meant to swim against alone.

On the flip side, when you intentionally place yourself in an environment of growth, spiritually, emotionally, and relationally, everything changes. Your confidence grows. Your ideas get sharper. Your faith deepens. You begin to stretch beyond old limits, not because you're trying harder, but because you're being pulled higher by the company you keep.

As Jim Rohn famously said, "You are the average of the five people you spend the most time with." I'd take that a step further. You are also shaped by the energy of your surroundings, the quality of your conversations, and the culture of your inner circle.

This chapter is about more than just choosing good friends or cleaning up your workspace. It's about creating a life environment that's in alignment with your calling. It's about surrounding yourself with voices that speak life, systems that support discipline, and communities that reflect the values you want to live by.

Whether you're walking through a period of isolation or already have a strong circle but want to refine it, this chapter will give you the tools to build an environment where growth isn't just possible, it's inevitable.

Let's dive into the power of environment, and how to build one that serves the version of you that you're becoming.

II. Why Environment Matters

"You are the average of the five people you spend the most time with." That quote from Jim Rohn may be one of the most repeated personal development truths of all time, but it's repeated because it's true. If you pause and take inventory of the voices you hear daily, the attitudes you're surrounded by, and the energy you absorb, positive or negative, you'll see a mirror reflecting your current trajectory. Your environment is not neutral. It's either lifting you up or pulling you down.

Think about it like this: no matter how great a seed is, it won't grow if it's planted in toxic soil. The same is true for your potential. You could have the right goals, a strong sense of purpose, and even faith in where you're headed, but if the environment around you is filled with negativity, drama, chaos, or complacency, it will slowly choke out your progress. It'll sap your energy, cloud your thinking, and dilute your commitment to growth.

On the other hand, when you surround yourself with people who challenge you to think bigger, live better, and act in alignment with your highest values, everything begins to shift. Suddenly, ideas seem more possible. Momentum builds. Confidence rises. Not because you're trying harder, but because you're aligned with a current that's flowing in the right direction.

Environment shapes mindset more than most people realize. If you're in a group of people who see problems as insurmountable obstacles, you'll begin to shrink your dreams to match their limitations. But if you're in a circle where challenges are seen as stepping stones to greatness, you'll start looking at your own roadblocks with fresh eyes. What used to intimidate you starts to look like an invitation to grow.

The influence of your surroundings isn't limited to people either. Your physical space matters. Is your home or workspace filled with clutter and distraction? Or does it reflect clarity, order, and purpose? Even your digital environment plays a role. What do you feed your mind with every day, news, gossip, mindless scrolling? Or do you deliberately curate content that feeds your spirit, expands your thinking, and calls you higher?

I've seen people completely transform, not because they changed who they were at their core, but because they changed their environment. They made new friends who thought differently. They joined mastermind groups or church communities that stretched their faith. They started their mornings with truth instead of stress. And the ripple effect was undeniable. They became more focused, more peaceful, more productive, and more resilient.

Environment isn't just a backdrop. It's a powerful force. The people you talk to most often, the conversations you engage in, the routines you follow, they're all either reinforcing your old identity or empowering the person you're becoming. There's no neutral ground.

If you want to reach the next level in any area of life, spiritually, emotionally, financially, or relationally, you have to get serious about evaluating and upgrading your environment. That might mean spending less time with people who constantly complain or criticize. It might mean organizing your space in a way that reflects your goals. It might mean setting boundaries, changing routines, or even changing locations.

The good news is, you're not stuck with the environment you have. You can create one that supports you, strengthens you, and aligns with your calling. You don't have to wait for permission. You just have to be willing to choose what feeds your growth instead of what comforts your stagnation.

The next step is learning how to identify the environmental toxins that may be holding you back and replace them with spaces, people, and practices that will help you thrive.

Let's dive deeper into that next.

III. Recognizing Toxic or Limiting Environments

Before you can build a life-giving environment, you have to be brutally honest about the one you're currently in. Some of the biggest barriers to growth don't look like threats. They're disguised as friends, habits, or even traditions. But they drain your energy, sabotage your focus, and subtly steer you away from the person you're called to become.

Toxic environments aren't always obvious. Sure, some relationships are clearly harmful, people who tear you down, manipulate you, or constantly spew negativity. But what about the subtle toxicity? The friend who always jokes about your goals but never takes you seriously? The family member who "means well" but discourages your new direction because it makes them uncomfortable? The coworker who thrives on gossip, pulling you into drama that leaves you emotionally exhausted?

Limiting environments can also be physical. A cluttered, chaotic space breeds distraction and confusion. The atmosphere around you can either amplify clarity or compound stress. If your daily surroundings reflect disorder, they'll likely influence your mental and emotional state in the same direction. Even the way your home is arranged can impact how motivated or calm you feel.

Then there are habits, routines we default to without questioning them. Scrolling social media the moment we wake up. Watching hours of mindless content before bed. Skipping quiet time with God because we're "too busy." These aren't just small choices. Over time, they shape our identity and influence what we believe is possible.

I've had to walk away from environments that were once familiar and even comfortable. Early in my journey, I was surrounded by people who operated in fear, small thinking, and scarcity. They weren't bad people, but their mindset kept them stuck, and by association, it kept me stuck, too. Every time I tried to talk about my vision, I got blank stares or passive resistance. I eventually realized I was trying to grow in soil that couldn't support my roots anymore.

And the Bible doesn't shy away from this topic either. Think about Lot's wife in Genesis 19. God was leading them out of a city filled with corruption, but she looked back, and that single glance tied her to the very place God was trying to free her from. Or consider the Israelites after they left Egypt. They had physical freedom, but their minds were still stuck in slavery. Their environment had conditioned them so deeply that they longed for the bondage they had known instead of embracing the promise ahead.

Jesus himself was limited by the environment in his hometown. In Mark 6:4-6, it says he could do no mighty works there because of their unbelief. The atmosphere didn't honor who he was, and as a result, his power was restricted. If even Jesus was affected by the environment around him, how much more should we be mindful of ours?

Recognizing a toxic or limiting environment takes courage. It requires you to stop making excuses for the things and people that no longer serve your growth. It asks you to choose discomfort over familiarity, and that's not always easy. But the cost of staying stuck is far greater than the cost of change.

Here's a simple but powerful exercise: Take inventory of the five people you interact with most. Write down how you feel after each encounter, energized or drained, supported or judged, aligned or conflicted. Then do the same for your routines and your physical spaces. Ask yourself: Does this environment reflect who I'm becoming, or who I've been trying to outgrow?

You can't heal in the same environment that made you sick. You can't thrive in a space that constantly triggers your fears or numbs your ambition. And you certainly can't build a purpose-driven life while clinging to environments that contradict your calling.

In the next section, we'll explore how to cultivate connections and community that breathe life into your journey and help you stay aligned with your highest purpose.

IV. The Power of Community and Connection

We were never meant to grow alone. One of the most powerful truths I've learned on this journey is that healing, transformation, and calling are amplified in the context of community. It's not just about having people around you. It's about being intentionally connected to people who challenge, support, and inspire you to rise into your full potential.

There's a kind of clarity that comes when you're around the right people. The ones who see beyond your current reality and speak to your potential. The ones who remind you of who you are when you forget. When you're in that kind of environment, growth isn't forced; it's organic. It becomes a natural byproduct of your relationships.

This is why belonging to a supportive group, whether it's a faith-based community, a mastermind, or a circle of intentional friends, is so vital. These environments create space for vulnerability and accountability. They offer encouragement on the days when your motivation falters and celebrate you when you hit milestones that used to feel impossible. They also hold up a mirror, lovingly showing you the blind spots you might otherwise ignore.

Graham Cooke often speaks about the idea that relationships are a divine training ground. According to him, our spiritual alignment isn't just cultivated in solitude; it's refined in connection. Growth, he says, is relational before it's functional. In other words, we become who we're meant to be through connection with others who are also on the path. This means that your environment isn't just something to manage, it's something that actively shapes your destiny.

If you're walking with people who only see your past, you'll struggle to step into your future. But if you're surrounded by people who speak life into your calling, challenge you to stay the course, and point you back to truth when you're wavering, everything changes. The right community acts like a greenhouse for growth, it creates conditions where even small seeds of faith can flourish into something extraordinary.

Jesus modeled this. Though He often withdrew to pray, He didn't live in isolation. He walked with twelve disciples, invested in them, and invited them into His process. His greatest lessons were often taught in the context of relationship. And when He sent His followers out, He sent them two by two, not alone. That was no accident. He knew the power of spiritual partnership.

We are wired for connection. Even in business and personal development, isolation breeds stagnation. If no one is stretching you, you're probably settling. If no one is speaking truth into your life, you might be listening to lies. That's why you have to get intentional about who you're building with.

It's not enough to hope for a supportive environment, you have to create it. Seek out groups that reflect the values and vision you want to embody. Get around people who are already living at the level you aspire to. Join Bible studies, entrepreneurial communities, support groups, or even online spaces that consistently reinforce your purpose and growth.

You'll know you've found the right environment when you feel both seen and stretched. Not coddled but called higher. Not judged but deeply encouraged. That kind of community doesn't just help you grow; it helps you stay grounded. It reminds you that you're not crazy for dreaming big, not weak for struggling, and not alone in your journey.

In the next section, we'll explore how faith-based support systems provide a spiritual backbone to your growth and how scripture confirms that walking with the right people is one of the wisest things you can do.

V. Faith-Based Support Systems

In a world that often promotes self-reliance and individual achievement, the Bible paints a very different picture of what true strength looks like. Scripture consistently emphasizes the value of walking in relationship with God and with others. Faith-based support systems aren't just helpful; they are foundational to long-term spiritual, emotional, and even practical growth.

Proverbs 27:17 says, "As iron sharpens iron, so one person sharpens another." That verse is more than poetic wisdom. It's a clear call to intentional, mutual development. Just as iron doesn't sharpen itself, neither do we. We need others to help refine us, shape us, and keep us sharp in the face of life's challenges.

Faith-based community provides something secular support systems can't: spiritual alignment and divine accountability. When you walk with others who share your core values and biblical worldview, your growth takes on a deeper dimension. You're not just being held accountable to goals; you're being encouraged to stay aligned with truth. You're being reminded of your identity in Christ when the world tries to label you with fear, failure, or comparison.

The early church modeled this beautifully. In Acts 2:42-47, we see a picture of believers gathering regularly, sharing meals, praying together, and meeting each other's needs. They were "devoted to the apostles' teaching and to fellowship." This wasn't a surface-level community. It was a shared life. A support system that carried each member through trials, celebrated victories, and kept their collective focus on God's purpose.

And that same structure still works today.

When you're surrounded by people who love the Lord, who know the Word, and who are committed to growing with you, your faith doesn't just survive, it thrives. These relationships anchor you when doubt creeps in. They challenge you when complacency sets in. They lift your arms when you're weary, just as Aaron and Hur did for Moses in Exodus 17.

Mentorship within faith-based environments also plays a huge role in this support structure. Paul mentored Timothy. Elijah mentored Elisha. Jesus mentored the disciples. Over and over, we see God using one generation to pour into the next, not just in knowledge, but in character, purpose, and faith. A godly mentor sees who you're becoming, not just who you are right now. They don't just teach you; they walk with you. They model integrity, discipline, and obedience.

Accountability is another vital piece of this equation. James 5:16 tells us to "confess your sins to one another and pray for one another, that you may be healed." That kind of vulnerability requires trust, and trust is built in the context of consistent, supportive relationships. In a faith-based group, confession isn't about shame, it's about freedom. You're not left to carry your burdens alone. You're supported, prayed for, and reminded of grace.

When these spiritual support systems are in place, everything else begins to shift. You stop feeling like you have to carry the weight of your growth alone. You're surrounded by others who speak life, hold you accountable to your purpose, and encourage your spiritual disciplines. Whether it's showing up for church, being faithful in prayer, or standing strong during a storm, you're not doing it in isolation.

In a world that often celebrates lone-wolf success, God's Word invites us to grow through connection. Faith-based support systems don't just help us succeed; they help us remain spiritually grounded while we do.

Next, we'll dive into how to build your own circle with intention, surrounding yourself with the kind of people who elevate, challenge, and support you on your journey.

VI. Building Your Circle Intentionally

If you're serious about personal growth, then it's time to get intentional about who you allow into your inner circle. You've heard it before, "You become like the people you spend the most time with." That's not just a nice motivational quote. It's a powerful truth rooted in both psychology and spiritual wisdom. And as Bob Proctor often emphasized, if you want to change your results, start by changing your environment, including your relationships.

When you're building a life of purpose, you can't leave your support system to chance. You need to build your circle with intention. That means evaluating who is currently in your life and asking, "Are these people lifting me up or pulling me down? Are they helping me grow, or are they keeping me stuck?"

That doesn't mean cutting off everyone who isn't goal-driven or spiritually aligned. But it does mean being honest about who has influence over your mindset, your energy, and your vision. If you're constantly around people who gossip, complain, or fear change, that energy rubs off on you, whether you realize it or not. On the flip side, when you're around people who speak life, chase growth, and encourage your purpose, it accelerates your transformation.

Napoleon Hill was one of the earliest voices to champion the concept of the "mastermind alliance." In his groundbreaking work Think and Grow

Rich, he explained that when two or more minds come together in harmony, they create a third, more powerful mind. It's not just collaboration, it's compound growth. Ideas get sharper. Vision becomes clearer. Doubts lose their grip. That's the power of a well-chosen circle.

Bob Proctor took that principle even further. He taught that your environment doesn't just reflect your self-image, it reinforces it. If you surround yourself with people who see your potential, who challenge your limiting beliefs, and who hold you to your higher standard, you start to believe it too. You begin to act like the version of yourself you're becoming.

So, how do you start building this kind of circle?

Begin with clarity. Define the kind of person you want to become. What are their habits? Their mindset? Their values? Then ask: who in your life already lives this way, or at least moves in that direction? Who challenges you to rise higher just by being who they are?

Next, start initiating more meaningful conversations. Don't wait for the "perfect" mentor or peer group to show up. Invite someone to coffee. Ask intentional questions. Look for small communities, faith groups, book clubs, mastermind meetups, where growth is the norm.

As you do this, stay open to divine connections. Some of the most life-changing relationships won't come from your careful planning. They'll come from following nudges. That person you meet in line at a conference. The friend of a friend who shares your vision. Be open. Be watchful. When your intention is aligned with growth, God often arranges the right people at the right time.

And finally, don't just seek value, bring value. The best circles aren't one-sided. Be the kind of person others want in their corner. Speak life. Show up consistently. Celebrate others' wins. Offer encouragement without judgment. When you become a growth-minded, faith-centered friend, you naturally attract others on the same path.

Your circle doesn't have to be big. But it does need to be intentional. A few solid relationships, deeply rooted in mutual respect, faith, and personal growth, are worth more than a hundred shallow acquaintances.

The people you allow close to you either water your vision or blur it. So, choose wisely, build prayerfully, and be willing to grow into the kind of person who belongs in the room you dream of entering.

VII. How Mentorship Elevates Environment

If you've ever experienced a breakthrough that seemed to come out of nowhere, chances are there was a mentor involved. Maybe not a formal one. Maybe it was a conversation, a course, or even a passing comment from someone who had already walked the road you were trying to navigate. Mentorship has the power to shift your trajectory because it brings clarity, correction, and belief at the exact moment you need it most.

I remember one such moment in my own journey. I was stuck, caught in the gap between what I knew and what I was doing. I had the vision, the drive, even the tools. But my results were flat. I was spinning my wheels, exhausted from trying to figure it all out alone. Then a mentor entered the picture. Not someone with flashy success, but someone with deep wisdom and a calm presence. Over coffee one morning, he said something that hit me like lightning: "You're not failing because you lack ability. You're failing because you're afraid to let go of the familiar."

That one sentence cracked something open in me. It was like someone turned the lights on in a room I had been fumbling through in the dark. That's the power of mentorship. It brings an outside perspective into your internal battles. It realigns your environment by introducing the energy, mindset, and habits of someone who's already living at the level you're reaching for.

When you position yourself around the right mentor, you get more than advice; you get alignment. You start to see how they structure their day, how they handle setbacks, and how they stay grounded in their faith. And when you witness that kind of living up close, something inside you rises. You start to believe that maybe you could live like that too.

This is what creating proximity is all about. Getting close to people who embody the growth, discipline, peace, and purpose you're pursuing. Not just admiring them from a distance, but intentionally seeking ways to learn from them. Sometimes that means reaching out and asking for a conversation. Sometimes it means investing in a program, a mastermind, or a coaching relationship. Other times, it means serving; showing up, adding value, and staying close enough to absorb their energy and wisdom.

And if you're thinking, "I don't know anyone like that", you're not alone. Many people come from environments where mentorship isn't modeled or available. That's why it's important to pray for divine connections. Ask God to bring the right voices into your life. Look for mentors in books, podcasts, sermons, and communities. You don't always need someone to sit across from you every week. You just need someone whose life pulls you higher and whose words awaken something in your spirit.

But mentorship isn't just about receiving. It's also about responsibility. As you grow, you'll be called to turn around and mentor others. And that's when you really realize the value of your environment, because you become part of someone else's support system. You become the proximity someone else needs to believe bigger.

A mentor doesn't have to be perfect. They just need to be one or two steps ahead, willing to share what they've learned. Their presence in your life can collapse time, accelerate breakthroughs, and protect you from unnecessary detours.

Your environment is a mirror. And mentorship helps you clean the smudges off that mirror so you can see clearly who you are becoming. So, seek proximity with humility. Honor the mentors who pour into you. And commit to being the kind of person who multiplies wisdom, not just receives it.

Because the truth is, you're not meant to grow alone. You're meant to grow in the presence of others who remind you of who you are and who you're becoming.

VIII. Creating a Physical and Digital Environment for Growth

Your environment is either pulling you forward or holding you back. It's not neutral. Whether you realize it or not, your surroundings, both physical and digital, are shaping your thoughts, habits, and decisions every single day. That's why it's so important to take inventory of your space and make intentional adjustments to reflect who you're becoming, not who you've been.

Let's start with your **physical space**. Look around the areas where you spend the most time: your office, your car, your kitchen, your bedroom. Do these spaces inspire you, or do they drain your energy? Are they cluttered and chaotic, or calm and purposeful? Creating a growth-friendly environment doesn't require luxury or perfection; it requires intention.

Your physical space should reflect clarity and direction. Begin by decluttering. Remove anything that feels outdated, heavy, or out of alignment with your current vision. This could be old paperwork, clothes that no longer fit your style or energy, or books that no longer serve your growth. Make room for what matters. A clear space invites a clear mind.

Next, add elements that elevate your mindset and reinforce your goals. That might mean posting your affirmations on the bathroom mirror, placing your vision board where you can see it daily, or setting up a designated prayer or meditation space. Keep tools within reach that support your habits: journals, planners, highlighters, devotionals, and business materials. Make it easy to succeed by designing your environment to support your best behaviors.

Now let's talk about your **digital environment**, the one most people overlook. Your phone, your computer, your email inbox, your social media feeds, they all contribute to your mental and emotional atmosphere. If your digital world is filled with distractions, negativity, or noise, it's no wonder you feel scattered and overwhelmed.

Start by limiting your digital intake. Unfollow accounts that drain your energy or trigger comparison. Subscribe to voices that speak life, truth, and inspiration. Limit your exposure to news and entertainment that keeps you stuck in fear, drama, or escapism. Remember, your input determines your output. If you want to think better and live bolder, you need to feed your mind accordingly.

Organize your digital tools for efficiency and clarity. Clean up your desktop. Archive or delete unnecessary files. Create folders that reflect your current goals. Use digital calendars, task managers, and reminders to automate what can be automated, so you're not wasting energy on things you could be managing smarter.

One powerful habit is to design a "digital morning routine." Before you check messages or scroll social media, begin your day with intention. Open your Bible app. Listen to a podcast that builds your faith or challenges your mindset. Write down three wins you plan to accomplish that day. Create a rhythm where your first inputs are aligned with growth, not noise.

Another strategy is to set boundaries on your tech usage. Turn off non-essential notifications. Use "do not disturb" during your most focused hours. Consider setting time limits for certain apps or implementing a Sabbath from digital input altogether, just one day a week to disconnect and reset.

The goal is not to eliminate digital tools. It's to make sure they're serving you, not enslaving you. Your devices can be powerful allies in your growth, but only if you're intentional about how you use them.

Ultimately, your environment is a declaration. It says, "This is who I am, and this is where I'm going." So, build one that reflects your next level, not your last one. Let every drawer, every screen, every corner of your life remind you of the mission you're on and the person you're becoming.

IX. Setting Boundaries with Love and Clarity

Setting boundaries is one of the most powerful and loving things you can do, for yourself and for others. It's not about creating walls or pushing people away. It's about defining the space where your values, energy, and purpose can thrive. It's about creating room to grow, without the guilt that often comes with saying "no."

The truth is, if you don't set boundaries, life will set them for you, and usually in the form of burnout, resentment, or broken focus. Especially when you're on a journey of personal growth, you need room to breathe, reflect, and execute. That room doesn't just happen. You have to claim it. And you have to protect it.

Many people struggle to set boundaries because they confuse it with rejection or selfishness. But that's a misunderstanding. Boundaries are not barriers. They are bridges; structures that make relationships healthier and more sustainable. They teach others how to engage with you respectfully, and they reinforce your own standards for what you will and will not accept.

From a biblical perspective, boundaries are wisdom in action. Even Jesus, who loved perfectly, still set boundaries. He withdrew from crowds to pray. He said "no" to demands that didn't align with His Father's timing. He didn't allow people's expectations to dictate His direction. That's not harshness, that's clarity.

Protecting your peace and focus starts with knowing what matters most to you. What are the non-negotiables in your life right now? Time for prayer and reflection? Energy for building your business or ministry? Emotional space to heal and grow? Once you identify what's sacred right now, you can build boundaries around it like a fence around a garden, keeping distractions out and protecting what's blossoming within.

But boundaries only work if they're communicated with love and clarity. That means having real conversations, not angry outbursts, silent withdrawals, or passive-aggressive behavior. Clarity is kind. When you tell someone, "I need this time to focus on what God's placed on my heart," or "I love you, but I won't participate in that kind of conversation anymore," you're not being difficult, you're being deliberate.

Here are a few faith-centered strategies for setting and communicating healthy boundaries:

1. **Pray before you speak**. Ask God for the right words, the right heart, and the right timing. You're not trying to win an argument, you're trying to honor your assignment.
2. **Be direct, but not defensive**. You don't need to over-explain or justify your boundary. A simple "That doesn't work for me right now" can be powerful when said with love.

3. **Use "I" statements**. Instead of accusing ("You always make me feel…"), take ownership of your needs ("I've realized I need more quiet time in the mornings to stay aligned.").
4. **Stay rooted in grace**. Some people won't understand your boundaries right away. That's okay. Your job isn't to control their reaction, but to remain kind and consistent.

It's also important to set **internal boundaries**, those limits you place on yourself to stay aligned. That might mean turning off your phone at a certain hour, choosing not to engage in gossip or negative thinking, or limiting exposure to media that disrupts your peace. Internal boundaries are just as vital as relational ones.

In the end, boundaries don't push people away; they teach people how to stay close in a healthy way. They don't shut down relationships; they refine them. And most importantly, they allow you to move forward in peace, purpose, and obedience to what God's called you to do.

Don't apologize for protecting your mission. The people who truly love and respect you will honor your growth, not resent it. And those who can't? They were likely never meant to go where God is taking you next.

X. Practical Exercises and Reflection

Creating a supportive environment isn't something that happens by accident; it's built with intention, clarity, and consistent action. Before you can construct a new environment that lifts you up, you have to get clear about what's working, what's not, and what needs to change. This section offers practical exercises to help you assess your current surroundings and begin reshaping your physical, emotional, and relational space to match the person you're becoming.

1. The Environment Inventory

Take out a journal or open a blank document and divide it into three sections labeled: **Physical, Emotional, and Relational.**

- Under **Physical,** list the spaces where you spend most of your time: your home, car, office, workspace, or digital devices. Ask: Does this space reflect who I want to become? Does it support focus, peace, and productivity?

- Under **Emotional,** evaluate what influences your mindset daily: music, media, conversations, or internal thoughts. Ask: Are these emotional inputs strengthening my identity or undermining it?

- Under **Relational,** list the people you spend time with regularly. Ask: Do these relationships lift me up, or do they drain my energy and confidence?

This exercise may reveal areas that are out of alignment. Don't judge yourself. The goal isn't perfection; it's awareness.

2. Define Your Ideal Environment

Now that you've assessed your current situation, imagine what your ideal environment would look and feel like. Get specific. Write it out in the present tense as if it already exists:

> "I wake up in a space that's clean, peaceful, and inspiring. My phone isn't the first thing I grab. I begin my day with prayer and gratitude. My workspace is organized and free of clutter. The people I speak to regularly challenge me to grow. I feel supported, focused, and energized."

This isn't just a visualization; it's a template. It becomes a compass for decisions about what to keep, change, or release.

3. Take One Step in Each Area

- **Physical:** Pick one small space and transform it today. Clear your desk. Create a prayer corner. Clean your car. Order that new journal. Change your phone wallpaper to an inspiring quote. Even one shift in your physical space can change how you show up.

- **Emotional:** Audit your daily inputs. Choose one thing to eliminate (e.g., scrolling toxic social media or watching the news first thing in the morning), and one thing to add (e.g., a five-minute devotional, gratitude journaling, or uplifting audio).

- **Relational:** Reach out to someone who inspires you. Set a boundary with someone who drains you. Join a community or group aligned with your values. Don't wait for the perfect tribe; start by connecting intentionally with one person who "gets" your vision.

4. Weekly Check-In Practice

Set aside 10–15 minutes each week to review the following:

- What felt good about my environment this week?
- What pulled me away from alignment?
- What can I adjust next week to stay on course?

You'll be surprised how quickly clarity compounds when you pause and reflect consistently. Progress builds through course correction, not constant intensity.

5. Speak Life into Your Space

Our words shape the atmosphere. Begin speaking blessings over your environment, literally. Say things like:

> "This space is a sanctuary for growth."
> "I attract people who support my purpose."
> "I am surrounded by peace and clarity."

Your voice carries authority; use it to declare what your environment is becoming, even before it fully manifests.

Creating a supportive environment isn't a one-time task; it's a rhythm. But with each conscious change, you'll feel more grounded, more energized, and more in alignment with your highest calling.

XI. Chapter Summary and Preview

If there's one truth that's become increasingly clear throughout this chapter, it's this: you can't become the person you're meant to be in an environment that keeps you small. Growth is not just about what you do; it's about where you do it, who you do it with, and what surrounds you every day.

We began with the reminder that isolation often breeds confusion and stagnation. Without community, accountability, or encouragement, it becomes easy to doubt your path or retreat back into familiar patterns. But when you're surrounded by people, spaces, and routines that echo your values and your calling, the journey forward becomes not only possible, it becomes sustainable.

You've now seen how powerful your environment truly is. We explored Jim Rohn's principle that "you are the average of the five people you spend the most time with." This idea alone should prompt serious reflection. The people you're around are either pulling you forward or holding you back. There's rarely any neutral ground. And that doesn't just apply to people. It extends to everything in your physical and digital world. Your environment is either reinforcing your growth or chipping away at it bit by bit.

We examined the subtle yet toxic impact of limiting environments. Draining relationships, disorganized spaces, and unfiltered media; these things often go unnoticed but have a profound impact on your energy, focus, and belief. We also dove into how to recognize those limiting forces and begin shifting them with purpose and compassion.

From there, we looked at the power of community and the value of surrounding yourself with faith-based support systems. Whether it's a church group, a mastermind alliance, or a trusted circle of growth-minded friends, your circle plays a direct role in shaping your progress. The right people will not only cheer you on, they'll call you higher. They'll remind you of your identity when you forget. They'll speak life into your dreams and tell you the truth when you drift.

We explored biblical principles of accountability, mentorship, and alignment. Scripture is clear: we are not meant to walk this journey alone. "As iron sharpens iron, so one person sharpens another" (Proverbs 27:17). The early church modeled this beautifully. They gathered in unity, shared resources, prayed together, and lifted one another up. That wasn't just a social practice; it was a spiritual strategy for sustaining purpose and power.

In practical terms, we covered how to evaluate your circle, set healthy boundaries, and even reframe your physical and digital environment to reflect your goals. We don't rise to the level of our intentions; we fall to the level of our systems. That's why making even small shifts to your surroundings can unlock a new level of focus and momentum.

Finally, we closed with actionable exercises to take inventory of your environment, envision your ideal space, and take tangible steps to align your surroundings with the life you're building. These are not one-time tasks. They're rhythms of reflection, adjustment, and intentional design.

As we turn the page to the next chapter, we'll begin exploring the importance of momentum. Once the right environment is in place, it's time to build consistent motion. You've probably felt it before: that sense that you're finally gaining traction, that your daily actions are building on each other, that progress is no longer a fight but a flow.

But momentum isn't magic; it's manufactured through intentionality, alignment, and consistency. In the next chapter, we'll look at how to maintain that momentum when life gets messy, how to stay on course when motivation fades, and how to keep showing up even when results don't come overnight.

You're not just building a dream, you're building a life. And the environment around you will either accelerate or choke that process. But now, you have the tools. And with that foundation set, it's time to keep moving forward, with clarity, conviction, and the support you've built.

Let's dive into momentum.

Chapter 11: The Momentum Effect: Keeping Your Progress Alive

I. Introduction

I remember working with a client who started off like a rocket. She was fired up after reading a few books, attending a couple of live trainings, and setting bold goals for her business. For the first few weeks, she was on fire, early mornings, consistent social media content, regular prospecting, and even a few sales right out of the gate. Everything was clicking. She was gaining traction.

But then... life happened. One week she had a family emergency. The next, she missed a couple of follow-ups. She told herself she'd catch up the next day, but the days turned into weeks. Her content slowed. Her energy dropped. Her self-talk shifted from "I've got this" to "Maybe I'm not cut out for this." What had started with so much promise began to stall out, not because she lacked skill or passion, but because she lost momentum.

And here's the thing that client isn't alone. You've likely experienced it too. You get excited about a new goal, start strong, and then somewhere along the way, the fire dims. You skip a day or two. You get distracted. You start second-guessing your abilities. Before you know it, you're back to square one, wondering where all that early energy went.

That's the momentum effect. Or in this case, the loss of it.

Momentum is one of the most underrated and misunderstood forces in personal growth. It's the invisible engine that powers your progress once you've begun. When you've got momentum, everything feels easier. Tasks that used to feel hard now flow. Confidence rises, clarity sharpens, and results start compounding. You stop thinking so much and just do. You're in motion, and motion creates more motion.

But momentum doesn't maintain itself. It has to be guarded, fed, and fueled. Think of it like pushing a car from a dead stop. The hardest part is getting it rolling. But once it's moving, keeping it moving takes far less effort. That's why the early days of any transformation matter so much. That's when you're generating your forward force. If you interrupt it too soon, you have to start over, pushing that heavy weight from a dead stop all over again.

That's why this chapter is so crucial. You've made it this far in the book, which means you've already gained some ground. You've learned about identity, fear, discipline, and action. You've started shifting how you think, how you work, and how you show up. But none of that will create lasting change without sustained momentum.

This chapter is about helping you protect that progress. It's about showing you how to turn short bursts of inspiration into long-term transformation. Because truthfully, that's what separates those who grow consistently from those who burn out. The ones who keep evolving are the ones who understand how to manage momentum; how to harness it, protect it, and ride it through the inevitable dips and distractions of life.

Think of this chapter as a momentum toolkit. We're going to walk through what momentum really is, how it works, and what kills it. You'll learn daily habits and thought patterns that fuel it. You'll understand how your environment, your support system, and your spiritual practices all contribute to your forward motion. And you'll gain clarity on what to do when things start to stall, because let's be honest, it's not a matter of if, it's a matter of when.

You don't have to be perfect to keep momentum alive. You just have to be consistent enough to stay in motion. That's what we're after. And it starts right here, right now, with a renewed commitment to not just start strong, but to keep going strong.

Let's explore how to make momentum your ally for life.

II. What Is Momentum and Why It Matters

Momentum isn't just a physics term; it's one of the most powerful, yet overlooked, forces in personal growth, business, and spiritual development. At its core, momentum is forward motion with increasing speed and ease. In practical terms, it's when the daily effort you've been applying starts to pay off not just once, but over and over, with compound effect.

In the early days of starting something new, whether it's a fitness goal, a business, a mindset shift, or a spiritual discipline, the effort feels heavy. It takes a lot to get going. You're building new habits, breaking old ones, dealing with resistance, and fighting off self-doubt. It feels like you're pushing a boulder uphill. But if you stay with it, something interesting happens: it gets easier.

Not because life becomes less demanding, but because you've changed. You've picked up speed. You've gained rhythm. Your actions begin to build on each other. One good decision leads to another. One win breeds the next. That's momentum.

Jim Rohn described it this way: "Success is nothing more than a few simple disciplines practiced every day." It's not the big leaps that matter most; it's the consistent, daily application of effort, thought, and discipline. And as those simple disciplines stack up, they begin to generate a kind of forward thrust in your life that's difficult to stop.

Napoleon Hill, in Think and Grow Rich, also emphasized this principle, though he didn't call it "momentum" directly. He talked about the power of persistence and the necessity of sustained effort, especially once you've built some initial traction. He observed that most people quit just before the tide is about to turn in their favor. They break momentum when they're right on the edge of a breakthrough.

That's the real danger of not understanding momentum; you can sabotage yourself simply by stepping away too soon.

Momentum is what turns ordinary effort into extraordinary results. It multiplies the impact of your actions. A single prospecting call leads to a referral. A simple social post opens a conversation that turns into a long-term business partner. A morning routine grounds you for an entire day of productivity. These things don't happen randomly. They happen because of momentum.

In business, momentum creates visibility and credibility. When you show up consistently, people notice. When you're consistent, your results begin to stack. You gain confidence, your message sharpens, and your reach expands. The marketplace responds to momentum because it recognizes it as stability and leadership.

In your personal life, momentum keeps your energy aligned with your goals. You're no longer trying to force your way through resistance every day. Instead, your habits carry you. You don't have to convince yourself to do the work; it's already part of who you are.

The spiritual parallel is just as clear. When you stay connected to God through regular prayer, reflection, and obedience, you begin to hear more clearly. You move more confidently. Your faith deepens, not because of a one-time experience, but because of steady, day-by-day walking. That's spiritual momentum.

So why does this all matter?

Because without momentum, you're constantly starting over. You're burning energy just trying to get back to where you left off. It's like resetting your progress every Monday. But with momentum, you're building upon what you did yesterday. You're not starting from zero; you're compounding your efforts. You're moving forward with less friction and more flow.

Whether you're working on your business, your health, your faith, or your relationships, momentum is the bridge between where you are and where you want to be. It turns effort into excellence. It rewards consistency. And once you understand how to build it, and more importantly, how to keep it, you'll become unstoppable.

III. The Science and Spiritual Law of Momentum

Momentum may feel mysterious at times, but it's rooted in very practical principles, both scientific and spiritual. At the core of momentum lies a powerful truth: small, consistent actions compound over time. That's not just motivational fluff; it's the way the world works.

Let's look at the science first. In physics, Newton's First Law of Motion tells us that an object in motion tends to stay in motion unless acted upon by an external force. In life, the same principle applies. When you begin taking action toward a goal, no matter how small, and you do it consistently, that action becomes easier to sustain. You build what psychologists call "behavioral momentum." Your brain wires those repeated behaviors into habits. What once took effort becomes automatic.

The beauty of momentum is that it doesn't demand perfection. It just demands consistency. If you do one small thing every day to grow, read five pages, make one phone call, record one video, say one prayer, you'll find that those small actions begin to stack. Each one becomes easier because you've already laid the groundwork. And eventually, the compound effect kicks in.

The compound effect, popularized by Darren Hardy, explains how small, smart choices, repeated over time, yield massive results. Most people underestimate what they can achieve in a year because they're too focused on what they can do in a day. But when you understand that progress isn't linear, it's exponential, you stop needing instant gratification. You trust the process, even when it feels slow, because you know it's building toward something big.

Spiritually, momentum follows the same pattern. Scripture is filled with stories of people who achieved a breakthrough not through one grand gesture, but through persistent obedience. The parable of the talents in Matthew 25 is a perfect example. In this story, Jesus describes three servants who are entrusted with different sums of money by their master. Two of the servants invest and multiply what they're given, while one buries his out of fear. When the master returns, he praises the two who produced more, saying, "You have been faithful with a few things; I will put you in charge of many things."

That phrase, faithful with a few things, is the spiritual law of momentum in action. God honors consistency. He multiplies what you manage well. If you show up daily with discipline, integrity, and faith, even in small ways, you're creating the conditions for blessing, growth, and expansion.

Another example is found in the story of Noah. He didn't build the ark overnight. It took years of consistent, obedient effort in the face of ridicule and doubt. But his momentum, rooted in trust and discipline, ultimately saved his family and changed the course of history.

Elijah, too, showed the power of persistent faith. After a long drought, he sent his servant to look for rain, not once, but seven times. Each time, the servant came back with nothing. Still, Elijah told him to keep looking. On the seventh time, a small cloud appeared. That small sign became the storm that ended the drought. Elijah's faith wasn't passive; it was persistent. That's spiritual momentum.

What these stories show us is that both science and scripture agree: growth is not about one-time miracles. It's about showing up daily and trusting that your faithful effort is never wasted.

You may not see immediate results. You might question whether your actions are making a difference. But trust this: every seed sown in faith and discipline is building something under the surface. Eventually, that harvest will break through.

Momentum is sacred. It is the fusion of consistency, belief, and obedience. When you understand and honor this principle, your progress will no longer feel like a grind; it will feel like grace in motion.

IV. Recognizing Momentum Killers

Momentum is fragile. It doesn't take a major crisis to derail it, just a little friction, distraction, or discouragement. You can be making real progress one week and feel completely off track the next, without any clear explanation. That's why it's critical to recognize and guard against the momentum killers that creep in subtly and silently.

Distractions are one of the most common culprits. In today's hyper-connected world, distraction isn't just a possibility; it's a constant invitation. Notifications, emails, endless scrolling, and interruptions don't just take your time; they steal your focus. And when your focus is gone, your momentum slows. Distractions don't always look like time-wasters either. Sometimes they show up as "good opportunities" that pull you away from your top priorities. Protecting your momentum means learning to say no, even to things that look valuable on the surface but aren't aligned with your highest priorities.

Then there's **discouragement**. It often sneaks in when progress feels slow or invisible. You've been putting in the effort, showing up day after day, but the results aren't coming fast enough. That's when your mind starts whispering lies: "This isn't working," "You're wasting your time," "Maybe you're not cut out for this." If you don't catch those thoughts early, they'll drain your energy and stop your momentum in its tracks. The key is learning to separate your feelings from the facts. Just because you feel discouraged doesn't mean you're off course. It may mean you're closer to a breakthrough than you realize.

Comparison is another stealthy thief. When you start measuring your progress against someone else's highlight reel, it creates unnecessary pressure and self-doubt. You lose sight of how far you've come and become obsessed with how far behind you think you are. Momentum is personal. You're not supposed to be running someone else's race. Stay in your lane, celebrate your pace, and remember, comparison kills both joy and progress.

Another major momentum killer is **lack of clarity**. When you're not sure what your next step is, it's easy to freeze. Confusion breeds inaction. That's why clarity is power. The clearer you are on your goals, your purpose, and your daily actions, the easier it is to maintain momentum. Take time regularly to revisit your vision, refine your plan, and recommit to your "why." Don't let ambiguity create inertia.

In addition to these external and mental blocks, you also have to watch for **emotional dips** and **mental fatigue**. These aren't signs of weakness; they're signs that you're human. Everyone has emotional valleys. You might feel drained, unmotivated, or even anxious without knowing exactly why. Sometimes it's your body calling for rest. Sometimes it's your mind processing internal resistance. The worst thing you can do is ignore it and try to "grind through" with no awareness.

When you recognize you're in a dip, pause. Don't panic. Get curious. Ask yourself, "What's really going on?" Is it physical exhaustion? Emotional overload? A buildup of negative thoughts? Often, a simple reset: a walk outside, a conversation with a trusted mentor, a few minutes in prayer or meditation, can restore your energy and focus.

Momentum doesn't mean you never slow down. It means you don't stay down. The most successful people don't avoid setbacks; they learn to bounce back quickly. They know how to course-correct before things spiral. They don't beat themselves up; they adjust, recalibrate, and keep moving.

Your job isn't to be perfect. Your job is to protect the flow of progress. That means being honest about what's pulling you off course and courageous enough to address it.

Keep your eyes open. Keep your heart grounded. Keep your schedule aligned. And remember: the more aware you are of what kills your momentum, the better equipped you are to preserve it.

V. How to Maintain Momentum Daily

Momentum isn't built in a day, it's built daily. While big wins and breakthroughs can make us feel inspired in the moment, it's the seemingly small, consistent actions that actually create lasting transformation. To keep your progress alive, you must establish daily rhythms that keep you anchored, focused, and connected to your goals.

Let's start with the **morning**. How you begin your day determines how you carry yourself through it. A chaotic or reactive morning leads to a scattered, unproductive day. But a focused morning routine helps you operate from intention instead of emotion. It sets the tone for confidence, clarity, and purpose.

That's why so many high performers have some form of morning ritual. For some, it starts with prayer or meditation, grounding themselves spiritually before facing the world. For others, it's movement: a walk, stretching, or a full workout. Many also include gratitude journaling, affirmations, or reading from a personal development book. These aren't just feel-good routines; they're anchors that remind you who you are, what you're committed to, and how you're going to show up.

One of the most powerful morning practices is **visualization**. Take five minutes to vividly imagine your goals as already accomplished. Picture yourself walking in your new identity, carrying out your mission with purpose and joy. This isn't fantasy; it's mental conditioning. As Bob Proctor often taught, when you hold the image of your goal with faith and emotion, you program your subconscious to move toward it.

Once your morning routine is done, momentum is kept alive through **daily focus**. Don't just create a to-do list, create a results list. Choose the top three actions that, if completed, will move you closer to your highest priorities. These are your non-negotiables. If nothing else gets done, these must. This level of clarity keeps your efforts from getting diluted by distractions and urgency.

Evening reflection is just as important. In the quiet of the night, you can reflect, reset, and recalibrate. Take a few minutes to ask yourself: "Did I live in alignment with my purpose today? Did I stay connected to who I want to become?" You're not looking for perfection, just awareness. Journaling your wins and lessons from the day helps you acknowledge progress, recognize patterns, and reinforce commitment.

This is where **the power of journaling** really shines. It's not just about venting thoughts or logging activities. It's about seeing yourself on paper. Journaling creates space for self-discovery and emotional regulation. When you're stuck or struggling, your journal becomes a conversation with yourself that reveals the next step forward. When you're thriving, it becomes a record of what works so you can repeat it.

Another key to daily momentum is **tracking your habits**. What gets measured gets improved. Use a simple habit tracker or checklist to build consistency. Whether it's drinking water, making calls, studying Scripture, or posting content for your business, track it. Not to create pressure, but to create evidence that you're showing up. Seeing those checkmarks stack up over time reinforces your belief that you are a disciplined, committed person.

Keep in mind that momentum doesn't always feel exciting. In fact, some of your most productive days may feel uneventful. But if you showed up, followed through, and stayed aligned with your values, that's progress. That's the path to compound growth.

There's a quote from Jim Rohn that says, "Success is nothing more than a few simple disciplines, practiced every day." That's what daily momentum is all about. It's not about trying harder. It's about living smarter. Aligning your routines with your vision. Turning intentional actions into automatic habits.

Protect your mornings. Reflect in the evenings. Stay honest with yourself in between. When you do this day after day, you won't just keep momentum, you'll multiply it.

VI. The Role of Focus and Clarity

Momentum isn't just about movement; it's about **direction**. You can be incredibly busy and still feel like you're getting nowhere if you're not clear on where you're going. That's why focus and clarity are essential ingredients to sustaining momentum. Without them, your energy gets diluted, your motivation fades, and even your best efforts fall short of real progress.

Let's start with clarity. One of the most powerful practices you can develop is regularly revisiting your "**why**." Your "why" is the emotional and spiritual fuel behind everything you're doing. It's the deeper reason you started in the first place. And when the days get long, when resistance kicks in, when you feel like quitting, that "why" is what pulls you forward.

Ask yourself often: Why does this matter to me? Who else benefits when I keep going? What does success look like, and how will it feel when I get there? The clearer your vision, the stronger your pull. When your "why" is big enough, the "how" becomes manageable.

But clarity alone isn't enough. You also need **focus**; the ability to block out distractions and concentrate your energy on what matters most. Jim Rohn used to say, "The key is not to prioritize what's on your schedule but to schedule your priorities." That's what focus really is: making your purpose non-negotiable in the face of competing demands.

Focus doesn't mean doing more. It means doing **less, better**. It means being willing to ignore the good so you can fully pursue the great. In a world that pulls your attention in a thousand directions, focused effort becomes a superpower.

This is where Bob Proctor's teachings become incredibly practical. He taught that your results always reflect the image you hold in your mind. If your focus is scattered, your results will be too. But if you can **hold a clear mental picture** of the life you want, the identity you're stepping into, and the impact you're here to make, your subconscious mind begins to align your behaviors to match that image.

Bob encouraged people to create what he called a "goal card", a small note with your main goal written in present tense. You'd carry it with you and read it multiple times a day. Why? Because repetition firmly plants the image into your subconscious, and once that happens, action starts to flow. You're no longer forcing discipline, you're being pulled by vision.

He also emphasized **acting in faith**, even before the path is fully visible. This ties directly into momentum. You don't build momentum by waiting until you have every step figured out. You build it by taking the next step you can see and trusting that clarity will expand as you move forward. Focus and clarity aren't passive; they're choices you make daily, through prayer, planning, reflection, and courageous action.

So, how do you build and protect focus and clarity in your life?

- **Start your week with vision**: Before Monday hits full speed, take 15 minutes to look at your goals and ask, "What matters most this week?" Then build your schedule around those priorities.
- **End each day with alignment**: Ask yourself, "Did I move closer to my vision today? What distracted me? What will I shift tomorrow?"
- **Use visual cues**: Vision boards, desktop backgrounds, or sticky notes can act as powerful reminders of who you're becoming and what you're building.
- **Guard your inputs**: Be selective about the voices and content you allow into your mind. What you feed your focus, shapes your future.

Remember this: **Momentum thrives in the presence of clarity**. When your vision is strong, and your focus is fixed, you stop second-guessing. You stop chasing. You start building, brick by brick, day by day, into the life you were designed to live.

Keep the image clear. Act in faith. Stay locked in on your purpose. That's how you protect momentum and move powerfully toward your destiny.

VII. Encouragement in the Dip

Every growth journey has a rhythm; ups and downs, forward strides and backward slides. If you've ever felt excited and unstoppable one day, then flatlined and full of doubt the next, you're not broken. You're human. This phenomenon is what I call **"the dip**." It's the emotional valley that often follows early excitement. And if you're not prepared for it, it can feel like failure. But the dip isn't failure. It's part of the process.

The dip shows up after you've made progress, when the novelty has worn off and the hard work sets in. It's when results are slower than expected, motivation is harder to find, and the voices of doubt start to get louder. It's the place where most people quit, not because they're not capable, but because they weren't expecting it.

Graham Cooke calls these times "hiddenness" or "process moments." He teaches that God often does His deepest work not in the spotlight but in the silence, when you feel unseen, unsure, or uninspired. It's during the dip that your roots grow deeper. It's where faith, character, and endurance are formed. These are not the moments to run from. They are the proving ground for greatness.

Think of a seed. Before it ever breaks through the surface, it must go through a dark, silent, invisible phase beneath the soil. That seed doesn't look like it's growing, but it's doing the most important work: establishing its roots. The same is true for you.

In your business, in your personal development, or in your faith journey, dips will come. Your job isn't to avoid them, it's to stay steady through them. To hold onto what you know, even when you don't feel it.

This is where encouragement becomes vital. And I don't just mean feel-good quotes or hype. I mean real, soul-level encouragement that reminds you: This dip is temporary. Keep going.

Start by talking to yourself instead of listening to yourself. Your feelings will try to convince you that you're not making progress, that it's not worth it, or that you're alone. But those feelings aren't facts. You can train your inner voice to speak truth in the middle of discouragement.

Declare out loud, "I am in process. God is at work. I am not turning back."

This is also where community becomes essential. When you're in a dip, you need voices that remind you of who you are, what you're capable of, and why you started. Graham Cooke often says, "The people you surround yourself with should see your process and still speak to your promise." Find those people. Stay close to them. And be that voice for someone else.

Practical encouragement tools can help you ride out the dip as well:

- **Keep a wins journal**: Record daily or weekly victories, no matter how small. When the dip comes, read back over those entries to remind yourself of how far you've come.
- **Create an "encouragement file"**: Save affirmations, messages from mentors, or Scriptures that speak life into you. Revisit them when you feel stuck.
- **Speak the Word**: Faith comes by hearing. Read and speak verses that anchor you in truth. Isaiah 40:31 says, "But those who hope in the Lord will renew their strength... they will run and not grow weary, they will walk and not be faint." That's not just poetry; it's a promise.
- **Accept the dip as part of growth**: Stop making it mean something negative. When you expect the dip, you won't panic when it arrives. You'll walk through it knowing momentum will return.

The dip is not your enemy. It's your invitation to deepen your trust, sharpen your focus, and solidify your commitment. The people who build extraordinary lives aren't the ones who never hit a low; they're the ones who don't let the low stop them.

So, if you're in the dip, take heart. Keep showing up. Keep sowing the right seeds. Your breakthrough isn't lost, it's just on the other side of your consistency.

VIII. Mentorship and Accountability for Ongoing Progress

If you've ever experienced a stall in your momentum, you know how sneaky it can be. One skipped task becomes two. Clarity starts to blur. Enthusiasm fades. Before you realize it, the progress you worked so hard to build feels like it's slipping away. That's why mentorship and accountability aren't just helpful, they're essential.

No one climbs to their next level alone. Even the most driven people hit walls. What separates those who break through from those who fall back is often the presence of a mentor or accountability partner who steps in to re-center, refocus, and reignite the mission.

Mentors offer more than just advice; they provide perspective. When you're caught in the weeds of your own challenges, a mentor sees the bigger picture. They remind you why you started, reflect the progress you may have forgotten, and help you course-correct without shame. They've walked the path ahead of you and can illuminate shortcuts, pitfalls, and blind spots you might otherwise miss.

I remember a time when I was stuck in a loop of over-planning and under-executing. I had goals, vision boards, and strategies, but little forward motion. It wasn't laziness; it was perfectionism wrapped in a disguise. A mentor of mine called it out. Not with judgment, but with clarity. He said, "Ray, you don't need another system. You need to move your feet. Action beats perfection." That wake-up call shifted everything.

Accountability does the same thing, especially when it's structured. Weekly check-ins, whether with a mentor, peer, or group, create a rhythm of reflection and forward movement. They force you to pause, evaluate your week, and make intentional choices about the next one.

In a group setting, this becomes even more powerful. Group calls or mastermind circles offer layered accountability. You're not just answering to a mentor, you're locking arms with others who are on the same path. Hearing someone else share a win reminds you what's possible. Hearing someone push through a challenge reminds you not to quit. And showing up to share your own update keeps you from drifting.

This isn't about pressure; it's about alignment. Consistent feedback keeps you aligned with your goals and your identity. Without it, it's easy to get lost in the noise or spiral into self-doubt. But with regular feedback, you gain clarity on what's working, what needs to shift, and how to take the next right step.

And don't overlook real-time feedback. Whether it's a mentor sending a voice message when you need a nudge, or a team chat that keeps energy high throughout the week, those small interactions add fuel to your fire. Momentum isn't always about big leaps; it's often sustained by these micro-adjustments, these check-ins that keep your vision sharp and your faith strong.

Biblically, this principle is rooted in wisdom and relationship. Proverbs 15:22 says, "Plans fail for lack of counsel, but with many advisers they succeed." And Hebrews 10:24-25 encourages us to "consider how we may spur one another on toward love and good deeds… encouraging one another."

You don't need to figure it all out alone. Find a mentor who sees your potential and holds you to it. Plug into a group that speaks your language of growth. Schedule weekly reviews, not as punishment, but as a gift to your future self. Surround yourself with people who won't let you shrink back.

Momentum doesn't happen in isolation. It's fueled in relationship, refined through accountability, and sustained through mentorship.

So, if you're serious about keeping your progress alive, don't just look inward; reach outward. The right voice at the right time can reignite your path and push you farther than you ever thought possible.

IX. Creating External Cues and Internal Drivers

One of the most overlooked secrets to sustained momentum isn't just willpower, it's structure. Specifically, the structure you create around yourself to remind, reinforce, and reenergize your commitment to progress. These structures come in two forms: external cues and internal drivers. Both play a critical role in making your momentum sustainable instead of situational.

External cues are the visual, auditory, and environmental signals that prompt action and keep your focus alive throughout the day. Think of them as reminders placed in your path on purpose. When life gets noisy and your goals start to blur, these cues help pull you back into alignment.

Something as simple as a vision board in your office, a daily affirmation on your phone lock screen, or sticky notes on your bathroom mirror can have a powerful effect. These aren't just motivational fluff. They are tangible anchors. Every time you see that image, phrase, or scripture, you're reminded of who you're becoming and why it matters.

Visualizations go a step deeper. Rather than just seeing something externally, you see yourself in it. Bob Proctor taught that our imagination is the workshop of the mind. If you want to build momentum, visualize yourself already operating from that place of power, purpose, and peace. See yourself finishing the project, having the difficult conversation, crossing the finish line. The clearer the image in your mind, the stronger the internal magnet that pulls you toward it.

But external cues alone aren't enough. You also need **internal drivers**, the deep, emotional reasons why you started in the first place. These are rooted in your identity and calling. When your actions are aligned with who you believe you are and what you're here to do, you move with energy and conviction.

Here's the key: your identity must come from truth, not past failure or fear. If you see yourself as undisciplined, inconsistent, or unworthy, your actions will reflect that belief. But if you begin to see yourself as called, equipped, and responsible for managing your gifts, momentum becomes a natural byproduct.

That's why I encourage you to revisit your internal "why" often. Write it down. Speak it aloud. Meditate on it in prayer. Ask: Who am I becoming, and what has God placed in me that the world needs? That internal connection is fuel. It pushes you forward on the days when motivation is low and distractions are high.

Pairing internal drivers with external cues creates a dynamic system of momentum reinforcement. Your environment reflects your focus, and your spirit stays anchored in truth. When those two are working together, you'll find yourself taking consistent action almost automatically.

Here are some practical ways to integrate this:

- **Morning Cue Stack**: Begin your day with a 5-minute sequence: affirmations, a short visualization, and reading your personal mission statement. This builds internal clarity before external chaos begins.
- **Environmental Engineering**: Design your workspace, phone background, and calendar alerts to keep your goals front and center. Don't let clutter or distraction hijack your energy.
- **Truth Reminders**: Keep a short list of scriptures, identity statements, or declarations nearby, places like your car

dashboard, bathroom mirror, or wallet. These redirect your mind when it starts to drift.

- **Weekly Reflection Prompt**: "Is my current pace aligned with my calling?" This one question can reset your focus and stir your internal motivation.

In Romans 12:2, Paul writes, "Be transformed by the renewing of your mind." That renewal happens through repetition; external cues and internal truths working in harmony until your actions reflect your highest identity.

Momentum isn't magic. It's a system. And when you structure your life with reminders that echo your calling and routines that support your growth, momentum becomes less fragile and more consistent.

You don't have to fight for progress every day. You just need to design for it. Let your surroundings speak truth. Let your spirit stay connected to your "why." That's how you build a life that moves forward by design, not by accident.

X. Practical Exercises and Reflection

Momentum doesn't happen by chance, it's built with intention, maintained through reflection, and refined through action. That's why this section is about taking inventory. Before you accelerate, you need to check the dashboard: What's fueling your growth? What's slowing you down? Where are the hidden leaks in your effort?

Let's start with a **Momentum Audit**. This exercise will help you identify what's actually supporting your forward motion, and what's quietly sabotaging it.

Momentum Audit: What's Working, What's Not

Doing What You Know

Take out a journal or open a document. Make two columns. On the left, write "What's Working." On the right, "What's Not."

Start by listing any actions, habits, mindsets, or systems that are actively helping you stay focused and moving forward. Be specific. This might include:

- Morning journaling that keeps your thoughts clear
- Regular calls with a mentor who holds you accountable
- Listening to faith-based podcasts that uplift your mindset
- Sticking to a content creation schedule
- Decluttering your workspace weekly

Then, shift to the right column. Write out what's not working. These are the habits, environments, or beliefs that are draining your energy, distracting you from your goals, or keeping you in a cycle of stop-and-start:

- Checking your phone first thing in the morning
- Avoiding uncomfortable tasks
- Saying yes to too many things out of guilt
- Comparing your progress to others
- Neglecting rest and proper recovery

Once the list is complete, don't just look at it; study it. Ask yourself:

- What patterns do I see?
- Where is my energy being multiplied, and where is it being stolen?
- What small change could create the biggest shift?

Remember, this isn't about self-criticism. It's about clarity. Without clarity, you'll repeat what you should be replacing.

30-Day Habit Commitment: Building an Action Plan

Now that you've identified what's helping and hindering your momentum, it's time to craft a 30-day plan based on three intentional habits. These habits should align with your identity, support your goals, and be sustainable, not overwhelming.

Step 1: Choose 3 Keystone Habits.

Pick one habit each in the areas of mindset, action, and environment.

Here's a sample breakdown:

- **Mindset**: Begin each day by speaking your top 3 affirmations aloud
- **Action**: Dedicate 60 minutes daily to your highest-priority task before checking email or social media
- **Environment**: Clean and reset your workspace every evening

Step 2: Create a Visual Tracker.

Use a printed calendar, habit-tracking app, or a whiteboard to mark off each day you complete the habit. Visibility increases consistency. When you see those boxes filling up, you'll want to keep the streak alive.

Step 3: Reflect Weekly.

Set a reminder every Sunday to evaluate your progress. Ask yourself:

- What helped me stay consistent this week?
- Where did I slip, and why?
- What adjustments do I need to make to stay aligned?

Include prayer and journaling in these weekly reviews. Invite God into your evaluation. Ask for wisdom, strength, and course correction.

Momentum isn't just about human effort; it's about partnering with divine guidance.

Step 4: Celebrate Small Wins.

Every seven days, take time to acknowledge your effort. Celebrate consistency, not perfection. Reward yourself with something life-giving: an inspiring book, a walk in nature, a dinner with someone who fuels your spirit. Let celebration reinforce the habit.

Closing Thoughts

The beauty of momentum is that it's self-reinforcing. Small wins build confidence. Confidence fuels action. Action creates more wins. But it all starts with awareness and commitment.

These exercises aren't meant to overwhelm you; they're meant to equip you. When you stop guessing and start auditing, you get clarity. And when you commit to a few habits, not ten, you gain traction.

You don't need a complete overhaul. You need a faithful plan and the willingness to work it. So, take a breath, grab your pen, and map out your next 30 days.

Your future self is already thanking you.

XI. Chapter Summary and Preview

Momentum isn't just a motivational buzzword. It's a living force that either propels you toward your purpose, or, if left unattended, slips away quietly, leaving you wondering where your progress went. In this chapter, we've explored the practical, spiritual, and emotional dimensions of keeping momentum alive, because without it, even the clearest goals and strongest intentions can lose steam.

We began by acknowledging a simple but often overlooked truth: early progress doesn't guarantee lasting change. Whether in your business, your spiritual walk, your relationships, or your personal growth, what you do after the initial spark matters far more than the excitement of getting started. Real transformation requires consistency, resilience, and the ability to adjust without losing sight of your direction.

We defined momentum as the cumulative effect of small, consistent actions. Drawing from the wisdom of thinkers like Jim Rohn and Napoleon Hill, we saw how effort compounds over time, creating exponential results. One action leads to the next, building confidence and clarity along the way. When you stay in motion, momentum works in your favor. But when you stop or hesitate too long, regaining traction can feel like starting over.

We also addressed the **science and spiritual law** behind momentum. Consistency doesn't just change your results, it changes you. It transforms your identity, aligns your beliefs with your actions, and begins to rewire your subconscious patterns. The Bible offers powerful affirmations of this principle, reminding us in stories like the parable of the talents that faithfulness in small things leads to greater increase.

But keeping momentum isn't easy. That's why we identified the **momentum killers** that most commonly trip people up: distractions, discouragement, comparison, and lack of clarity. We talked about how these forces can subtly drain your energy and cause emotional dips that masquerade as "just being tired" or "losing interest," when really, they're indicators of disconnection from your vision or purpose.

To protect against those dips, we introduced daily and weekly practices: morning routines, evening reflection, gratitude journaling, and centering back on your "why." These rituals aren't just tasks, they're anchors. They stabilize you when motivation fades and keep your internal compass pointed toward your calling.

We also emphasized the **role of faith** and the emotional cycles of growth. Every person who steps out to pursue something greater will face a valley, what Graham Cooke calls the "hidden season," where progress seems invisible. But it's often in those quiet, unseen moments that the deepest transformation occurs. Encouragement in those seasons isn't a luxury; it's a necessity.

Then we explored **the power of mentorship and accountability**. Progress rarely happens in isolation. People grow best in relationships, especially when those relationships challenge and support them. Whether through weekly check-ins, group calls, or one-on-one coaching, mentorship is what helps you reset when you stall and keep moving when you're tempted to give up.

You also learned about **external cues and internal drivers**, how your physical environment, digital intake, and spoken affirmations can either amplify your momentum or steal it. By creating spaces that support your focus and routines that reinforce your identity, you reduce resistance and build flow.

And finally, in the last section, we walked through **practical exercises** to do a momentum audit and commit to three keystone habits for the next 30 days. These small steps, done with consistency, create waves of change that eventually turn into a lifestyle of inspired, purpose-driven action.

Preview: Aligning Your Growth with a Greater Purpose

In the next chapter, we're going to zoom out. Up to this point, we've focused on getting aligned with your identity, conquering fear, creating discipline, managing emotions, and building momentum. But here's the big question that sets everything else in motion: What's it all for?

Chapter 12 is about aligning your growth with a greater purpose. It's one thing to grow for your own success, but when your growth becomes part of a divine mission, when your progress starts serving others, it changes everything. You stop chasing goals and start answering a calling. You shift from performance to purpose. And that's when your journey becomes unstoppable.

Get ready to connect the dots between your inner transformation and the impact you're meant to have in the world.

Let's go there together.

Chapter 12: Purpose-Driven Living: Aligning Actions with Values

I. Introduction

I remember a time in my life where, on paper, everything looked successful. I had a growing business, consistent income, recognition from my peers, and a schedule packed with opportunity. Yet, underneath the surface, I felt strangely hollow. The fire that once fueled my ambition had dulled into a low flicker. I was getting things done, hitting my targets, and staying productive, but I wasn't fulfilled.

It was during this time that I began to question what "success" really meant to me. Was it simply checking off boxes, building income streams, or achieving recognition? Or was there something deeper calling to me, something more lasting and life-giving than just performance and results?

This is the tension many of us face in the pursuit of our goals: the tug-of-war between outer achievement and inner alignment. We may be doing all the right things outwardly, but if our actions aren't connected to our values, if our path isn't guided by purpose, we eventually run dry. No matter how disciplined or productive you are, if you're out of alignment with what truly matters to you, burnout is inevitable.

Burnout doesn't always show up as exhaustion. Sometimes it shows up as restlessness, cynicism, or a persistent sense that you're meant for more, even when you're already "doing a lot." It's that quiet voice inside that whispers, "This isn't quite it," even though everyone else is applauding your progress.

This disconnect is often the result of what I call "success without substance." It happens when we pursue goals based on external expectations rather than internal conviction. We chase metrics,

243

milestones, and admiration, but lose connection with who we are, what we stand for, and why we started in the first place.

In contrast, when your daily actions reflect your values, something shifts. Your work gains meaning. Your energy multiplies. You stop striving and start flowing. You feel anchored, no longer tossed by every opportunity or shiny object. Instead of chasing more, you begin living your mission.

This chapter is about realignment. It's an invitation to pause and ask deeper questions. Are the things you're doing each day aligned with the person you want to become? Is your business, your work, and your relationships an honest reflection of your purpose? Or are they echoes of someone else's priorities?

Living purposefully doesn't mean abandoning ambition. It means refining it. It means running after your goals with clarity and conviction, knowing they're rooted in who you are and what you're here to contribute.

As we walk through this chapter, we'll explore what it really means to live a purpose-driven life. We'll define the difference between chasing goals and living on purpose. We'll walk through ways to clarify your core values, align your habits with those values, and create a rhythm of life that supports sustainable growth, not just success.

We'll also look at how faith plays a role in revealing and anchoring your purpose, and how mentorship can help you stay aligned when life or business gets noisy. Whether you're at the beginning of your journey or in the middle of a major pivot, this chapter will help you root your actions in something deeper, something that lasts.

Because when you live from purpose, everything changes. Your energy shifts, your results compound, and most importantly, your fulfillment deepens, not because everything goes perfectly, but because you know you're walking in alignment with who you're meant to be.

II: Defining Purpose-Driven Living

Many people spend their lives chasing goals: career milestones, income targets, social status, or even material possessions. These pursuits often come from a desire to achieve or prove something, and while they may bring short-term satisfaction, they rarely offer long-term fulfillment. The truth is, goals are important, but they're not enough on their own. Without a deeper purpose guiding them, goals can become exhausting, even hollow.

Living on purpose is fundamentally different. It's not about what you're chasing; it's about what's pulling you forward from the inside. Purpose-driven living means that everything you do is aligned with who you are and what you truly value. It's not motivated by ego, fear, or external pressure. It flows from your identity, your beliefs, and your deepest "why."

Jim Rohn once said, "If you don't design your own life plan, chances are you'll fall into someone else's. And guess what they have planned for you? Not much." That's a sobering truth. Many people are running on someone else's script, living lives shaped by culture, family, or fear rather than clarity and conviction. Purpose-driven living is about tearing up that old script and writing your own.

Bob Proctor added another layer when he emphasized that our actions must align with our paradigms, our internal belief systems. He taught that purpose isn't just a nice idea; it's the fuel that activates the best version of ourselves. When our purpose is clear, it becomes easier to say no to distractions and yes to growth. When we act in alignment with our values, we gain momentum, confidence, and peace of mind.

Here's the real distinction: chasing goals is usually outcome-focused. It says, "I'll be happy when…" Living on purpose is process-focused. It says, "I'm fulfilled now because I'm doing what I was made to do." One is conditional. The other is rooted in identity.

This doesn't mean goals are bad. In fact, when they're built on a foundation of purpose, goals become powerful tools for growth and contribution. They become expressions of who you are, not just boxes to check off. That's what transforms hustle into harmony and effort into impact.

Purpose-driven living also simplifies decision-making. When you know what matters most to you, it's easier to filter out noise and focus on what aligns. You stop being reactive and start being intentional. Your yeses and noes carry more weight. Your schedule reflects your values, not just your obligations.

And here's what's beautiful about purpose: it evolves. It deepens as you grow. What felt purposeful ten years ago may not serve you now. That's okay. The goal isn't to lock in one version of purpose forever, but to remain in constant relationship with it. Check in with it. Let it guide you. Let it shape how you build, lead, and live.

If you find yourself busy but not fulfilled, productive but not passionate, it may be time to pause and ask, "Is what I'm doing aligned with what I value?" That's the question that flips the switch from goal-chasing to purpose-living.

In the next section, we'll dig deeper into how to clarify your core values so you can begin building a life that not only looks good from the outside but feels deeply aligned on the inside.

III: Clarifying Your Core Values

You can't live a purpose-driven life if you haven't first defined what actually matters to you. Core values are the non-negotiables, those deeply held beliefs that guide your decisions, shape your behavior, and determine what "success" truly looks like for you. Without clarity on these values, it's easy to drift, chase empty goals, or allow the world to define your direction.

Start here: What principles are so important to you that compromising them would make you feel like you've lost a piece of yourself?

Maybe it's integrity. Maybe it's faith. Maybe it's contribution, family, excellence, or freedom. These aren't just lofty ideals, they're the compass points of a life well-lived. They help you measure not just what you're doing, but why you're doing it and who you're becoming in the process.

Exercise 1: The Values Inventory

Take 10 minutes and list the top 10 things that matter most to you. Don't overthink it. Include both internal qualities (like courage, creativity, or patience) and external priorities (like your family, calling, or legacy).

Next, narrow it down to your top five. These are your non-negotiables. If life was stripped down to just these five values, you'd still feel fulfilled.

Now, ask yourself: How aligned is my current daily life with these five values?

That one question alone can be eye-opening. You may discover that while you say you value freedom, your schedule is crammed with obligations. Or that while you value connection, you've been isolated. The goal isn't guilt, it's awareness. Because with awareness comes power.

Exercise 2: The "Hard Decision" Test

Think back to a time when you had to make a hard decision. What value ultimately guided you? Was it a commitment to truth? A sense of responsibility? A desire to grow?

Now flip it. Recall a moment when you made a decision that left you unsettled afterward. Which value did you ignore or compromise in that moment? These situations shine a light on your real value system, not the one you talk about, but the one you live by. That's where transformation begins.

Faith and Spiritual Identity

For many people, including me, faith plays a central role in defining purpose and values. Scripture gives us a blueprint of what a values-centered life can look like. Take Micah 6:8: "What does the Lord require of you? To act justly and to love mercy and to walk humbly with your God." That's not just a command, it's a value system: justice, mercy, humility.

Or consider the fruit of the Spirit listed in Galatians 5:22-23: love, joy, peace, patience, kindness, goodness, faithfulness, gentleness, and self-control. These aren't just admirable traits. They are spiritual values that shape how we treat others, how we show up, and how we build our lives.

When you root your values in your identity as a child of God, they don't shift with moods, circumstances, or culture. They become stable anchors. Graham Cooke often says, "Your identity is the starting point, not your behavior." In other words, you're not trying to earn your way into being a good person. You're choosing to live out of the truth of who God says you already are.

So, when you sit down to clarify your core values, don't just look inward. Look upward. Ask God to reveal the principles He wants you to live by.

Then ask yourself: What would my life look like if these values were visible in everything I do, from my business to my relationships to my private moments?

When you define and align with your core values, both personal and spiritual, you'll experience clarity, peace, and power. You'll begin to live not from pressure, but from purpose.

Next, we'll look at how to align your everyday actions with those core values, so you can live in true integrity and momentum.

IV: Aligning Daily Actions with Core Values

It's one thing to identify your core values. It's another to actually live them. Many people say they value health, but they don't move their bodies. Others claim to value financial freedom, but they spend impulsively. Someone might believe in the importance of faith, but rarely engage in prayer, worship, or study. The disconnect isn't always conscious, but it's costly.

Living in alignment with your values is about congruence. It's the ability to look at your calendar, your habits, and your energy and say, "This reflects what matters most to me." That kind of alignment builds confidence, reduces stress, and multiplies impact.

So, the real question becomes: Do your daily actions support or sabotage your stated values?

Let's say one of your core values is family. How often are you fully present when you're with them? Are you carving out intentional time, or just fitting them in between work and social media?

Maybe one of your values is contribution. Do your routines include time to serve others, or are you so caught up in survival mode that giving back feels like a luxury?

When your actions and values don't match, it creates inner conflict, what psychologists call "cognitive dissonance." That friction might show up as anxiety, guilt, burnout, or procrastination. You know you're meant to live one way, but you're operating on autopilot in another.

The Daily Alignment Audit

Try this simple tool: for the next three days, track how you spend your time. You don't need a fancy system, just note your activities every hour. At the end of each day, review your log through the lens of your top five core values (from the previous section). Ask:

- What percentage of my time today reflected my values?
- Where did I drift into misalignment?
- What is one thing I could do differently tomorrow?

Even subtle misalignments add up. But so do small, intentional shifts.

The Power of Micro Shifts

You don't need to blow up your life to live with integrity. In fact, big changes often fail because they're unsustainable. The goal here is integration, not interruption.

For example:

- If you value growth, replace 15 minutes of scrolling with reading.
- If you value peace, start your day in silence or prayer before checking your phone.
- If you value excellence, clean your workspace at the end of the day.
- If you value health, prep water and snacks before diving into your work block.

Small hinges swing big doors. The shift doesn't have to be dramatic. It just has to be intentional.

Spiritual Alignment and Obedience

Faith plays a major role in alignment. Romans 12:2 reminds us to be "transformed by the renewing of your mind." That means transformation starts with what you think, and flows into what you do. Faith without works is dead, and values without action are just nice ideas.

Graham Cooke says, "You are a new creation. Live like it." That's alignment. Not just believing you are purposeful, valuable, and anointed, but arranging your life to reflect that truth.

Ask yourself:

- If I truly believed I was called to greatness, how would I structure my day?
- If I truly valued peace, how would I protect it in my schedule?
- If I truly prioritized faith, where would it show up in my routines?

When your outer life matches your inner convictions, everything flows more freely. Integrity isn't just about morality, it's about wholeness. It's about no longer living in fragments, no longer presenting one version of yourself in public and another in private.

Living aligned means you can look in the mirror without flinching. It means your habits and your heart are finally walking the same path.

Next, we'll explore how faith can act as your compass for making those aligned decisions, especially when the road isn't clear.

V: Faith as a Compass for Purpose

Purpose isn't something you randomly stumble upon. It's not buried treasure you dig up after years of trying to "find yourself." In the kingdom of God, purpose is revealed, not through striving, but through surrender.

At the heart of purpose-driven living is faith. Without faith, all the goals and plans in the world still feel hollow. With faith, your steps may not be certain, but they are guided. And that makes all the difference.

Jeremiah 29:11 says, "For I know the plans I have for you," declares the Lord, "plans to prosper you and not to harm you, plans to give you a future and a hope." That's not vague encouragement, that's a divine guarantee. God already has a purpose for your life. He isn't improvising as you go. Your job isn't to invent your purpose, it's to receive it, align with it, and walk it out.

But here's the challenge: we often try to figure it all out before we take the first step. We want the full map, not just the next turn. That's where Proverbs 3:5–6 becomes essential: "Trust in the Lord with all your heart and lean not on your own understanding; in all your ways submit to Him, and He will make your paths straight." Your understanding is limited. God's vision is not.

When you truly trust that God has your future covered, you stop forcing outcomes. You stop hustling for identity. You stop comparing your pace to someone else's highlight reel. Faith becomes the compass that keeps you on track when your emotions try to pull you off course.

Discovering Purpose Through Intimacy

Graham Cooke teaches that purpose is best discovered in the presence of God. Not in a boardroom, not in a brainstorming session, not even on a retreat. True purpose is revealed through intimacy, in the quiet, unseen places where your identity is affirmed and your calling begins to take shape.

He puts it this way: "God is not in a hurry to give you answers. He wants to walk with you long enough that you become the answer." That shift in perspective is everything. Your purpose isn't just a task. It's not just what you do, it's who you become in the process of knowing Him.

In intimacy with God, you learn that you're not defined by your productivity. You're not validated by your results. You are called; simply because He says so.

So instead of anxiously asking, "What should I be doing with my life?", the faith-centered question becomes, "Who am I becoming in partnership with God?"

From that space of intimacy, your actions begin to align naturally with divine purpose. You stop looking for formulas and start listening for direction. You stop striving to create meaning and start receiving it as a gift.

When Purpose Feels Distant

There will be times when your purpose feels unclear. Maybe your circumstances don't make sense. Maybe the fruit of your obedience is delayed. This is where many people get discouraged and default to self-made plans.

But faith says: "Even when I don't see the whole picture, I'll trust the One who does." Like Abraham being called out without knowing the destination. Like Moses stepping into leadership even when he felt unqualified. Purpose always requires faith. And faith always requires obedience without full understanding.

When you lean into faith as your compass, you start moving not just toward what you want, but toward who you're meant to be.

Let God's voice be the loudest in your life. Let His Word be your foundation. Let His presence be the source of your confidence. Purpose doesn't come from figuring everything out; it comes from following the One who already has.

Next, we'll look at what happens when we ignore this alignment, when we chase success but lose ourselves in the process.

VI: The Cost of Misalignment

Success without alignment is a recipe for burnout. Many people climb the ladder of achievement only to realize it's leaning against the wrong wall. They hit milestones, earn promotions, or build businesses, but feel hollow when the applause fades. That's the high cost of misalignment, when what you're doing no longer resonates with why you're doing it.

At first, you might not even notice it. You're busy. You're productive. You're checking all the boxes. But somewhere along the way, your energy begins to dip. Your motivation becomes forced. You dread the very work that used to light you up. That's not laziness, it's often your soul trying to send a message: "You've drifted too far from your true north."

The Emotional and Physical Toll

Living out of alignment with your values slowly corrodes your joy, your clarity, and even your health. Stress becomes chronic. You feel constantly behind, no matter how much you accomplish. And perhaps worst of all, your confidence starts to erode, not because you're failing, but because deep down, you know you're not where you're supposed to be.

This is the point where many people either double down on the hustle or completely shut down. Neither is the answer.

True fulfillment isn't found in achieving more. It's found in aligning more deeply with your God-given purpose. When that alignment is missing, you might succeed outwardly but feel like a fraud inwardly. That internal dissonance will always surface, whether in your relationships, your health, or your peace of mind.

A Personal Story of Burnout and Realignment

Several years ago, I found myself hitting all my "success" targets: steady income, growing influence, and external recognition. But inside, I was empty. I was grinding through tasks I no longer believed in. I'd become an expert at masking exhaustion and pushing through the fog, but at some point, the cracks became impossible to hide.

I remember sitting at my desk late one night, staring at a glowing screen with a to-do list that never seemed to shrink. My chest was tight. My thoughts were scattered. And for the first time in years, I asked myself a hard question: "If this isn't it... then what is?"

That was the beginning of realignment.

Through prayer, journaling, and mentorship, I began peeling back the layers. I reconnected with the original why that launched my journey. I realized that I had allowed busyness to replace intimacy with God. I was running a race He never told me to enter.

And when I finally surrendered, something powerful happened. The fog lifted. Peace returned. Not because my circumstances changed overnight, but because I changed. I was no longer running on fumes; I was moving in sync with purpose again.

Faith and Mentorship: Keys to Course Correction

Realignment requires two powerful forces: faith and mentorship.

Faith allows you to pause and listen to the still, small voice that's been drowned out by activity. It gives you permission to stop striving and start seeking. God doesn't just want you to be effective; He wants you to be fulfilled. And He will guide you, if you're willing to follow.

Mentorship is the mirror you sometimes need when you can't see clearly. A good mentor won't just applaud your results; they'll ask the tough questions. They'll help you see the bigger picture, recalibrate your motives, and remind you who you really are.

Whether it's a trusted spiritual advisor, a coach, or a seasoned leader, the right voices in your life can help you rediscover your true path and give you the courage to walk it.

Misalignment is costly, but it's also reversible. When you're brave enough to stop and ask whether your actions still reflect your values, you give yourself the chance to pivot. That pivot may feel uncomfortable at first, but it leads to peace, clarity, and a deeper sense of calling.

In the next section, we'll explore how to create rhythms and habits that keep you anchored in purpose, so you don't drift again.

VII: Cultivating Purposeful Habits

Living on purpose doesn't happen by accident. It's not just about having grand visions or waiting for inspiration to strike. It's about creating a rhythm, a daily cadence, that reinforces meaning over motion. Many people spend their days spinning in constant activity but never move closer to the life they were designed to live. That's because motion without meaning eventually leads to burnout, while even small steps taken in alignment with purpose build lasting momentum and deep fulfillment.

Meaningful Rhythm Over Mindless Routine

The first step in cultivating purposeful habits is to evaluate your current rhythm. Is your day driven by reaction or intention? Do your routines reflect your highest values or simply your most urgent distractions?

A purpose-driven rhythm begins before the day even starts. The way you begin your morning sets the tone for everything that follows. Instead of grabbing your phone and scrolling through other people's agendas, imagine starting your day in silence, aligning with your Creator, grounding yourself in truth, and declaring your intentions before the world tries to impose its demands.

That's not idealistic. That's strategic.

Purpose isn't about adding more to your plate; it's about structuring your life so that the most important things always come first. And when they do, everything else starts to find its place.

Journaling as a Tool for Awareness

One of the most powerful tools for cultivating purposeful habits is journaling. Not a daily diary of everything you did, but a place to process who you're becoming. When you journal consistently, you create space to reflect on your actions, evaluate your motives, and redirect your focus when you drift.

Try using prompts like:

- "What did I do today that aligned with my purpose?"
- "Where did I compromise or shrink back?"
- "What lesson is God trying to teach me right now?"

The clarity that comes from writing things down is unmatched. It takes your swirling thoughts and gives them shape. It allows the subconscious to surface and gives your spirit a voice in the chaos.

Prayer as a Centering Habit

Purposeful people don't rely solely on intellect or hustle. They lean into divine wisdom. Prayer isn't just about asking for things, it's about aligning your will with God's. It's about receiving guidance, building intimacy, and staying sensitive to spiritual promptings.

When prayer becomes a non-negotiable part of your rhythm, you stop running in the wrong direction. You start catching divine ideas, sensing what's urgent and what's not, and making decisions from a place of peace instead of panic.

Your purpose will always be bigger than your own capacity; that's why partnering with God daily is essential. It keeps you grounded, focused, and connected to a source greater than yourself.

Intentional Goal Setting

Too many people set goals based on what they think they should want, not what truly matters to them. Purposeful habits include aligning your goals with your values. If family is a core value, your schedule should reflect that. If faith is foundational, it should shape your calendar.

Set goals that flow from your purpose, not just your ambition. Use the SMART method, Specific, Measurable, Achievable, Relevant, and Time-bound, but anchor each one in a deeper why. Then break those goals into daily habits and checkpoints.

Don't underestimate the power of tracking. What you track improves. Whether it's in a journal, an app, or a sticky note on your desk, keep your purpose in front of you. Make it harder to forget what matters most.

Cultivating purposeful habits isn't about perfection. It's about intentionality. When you build a rhythm that includes reflection, connection, and action, your life begins to reflect the person you were created to be, not just in moments of clarity, but in the consistency of everyday living.

VIII: Mentorship for Staying on Track

Pursuing a purpose-driven life is one of the most rewarding and challenging decisions a person can make. But staying on track, especially when distractions, doubts, and detours show up, often requires more than willpower; it requires wisdom. That's where mentorship becomes essential.

No one fulfills their purpose alone. Even the most self-motivated individuals benefit from the clarity, accountability, and elevation that come from walking with someone who's further down the road. Mentors help you see what you can't yet see, believe when your faith wavers, and act when you're tempted to stall. In short, they help you stay aligned with who you're becoming.

The Biblical Blueprint for Mentorship

Scripture is full of examples of mentorship: Moses had Jethro, Joshua had Moses, Paul had Barnabas, and Timothy had Paul. The model is clear: God often works through people to guide and grow us.

Proverbs 15:22 says, "Plans fail for lack of counsel, but with many advisers they succeed." Mentorship isn't just helpful, it's biblical. When you open your life to wise counsel, you tap into a divine strategy for growth and guidance. It's not a sign of weakness. It's a mark of maturity.

Purpose without feedback can easily drift into ego. Mentors help strip away the noise and highlight what's really aligned with your core values and calling. They speak truth in love, not to flatter you, but to forge you.

Discovering Purpose Through Guided Insight

One of the most powerful things a mentor brings to the table is perspective. When you're in the trenches of your own journey, it's easy to miss patterns or fall into self-sabotage. A good mentor has the ability to spot your blind spots and help you correct your course without shaming you for drifting.

They ask better questions. They challenge you to dig deeper. They help you articulate your "why" when you've lost touch with it. Many people spend years chasing goals that were never theirs to begin with; goals handed down by culture, family, or fear. Mentors help you filter those ambitions through the lens of your values and faith.

Realignment Through Relationship

Living on purpose doesn't mean you'll never wander. Life gets noisy. Circumstances shift. Emotions cloud judgment. In those moments, a mentor acts like a compass, helping you realign with what matters.

Whether it's a spiritual leader, a coach, or a trusted elder, a good mentor reminds you of your identity when you're tempted to shrink or stray. They don't just hold you accountable to tasks; they hold you accountable to your calling. They don't let you forget who you are or why you started.

They can also help you discern between good ideas and God ideas, between distractions dressed up as opportunities and the real assignments that require your obedience. That discernment becomes crucial as your influence and options grow.

Choosing the Right Mentors

Not all advice is created equal. Just because someone is successful doesn't mean they're equipped to mentor you. Look for people who:

- Live in alignment with their own values
- Have fruit in the areas you want to grow
- Walk with humility and integrity
- Challenge you, not just cheerlead you

Mentorship is sacred. Choose your guides wisely and be open to the unexpected. Sometimes God sends mentors in forms you didn't anticipate.

If you're serious about living purposefully, surround yourself with people who refuse to let you settle. Let their insight stretch you. Let their wisdom correct you. Let their example inspire you.

In the next section, we'll explore how to live out that purpose both in business and in life, so that your mission becomes not just a personal conviction but a public impact. Let's keep moving forward.

IX: Living Purposefully in Business and Life

Living purposefully isn't something you turn on when you're journaling or sitting in a quiet devotional moment; it's something that needs to run through everything you do, especially your work. If your business and lifestyle are divorced from your deepest values, you'll always feel that inner tension. You may look successful to others, but inside, you'll know something's off.

When you begin integrating your mission, message, and marketplace, everything changes.

Your Mission: The Why Behind the Work

Purpose-driven living starts with clarity of mission. What are you here to do? What's the bigger picture behind your brand, your offer, and your outreach?

Your mission isn't just about making money. It's about making meaning. It's about serving others in a way that feels congruent with your spiritual DNA. Whether you're leading a team, coaching clients, selling products, or building a platform, your mission should reflect your heart.

When your business decisions are filtered through your purpose, you won't chase every shiny opportunity. You'll become more focused, more intentional, and more magnetic to the right people.

Your Message: The Voice of Your Values

Your message is how you communicate your mission to the world. It's not just your marketing, it's your tone, your presence, and your integrity. Your message says, "This is who I am. This is what I believe. And this is how I show up."

Far too many entrepreneurs adopt a voice that doesn't sound like them. They dilute their convictions because they're afraid of losing followers or sales. But when you lose your voice, you lose your power.

A purpose-driven message is bold, clear, and authentic. It speaks to a specific audience, not to the masses. It resonates with those who share your values and attracts the kind of tribe that aligns with your long-term vision.

Remember, your message should never contradict your mission. The two must walk hand in hand, or people will sense the disconnect.

Your Marketplace: Where You Serve and Solve

Now let's talk about the marketplace. This is where your mission and message get tested in the real world. This is where you earn trust and income by solving real problems for real people.

Too many people treat business like a separate realm from their values. But in truth, your marketplace is the most tangible expression of your purpose. When you bring faith, integrity, and intention into your business decisions, how you price, how you serve, and how you follow up, you begin building something bigger than a paycheck.

Bob Proctor often said, "The purpose of a goal is not to get, it's to grow." The same is true in business. If your marketplace activity is growing you closer to your purpose and deeper into service, you're doing it right.

Alignment = Influence + Fulfillment

When your mission, message, and marketplace align, something powerful happens. You begin to build not just a business, but a movement. You become someone others trust, not because you're loud, but because you're consistent. You're not just saying the right things; you're living them.

That alignment builds credibility. People can feel when someone is walking in integrity. They sense the difference between hype and heart. And when your work matches your walk, your influence grows naturally.

Even more important than influence is fulfillment. There's a kind of peace that comes from knowing you're showing up as your whole self, in business, in life, and in relationships. You're not performing. You're not pretending. You're living aligned.

As we approach the final sections of this chapter, I want to encourage you to ask yourself: Am I integrating my values into every area of my life and business? If the answer is no, that's not a failure. It's a signal A signal that it's time to realign.

And the good news? It doesn't take a massive overhaul. It starts with one courageous decision at a time.

Let's keep going.

X: Practical Exercises and Reflection

Reading about purpose is one thing, living it is another. Many people get inspired after reading a book, hearing a podcast, or attending a seminar, only to slip right back into old routines. Why? Because inspiration without aligned action fades fast. That's why this section isn't just a feel-good moment. It's a call to evaluate, engage, and adjust.

It's time to do the work.

Below, you'll find a series of exercises and reflection prompts designed to help you identify gaps between your stated values and your daily behavior, so you can start closing those gaps, on purpose.

Exercise 1: The Purpose Alignment Worksheet

Take a piece of paper (or open your journal) and draw two columns.

Column 1: My Core Values

Write down your top 5–7 core values. These might include faith, honesty, family, service, growth, health, creativity, generosity, or discipline. Don't overthink it. Just go with the values that feel immovable for you, the non-negotiables that shape who you are.

Column 2: My Daily Actions

Now list your typical daily routines and behaviors, how you spend your mornings, how you treat others, how you spend money, who you interact with, how you talk to yourself, how you rest, and how you pursue your goals.

Next, draw lines connecting your values to the actions that support them.

Now look again.

Where are the gaps?

Which actions don't align with any core value?

Which values are neglected altogether?

This exercise often reveals misalignment you've sensed but couldn't clearly identify. Maybe you value connection, but spend your free time scrolling in isolation. Maybe you value health, but constantly skip workouts or eat in ways that don't honor your body. Maybe you say you value faith, but never set time aside to connect with God.

This awareness is powerful. Not for judgment, but for correction.

Exercise 2: Stop/Start Commitment Prompt

Now answer these two questions:

1. **What's one thing I need to STOP doing to live more aligned with my purpose?**
    Be honest. Is it a habit, a relationship, a mindset, a routine, or a compromise you've been justifying? Stopping something doesn't mean you're a failure. It means you're growing. Write it down. Make it specific.

Examples:

- I will stop saying yes to things I no longer feel called to.
- I will stop surrounding myself with people who tear down my faith or dreams.
- I will stop scrolling through social media when I feel stuck.

2. What's one thing I will START doing this week to live more aligned?

This doesn't need to be monumental. Small steps create momentum. The key is that it reflects a true value of yours and brings your behavior closer to your belief.

Examples:

- I will start a 15-minute morning journaling practice focused on gratitude and clarity.
- I will start reaching out to one new person a week aligned with my purpose.
- I will start reading scripture daily to center my decisions in faith.

Daily Reflection Practice: The 5-Minute Alignment Check-In

End your day with these simple questions:

1. What did I do today that aligned with my values?
2. Where did I feel out of alignment?
3. What do I need to adjust tomorrow?

This practice builds self-awareness and keeps your growth on track. Remember, alignment doesn't mean perfection; it means attention. It means you're living on purpose, not on autopilot.

Final Word on Integration

You were never meant to separate your purpose from your actions. True fulfillment comes when the way you live matches the reason you're here. These exercises aren't just boxes to check; they're bridges from who you've been to who you're becoming.

And the more aligned you become, the lighter you'll feel, the clearer your path will look, and the more effective your actions will become.

Let's move forward, on purpose.

XI: Chapter Summary and Preview

As we close this chapter on purpose-driven living, let's pause and reflect on the journey we've just taken together. This chapter wasn't about motivational hype or lofty ideals; it was about alignment. And alignment, when lived out daily, becomes one of the most powerful forces in your personal transformation.

We started by looking at the subtle but critical tension between success and meaning. Many people chase achievement, hoping it will fill a deeper void, only to arrive at their goals feeling empty, unfulfilled, or lost. Why? Because when your actions are misaligned with your values, the outcome may look good on paper, but it won't feel good in your soul.

Living purposefully means stepping away from surface-level success and choosing a deeper, more intentional way of showing up in the world. It means making decisions, big and small, based on who you truly are, not just what the world says you should be chasing.

Recapping the Key Insights

1. Purpose isn't just a destination; it's a way of living.

You don't need to have it all figured out to live on purpose. You just need to keep showing up every day with integrity, intention, and a commitment to honoring your core values. This creates a rhythm of fulfillment that no amount of hustle or external success can replace.

2. Core values are your internal compass.

We explored how to identify the non-negotiables in your life: the beliefs, principles, and convictions that define who you are. These values aren't just words on a wall; they're the foundation of every decision that leads to peace, progress, and purpose.

3. Alignment is visible in your habits.

Your calendar and your behavior tell the real story. If your daily routines don't reflect your values, the result will be misalignment, and eventually, burnout or regret. Small shifts in how you manage your time, energy, and focus can realign you with what matters most.

4. Faith anchors purpose.

When you align your life with God's plan, things start to move with a clarity and grace that can't be forced. We looked at biblical foundations for purpose, such as Jeremiah 29:11 and Proverbs 3:5–6, and how intimacy with God reveals direction. Faith isn't a side-note to purpose; it's the source of it.

5. Mentorship matters.

Purpose isn't something you chase alone. The right mentors help you refine your vision, challenge your blind spots, and walk with you as you become the person you were created to be. Community strengthens clarity.

6. You need practical tools, not just philosophy.

This chapter gave you worksheets, reflection questions, and exercises to evaluate how closely your current life reflects your deepest values. Awareness is the first step. Action is what makes it real.

Looking Ahead: Sustaining Transformation Through Faith

Now that you've begun aligning your actions with your purpose, the natural question becomes: **How do I sustain it?** How do I stay anchored when life gets noisy again, when setbacks come, motivation dips, or distractions creep back in?

That's exactly what Chapter 13 is here to help you do.

But make no mistake, this isn't the final chapter. It's the **launchpad** for the final phase of your journey. The next few chapters will guide you deeper into sustainable transformation. They'll show you how to walk this out with resilience, grace, and faith; not for a season, but for a lifetime.

In Chapter 13, we'll dive into:

- How to anchor your identity so deeply in God that life's storms can't shake your core
- Building spiritual disciplines that support your progress long after the initial fire fades
- Creating systems of accountability and grace to carry you through the highs and lows
- And stepping forward in your calling with clarity, courage, and a deeper sense of peace

Because lasting change isn't just about what you do once. It's about **who you become over time** and how well you protect, nurture, and honor that person daily.

So, pause for a moment. Let what you've just worked through settle in.

Then take a deep breath, because you're not winding down, you're leveling up.

You're stepping into the part of the journey where change becomes lifestyle… and lifestyle becomes legacy.

Let's keep building it together.

Chapter 13: The Role of Faith in Lasting Change

I. Introduction: From Temporary to Transformational

I've had times when I made big promises to myself. You probably have too. I'd get fired up from a seminar, inspired by a book, or convicted after hitting a low point. And for a few weeks, maybe even a couple of months, I'd stay on track. I'd do the thing. I'd show up, stick to the plan, say all the affirmations, and act like I was in control.

But then... life.

Distractions crept in. Old habits started whispering again. The momentum faded. And before I knew it, I was back where I started: frustrated, spinning my wheels, and wondering why the change didn't last. It took me a while to see it, but looking back, I realize those shifts were missing something critical: **a foundation of faith.**

Here's what I've come to believe, and it's not based on theory, it's based on experience: **You can't create lasting transformation without rooting your growth in something deeper than motivation.** Motivation is loud, but it's short-lived. Inspiration is great, but it fades. Even discipline, if built on willpower alone, eventually hits a wall.

But faith? Faith digs deep. Faith doesn't just prop you up when you're strong, it holds you when you're weak. It keeps speaking when everything else is silent. Faith is the anchor that keeps you from drifting and the fuel that keeps your fire alive when the winds of life try to snuff it out.

There's a huge difference between changing a behavior and transforming a life. One is external. The other is rooted in identity. And your **identity is shaped by what you believe** about yourself, about your purpose, and about the God who created you.

That's why this chapter matters.

If you've made progress already in your mindset, your discipline, your clarity, or your consistency, I want to assure you that's real. You've done the work. But I also want to challenge you to go deeper. Because if you don't anchor that growth in something unshakable, it'll always be vulnerable to disruption.

I've walked this road. I've seen what happens when people build on hype, on hustle, or even on fear. And I've also seen what happens when people build on truth, on trust, and on the quiet, powerful confidence that comes from knowing you're walking with God.

That's what this chapter is about.

You're going to see how faith isn't just something you "add" to your growth journey. It's the source of strength, wisdom, peace, and direction. It's not about being religious, it's about being rooted. Because when you're rooted in faith, your growth doesn't depend on perfect circumstances or constant motivation. It flows from a deeper place, a place that doesn't run dry.

We're going to talk about:

- Why temporary change fails without spiritual depth
- What it means to build your transformation on a foundation of faith
- How to lean on God for daily strength and long-term breakthrough
- Stories, from scripture and real life, that reveal how faith sustains growth through storms, setbacks, and silence

So, if you've ever felt like you start strong but fade fast, or like you're constantly reinventing yourself without ever feeling settled, this chapter is for you. You're not alone. And you're not broken. You just haven't been shown how to root your growth in something that lasts.

Let's change that, together.

This is where short-term motivation ends... and lasting transformation begins.

II. Defining Lasting Change: Anchored, Not Just Inspired

There's a big difference between being inspired and being transformed.

Inspiration can spark a fire, but transformation builds the furnace. One gives you a rush of adrenaline; the other rewires the way you think, believe, and live. Most people spend their lives chasing that initial spark, hoping it'll carry them all the way to the finish line. But sparks don't last. And without something deeper, neither does the change.

How many times have you felt fired up after watching a video, reading a book, attending a seminar, or even hearing a powerful sermon, only to feel completely deflated a week later?

That's not failure. That's human nature. We weren't designed to run on emotional highs. And we definitely weren't meant to build our future on excitement alone. Motivation, by itself, is like sugar. It gives you a quick hit of energy, but it doesn't sustain you. What we need is something that feeds us on the soul level. Something that keeps us grounded when the emotional rush fades. That something... is faith.

Lasting change isn't about what you do in moments of excitement. It's about who you become when no one's watching. It's about being consistent when it's hard, when it's boring, and when it's inconvenient. That kind of consistency doesn't come from hype; it comes from alignment. And alignment only happens when your identity, your beliefs, and your actions are rooted in something unshakable.

Jim Rohn used to say, "Discipline is the bridge between goals and accomplishment." But what powers that discipline when you're tired, when you're overwhelmed, or when your circumstances scream for you to quit?

That's where faith steps in.

Faith gives you an **inner anchor**. It connects your temporary effort to eternal purpose. It reminds you that your work has meaning, even when there are no quick results. When motivation says, "Push harder," and burnout says, "Give up," faith whispers, "Keep going. You're not alone. This matters."

And let's be honest: life is unpredictable. You'll have great days, and you'll have days that gut-punch your confidence. If your change is built only on external conditions, a perfect morning routine, an easy month in business, or a supportive environment, it won't survive the pressure. But when your change is anchored internally, especially in your connection to God, it becomes resilient. It grows roots.

Transformation that lasts doesn't come from what you feel. It comes from what you believe.

It's what happens when you choose consistency over convenience. When you surrender the outcome and commit to the process. When you stop measuring success by the size of your results and start measuring it by the strength of your alignment.

That kind of transformation can't be shaken, because it's not dependent on how loud the world is; it's built on the still, steady voice of truth inside you. The voice that says, "You were made for more." The voice that calls you forward, even when your circumstances try to pull you back.

So, if you've ever asked yourself why your change hasn't lasted in the past, maybe it's not because you lacked discipline, or strategy, or intelligence. Maybe it's because you didn't yet have an anchor.

This chapter is here to help you plant one.

Because lasting change doesn't begin with a plan, it begins with a **foundation.**

Let's build it.

III. Faith as the Foundation: Building from the Inside Out

There's a reason Hebrews 11:1 defines faith like this:

"Now faith is the substance of things hoped for, the evidence of things not seen."

Faith isn't wishful thinking. It's not just blind optimism or religious jargon. According to scripture, faith is substance, something solid. Something you can stand on when the ground around you is shifting. It's also evidence, proof that even though you can't see the outcome yet, it's already real on the inside.

In other words, **faith is the foundation you build from,** not the cherry on top once everything works out.

Here's the thing. You can rely on willpower for a while. It can help you push through hard mornings and power through to-do lists. But here's the catch: willpower is limited. It burns out. It's a finite resource, kind of like a battery. You can recharge it with motivational videos, energy drinks, or positive affirmations, but eventually, it drains again.

Faith is different.

Faith is not just a mental trick or emotional boost. It's a **spiritual power source**. It's the voice that says, "There's more for you," even when your current results don't show it. It's the unseen conviction that God is working behind the scenes, even when the scene in front of you looks messy. And it's the fuel for change that outlasts emotion, excitement, or effort alone.

You can muscle your way through change for a little while, but you can't sustain transformation without being spiritually anchored.

Bob Proctor often said, "Faith and fear both demand you believe in something you cannot see. You choose." That hits hard. Every day, you're choosing to put your belief in one direction or the other. Faith believes in possibility. Faith believes in growth. Faith believes that your future doesn't have to look like your past.

Fear believes in limitation. Faith believes in transformation.

But here's the thing: faith isn't passive. It's not sitting back and hoping things work out. Faith requires action, **spirit-led action**. That means tuning into your Creator, following divine guidance, and stepping out before you have it all figured out. It's being obedient, even when it's uncomfortable. It's trusting the process when you don't see the full picture.

This is where faith separates itself from willpower. Willpower tries to control the outcome. Faith learns to surrender control and take bold steps anyway. Willpower is about pushing forward in your own strength. Faith is about walking forward with divine strength. It's knowing that even if your feet shake, your foundation won't.

And when you're building lasting change, that's exactly what you need.

One of the biggest traps people fall into is thinking that lasting success is all about hustle. And yes, effort matters. Discipline matters. But when those things are built on fear, ego, or insecurity, they eventually collapse. Why? Because you're building on sand.

Faith is rock. It's the foundation that allows you to build a life that lasts. Not a performance-based life, but a purpose-driven one. Not a life defined by what people think, but a life led by what God says.

When you lead with faith, your transformation isn't fragile; it's fortified.

So, ask yourself: Are you trying to change by force... or by faith? One burns out, the other breaks through.

And here's the good news: if you've built on willpower before and it didn't last, that doesn't mean you failed. It just means you hadn't yet tapped into the true foundation.

Now you can. Let's keep building from there.

IV. How Faith Transforms Identity

If you try to change your behavior without changing your identity, you'll eventually snap back to who you think you are. That's why so many people make short-term progress and then sabotage it. They're trying to build a new life using the blueprint of the old self.

But faith gives you a new blueprint.

One of the most powerful things Graham Cooke teaches is that God is not in the business of fixing your old self; He's in the business of **replacing it** with a new one. In Christ, you are a new creation (2 Corinthians 5:17). Not upgraded or slightly improved, but new.

Let that sink in.

Faith doesn't just give you the strength to act differently; it gives you the vision to see yourself differently. And once you see yourself differently, your actions will naturally start to line up.

Behavior modification says, "Try harder to be good."

Identity transformation says, "You are already good, because God made you new."

This isn't some motivational fluff or spiritual hype. It's truth. And it's the difference between hustling for your worth versus living from it.

Think about how most people approach change. They try to fix their habits. They try to be more disciplined. They white-knuckle their way through temptation, or procrastination, or fear. But underneath all that effort is a limiting belief that says, "This is just who I am."

That's the trap.

Faith breaks the trap wide open by introducing a new truth: Who you are in Christ is not who you were. You're not bound by your past, your mistakes, or even your current mindset. Faith says there's something deeper at play, something already established in Heaven that you're now learning to walk out on Earth.

This is what Graham Cooke calls "living from your identity instead of towards it."

You're not striving to become someone new. You're learning to live from the truth that you already are someone new. And as that revelation sinks in, your behavior begins to follow.

That's why true transformation lasts. Because it's not behavior-first. It's identity-first.

Let me give you a real-world example. I've mentored people who would make huge progress in their business, start building teams, creating content, showing up with energy, and then out of nowhere, they'd self-destruct. They'd stop showing up, doubt themselves, and go right back to square one.

Every time, the root issue wasn't their habits. It was their identity. Deep down, they still saw themselves as inconsistent, not enough, or "just not that kind of person." No matter how many systems or strategies we gave them, their identity pulled them back to their default settings.

Faith changes that.

When you begin to see yourself as God sees you, capable, equipped, loved, and called, you no longer need to strive for validation. You act in alignment with who you know you are. You stop chasing worth and start living from it.

This is the secret to real, lasting transformation.

You're not called to "fake it till you make it." You're called to believe it till you become it, because belief is what allows you to embody truth. And faith is the vehicle that makes it real.

So, here's your question for this section: Are you trying to improve your behavior, or are you allowing God to upgrade your identity?

If you want change that lasts, start where He does: in the heart, not the habits.

You're not who you used to be, you're not what you've done, and you're not what others say you are. You are who God says you are.

And once you accept that... the transformation becomes inevitable.

V. The Role of Grace and Surrender

If you've ever tried to change your life purely through effort, you already know how exhausting it is. You push, grind, hustle, and maybe you even make a little progress, until something throws you off. You slip, you stumble, or life blindsides you, and all that hard-won progress feels like it evaporates overnight.

That's because effort alone can't sustain transformation.

Don't get me wrong, discipline and drive matter. But if they're not rooted in something deeper, they'll only take you so far. Eventually, you'll hit a wall. And at that wall, you'll be faced with a choice: keep striving in your own strength or surrender to something greater.

That's where grace comes in.

Grace is the game-changer. It's the divine power that picks you up when you fall, strengthens you when you're weak, and carries you when you've got nothing left in the tank. It's not a license to be lazy. It's the fuel that makes consistent growth possible.

One of the most freeing truths I ever learned is that transformation isn't something you have to force. It's something you partner with. You're not doing this alone. You were never meant to.

When you surrender, truly surrender, you're not giving up. You're giving over. You're saying, "God, I'm done trying to control every outcome. I'm ready to trust You with the process."

And that shift? That surrender? That's where the real power begins to flow.

Letting go of control doesn't mean abandoning responsibility. It means acknowledging that your transformation isn't just a project, it's a relationship. One that requires trust, obedience, and a whole lot of grace.

Think of it this way: effort is rowing the boat with everything you've got. Surrender is hoisting the sail and letting God's wind carry you farther than you ever could have rowed alone.

You still have a role to play. You still show up, do the work, and stay consistent. But your source shifts. You're no longer drawing strength from your willpower; you're drawing from God's power.

That's what Paul meant when he said, "When I am weak, then I am strong" (2 Corinthians 12:10). He wasn't glorifying weakness. He was highlighting the supernatural strength that shows up when you acknowledge your need for God and stop pretending you can do it all yourself.

Grace fills the gaps your effort can't reach.

You'll never outgrow your need for it. Whether you're just getting started on this journey or you're years in, you're going to have moments where you fall short, when fear creeps in, or when you take your eyes off the goal. In those moments, grace catches you.

That's what makes this a lasting change, not because you're perfect, but because you're anchored in a relationship that won't let go when you mess up.

So, ask yourself: Where am I still holding on too tightly? Where am I relying more on willpower than on partnership with God?

When you can identify those areas and consciously surrender them, you create space for grace to flow. And when grace flows, transformation accelerates.

Let grace carry what your strength can't. Let surrender invite in the supernatural. And remember, you don't have to do this perfectly, you just have to keep showing up with an open heart and a willingness to trust.

Because lasting change isn't about trying harder, it's about trusting deeper.

VI. Walking by Faith, Not by Sight

One of the hardest lessons in personal growth and transformation is learning to trust the process, especially when you can't see immediate results. That's where faith becomes more than a nice idea. It becomes the foundation you stand on.

The Apostle Paul wrote, "We walk by faith, not by sight" (2 Corinthians 5:7). And that one line separates those who experience real, lasting change from those who quit when things get hard or slow. Because make no mistake, transformation is rarely instant. It's a long, often invisible process. Progress might be happening beneath the surface, but to your eyes, it might look like nothing's moving.

This is the part where people give up, not because they weren't capable, not because the plan was wrong, but because they couldn't see anything yet.

Faith says, "I'm going to keep going anyway."

When God gave Joseph a vision of leadership, influence, and favor, Joseph didn't walk straight into a palace. He got thrown into a pit, sold as a slave, and imprisoned for a crime he didn't commit. From the outside, it looked like failure. But in reality, it was preparation. Every delay, every setback, and every injustice was refining him for the very position he'd been promised.

Joseph walked by faith, not by what he saw, but by what he believed God said.

Same with Abraham. God promised him a son, even though Abraham was old and Sarah's womb was barren. For years, there was no evidence that anything was changing. Yet Romans 4 tells us that Abraham "did not waver through unbelief regarding the promise of God, but was strengthened in his faith" (Romans 4:20). Why? Because he chose to believe that God was faithful, even when reality didn't look like it.

And then there's Paul. Talk about a guy who had every reason to doubt the process. He gave his life to preaching the gospel and ended up shipwrecked, beaten, imprisoned, and misunderstood. Yet he kept going. He wrote letters from prison that still shape our lives today. That's the power of someone who walks by faith.

Faith isn't blind optimism. It's anchored trust.

It's saying, "God, even though I don't see it, I believe You're working. Even when I feel forgotten, I trust that You remember. Even when the doors don't open, I know You haven't stopped preparing me."

You can have all the right strategies in place, goals, routines, and accountability, but if you don't learn to walk by faith, you'll be tempted to quit when the results are delayed. You'll let your emotions lead instead of your conviction. And that's where people get stuck, looping through the same cycle, starting over again and again.

But if you'll stay the course, if you'll trust God's timing over your own timeline, you'll see things shift in ways you couldn't have predicted.

Walking by faith means showing up every day, doing what you know to do, even if nothing looks different yet. It's trusting that obedience before the outcome is what actually invites the outcome.

It's what Joseph did, it's what Abraham did, and it's what Paul did.

It's also what you're being called to do.

So, ask yourself: Where have you been waiting to see something before moving forward? What would it look like to walk by faith instead?

If you keep watering the seed, even when there's no sprout above the ground, eventually the roots will break through. Eventually, the fruit will come. Not by force, but by faithfulness.

Faith is the bridge between what God has spoken and what you're still waiting to see.

Don't let the delay convince you that the promise isn't real.

Walk by faith.

Keep walking.

VII. Faith-Fueled Habits and Discipline

If lasting transformation is the destination, discipline is the vehicle, and faith is the fuel that keeps it moving.

There's something powerful that happens when your daily routines stop being just about willpower and start being anchored in something deeper. When your habits flow from your relationship with God, they carry a weight of purpose that's hard to shake, even on the hard days.

Discipline on its own can feel rigid, like another task on a to-do list. But when your discipline is spiritually grounded, it becomes sacred. It's not just about what you're doing, it's about who you're becoming through the process.

Most people try to build new habits using motivation. They wait until they feel like doing the right thing. But feelings are fickle. Faith, on the other hand, is stable. Faith doesn't ask how you feel today. Faith says, "Show up anyway."

And that's where routines rooted in faith come in.

1. Prayer as a Daily Anchor

Prayer isn't just a spiritual obligation; it's a lifeline. It's your direct connection to wisdom, strength, and perspective you won't find scrolling social media. Prayer reminds you that you're not in this alone, and it resets your mind when it starts to wander back toward fear or distraction.

Make prayer part of your daily rhythm, not as a checkbox, but as a conversation. Morning prayer can set the tone for your day. Midday prayer can recenter you. Evening prayer can help you release what you're carrying. No matter what time, it's about intentional connection.

2. Scripture as a Source of Renewal

Romans 12:2 tells us to "be transformed by the renewing of your mind." That's not a one-time event; it's a daily decision. And scripture is the key.

Reading God's Word daily isn't just about gaining knowledge. It's about aligning your thoughts with truth. It's about reprogramming the internal dialogue that used to sabotage you. When you fill your mind with God's promises, you push out fear, shame, and limitation.

Choose a few key scriptures that speak directly to the season you're in. Write them on note cards. Post them on your mirror or your desk. Let the Word shape your identity, your decisions, and your perspective.

3. Declarations That Shift Identity

Here's something most people don't do, but should: speak life over yourself out loud.

Declarations are more than positive affirmations. When rooted in scripture, they're a faith-filled declaration of truth, whether you feel it yet or not. You're not just hoping to become disciplined, focused, or free from fear. You're declaring it as if it's already true, because in Christ, it is.

Examples:

- "I am disciplined and diligent because the Spirit of God lives in me."
- "I walk in peace and confidence, not fear and chaos."
- "I am called, chosen, and fully equipped for every good work."

Say it until you believe it. Say it until your behavior starts catching up to your identity.

Faith-fueled habits aren't just about doing the right things; they're about becoming the kind of person who naturally lives aligned with God's purpose. That's what real transformation looks like. It's not driven by pressure, it's nurtured by presence.

So, as you build your routines, ask yourself: Are they rooted in striving, or are they anchored in grace? Because when discipline is powered by faith, it doesn't burn you out, it builds you up.

This is how you sustain the progress you've made. This is how you keep growing when motivation fades. You don't rely on hype. You rely on Him.

And that changes everything.

VIII. Overcoming Setbacks with Spiritual Strength

Setbacks aren't a sign that you're off track; they're part of the path. Every single person who's ever made lasting change has stumbled along the way. The difference isn't whether they fell. The difference is how they got back up.

And that, my friend, is where spiritual strength makes all the difference.

When your strength is rooted in your own willpower, setbacks can feel like permanent stops. You mess up, miss a goal, slip into old patterns, and suddenly the inner critic shows up with a megaphone: "See? You'll never change." That's human discouragement talking. And if you buy into it, you'll start reinforcing the very cycle you were trying to break.

But faith offers you another lens entirely.

Faith says, "You're not defined by your worst day."

Faith says, "My grace is sufficient for you" (2 Corinthians 12:9).

Faith says, "Though the righteous fall seven times, they rise again" (Proverbs 24:16).

That's a promise you can stand on. Not a motivational quote. A promise.

Failure Isn't Final

One of the biggest lies people believe is that a setback equals failure. But in God's economy, setbacks are setups for something greater. They're opportunities to re-center, re-align, and often go deeper than you would have if everything had gone smoothly.

Think about Peter. The guy literally denied Jesus three times when it mattered most. But that wasn't the end of his story; it was the start of a radical transformation. Jesus didn't write him off. He restored him. And Peter went on to become a foundational leader in the early church.

That's what God does. He meets you in the aftermath and rebuilds you stronger.

Leaning on Promises, Not Pressure

When you face a setback, your reflex might be to fix it, figure it out, or muscle through. But spiritual strength isn't about tightening your grip; it's about loosening it. It's about leaning, not striving.

Psalm 46:1 says, "God is our refuge and strength, an ever-present help in trouble." Not used-to-be help. Not maybe-someday help. Ever-present. Right now. In the middle of your mess.

When you mess up, pause. Don't rush to "fix" it. Get quiet. Ask, "Lord, what do You want to show me here?" Sometimes the setback is simply revealing an area that needs healing. Sometimes it's showing you where you were relying on your own strength instead of His.

And sometimes, it's just life being life. No deep reason. No cosmic lesson. Just another opportunity to practice resilience through grace.

Responding Instead of Retreating

Here's where it gets real: when you fall down, you have two choices. You can retreat into shame and old patterns, or you can respond in faith. Responding means you don't pretend it didn't happen, and you don't beat yourself up either. You acknowledge it, surrender it, and step forward anyway.

Faith says, "I'm not what I did. I'm who God says I am."

Faith says, "His power is made perfect in my weakness."

Faith says, "This setback is just part of the story, not the end of it."

Build a Bounce-Back Strategy

You don't need a perfect plan. But you do need a bounce-back strategy, a go-to spiritual routine when things go sideways.

Open the Word. Start with Psalms or Romans. Let truth cut through the noise.

Pray honestly, without filters. Tell God exactly how you feel.

Reach out to a mentor or accountability partner who can speak life back into you.

Declare who you are, even when you don't feel it.

The sooner you respond in faith, the faster you break the shame spiral. The key isn't perfection, it's presence. Keep showing up. Keep leaning on Him. Keep walking, even with a limp.

You're not sustained by your performance. You're sustained by your position, as a beloved child of God.

And that never changes, even when you fall.

IX. The Power of Faith in Community

When you're walking the path of transformation, isolation can be one of the greatest threats to your growth. It's in solitude that doubt creeps in, old patterns reemerge, and the whispers of fear grow louder. But when you surround yourself with faith-filled voices, people who see the gold in you, speak life over your vision, and refuse to let you settle, you become nearly unstoppable.

Faith isn't meant to be lived out in a vacuum. It thrives in connection. Scripture reminds us that "iron sharpens iron, so one person sharpens another" (Proverbs 27:17). That's not just a poetic metaphor; it's a blueprint for growth. The right people can pull you out of your lowest moments, challenge you to rise higher, and remind you of your identity when you start to forget who you are.

In my own life, I've seen the power of community show up in ways I couldn't have orchestrated on my own. There were times when I was holding on by a thread, when I questioned whether I was truly called or just fooling myself. It wasn't a podcast, a course, or another motivational quote that shifted me, it was a conversation. A friend who said, "I still believe in you." A mentor who said, "This setback doesn't define you." A prayer circle that refused to let me walk away from what God had clearly put in my heart.

That's the kind of spiritual circle I'm talking about.

Mentorship matters. A mentor doesn't just teach you; they reflect back to you the version of yourself that God sees. They call you higher without judgment. They give you strategies, yes, but more than that, they give you hope wrapped in experience. A good mentor has been through the fire and lived to tell the story, and they help you navigate your own storms without losing your faith in the process.

Fellowship matters too. There's something powerful about locking arms with people who are walking the same road. People who may not have it all figured out but are showing up anyway. Whether it's a small group, a Bible study, a mastermind, or even a few committed friends, those shared moments of worship, reflection, and prayer can breathe new life into your journey. You begin to realize you're not alone in your battles. And that knowledge alone can be enough to keep you moving forward when everything in you wants to quit.

Accountability matters. Not the kind that shames you for slipping, but the kind that loves you enough to tell you the truth. Faith-filled accountability says, "I see your potential, and I'm not going to let you settle for less." It's firm, but it's kind. It holds space for grace while still pushing you to grow. And when it's rooted in love, it becomes one of the most powerful forces for lasting change.

We were never meant to do this alone. The early church in Acts is a perfect example. They broke bread together, prayed together, shared resources and carried each other's burdens. That wasn't just a logistical model, it was spiritual strength in action. And it's still available to us today, if we'll seek it out and commit to it.

So, if you're serious about sustaining the changes you're making, if you want to walk in lasting transformation, take a look at who's in your circle. Are they fueling your faith or feeding your fear? Are they calling out your potential or keeping you comfortable? This isn't about judgment; it's about alignment.

The right community won't just encourage your progress, they'll multiply it.

And if you don't have that kind of support yet, start praying for it. Start being that kind of voice for someone else. You'll be amazed how God meets you in that space.

Transformation was never meant to be a solo journey. It's a team effort, and a faith-filled community is the secret weapon.

X. Practical Exercises and Reflection

You've come a long way in this journey of personal transformation, and now it's time to get practical. Faith is not just a feeling; it's a muscle. And like any muscle, it has to be exercised regularly to stay strong. This section is about doing the internal work that keeps your spiritual foundation solid, especially when the world around you starts to shake.

Let's start with a **Faith Inventory**. Think of this like a diagnostic check-up for your belief system. If your results are inconsistent, if your growth feels start-and-stop, there's a good chance your faith is being pulled in different directions. Don't judge it, just notice it.

Take out a journal or open a blank document and write down your answers to the following questions:

1. **What do I say I believe about God, myself, and my future?**
2. **What do my daily actions say I actually believe?**

3. **Where do I tend to default to fear, control, or self-reliance instead of trusting God?**
4. **What promises from Scripture have I been avoiding or doubting?**
5. **Which beliefs do I need to reinforce, revisit, or replace?**

This exercise isn't about guilt; it's about clarity. Sometimes we're walking around with subconscious beliefs that are completely out of alignment with what we say we stand for. And that disconnection creates frustration. Once you spot the disconnect, you can start doing something about it.

Now, let's build in some **exercises for anchoring habits in faith instead of fear.**

1. Start Your Day with a Declaration Routine

Create 5–7 personal, faith-filled declarations that you speak aloud every morning. These should reflect the truths you want rooted deep in your heart. For example:

- "God is guiding my steps today."
- "I walk in clarity, not confusion."
- "My identity is secure in Christ, not in my performance."
- "What God started in me, He will finish."
- "I act in boldness, not fear, because I trust His plan."

Don't just whisper these. Speak them out loud with conviction, even if you don't feel it yet. Faith often starts in the speaking before it ever settles in the heart.

2. Create a Faith-Focused Habit Tracker

Take one or two spiritual habits, like journaling, scripture reading, prayer walks, or evening gratitude, and track them for 30 days. Your goal isn't perfection. It's consistency. Make it visible. Put it on your mirror, fridge, or phone wallpaper. Keep it in front of you.

This works because discipline strengthens faith. When you see yourself following through, your trust in God, and in your own ability to walk it out, increases.

3. Rewrite a Fear-Based Script

Take one fear you've been holding onto. Maybe it's fear of failure, fear of rejection, or fear that you're not enough. Write it down in detail.

Now, across from it, write a new faith-based narrative rooted in God's truth.

For example:

- **Fear-Based Thought:** "If I really go all in, I might fail and disappoint everyone."
- **Faith-Based Rewrite:** "God didn't call me to be perfect, He called me to be faithful. My job is obedience. The outcome is His."

When fear shows up again (and it will), go back to your faith-based script and speak it out loud. Let it become your go-to response.

4. Anchor Your Faith to a Scripture Promise

Choose one verse that speaks to the season you're in. Write it out by hand. Memorize it. Post it where you'll see it often. Make it your anchor. Whenever your mind starts to spin, come back to that verse.

Examples:

- **Philippians 1:6:** "He who began a good work in you will carry it on to completion."
- **Isaiah 41:10:** "Do not fear, for I am with you... I will uphold you with my righteous right hand."
- **2 Timothy 1:7:** "God has not given us a spirit of fear, but of power, love, and a sound mind."

You don't have to do all of these at once. Pick one, start small, and let your faith grow in the soil of intentional action. When fear tries to take the wheel, come back to these tools. Come back to truth.

This is how you move from inspired to anchored, from temporary change to lasting transformation.

Ready to lock it in? Let's go.

XI. Chapter Summary and Preview

Faith isn't just a nice sentiment, it's the cornerstone of lasting transformation.

In this chapter, we've explored the difference between momentary motivation and sustained growth. We've seen how **faith anchors us when excitement fades,** when life gets complicated, and when our old patterns try to resurface. Without that anchor, even the best systems and strategies will start to unravel the moment pressure shows up.

We walked through what it means to let faith shape not just your goals, but your **identity.** You've seen that lasting change doesn't come from gritting your teeth or trying harder, it comes from **living out of who you are in Christ.** That's the shift. That's the game-changer. Because when you live from a place of truth, grace, and divine partnership, your transformation isn't just sustainable, it's inevitable.

You learned that **willpower has limits**, but spirit-led change taps into a source that doesn't run dry. Whether it was Graham Cooke's reminders that you're not working toward your identity but from it, or Paul's encouragement to walk by faith and not by sight, the message is the same: lasting change flows from spiritual truth, not emotional hype.

We talked about how **grace meets you when you fall**, and how surrendering control to God isn't weakness; it's where your real strength is born. You've been given **tools to reinforce your faith daily**: scripture declarations, journaling, habit trackers, and reflection exercises. These aren't spiritual chores; they're spiritual reinforcements.

And let's not forget the role of **community**. Faith isn't meant to be lived in isolation. There's power in surrounding yourself with mentors, truth-speakers, and fellow travelers who can lift your arms when they get tired. Faith grows best in the soil of fellowship, accountability, and grace-filled encouragement.

So, here's the big takeaway: **faith is the fuel that keeps the fire burning when the spark of motivation flickers**. It's not about avoiding obstacles, it's about having the spiritual stamina to press through them without losing your way. It's about trusting that even when you can't see the path clearly, the One who called you is still leading the way.

But here's the thing: transformation doesn't happen in a vacuum.

It's easy to walk in faith when everything feels aligned. But what happens when it doesn't? What happens when people criticize you, when circumstances shift, when the pressure ramps u,p and the easy path is the one that takes you backward?

That's what we're digging into next.

Chapter 14: Staying True Under Pressure: Faithfulness in the Journey is about standing firm when the ground starts to shake. It's about resilience, loyalty to your purpose, and spiritual grit. You'll learn how to recognize opposition for what it is, how to respond with wisdom instead of fear, and how to stay true to the course you've chosen, even when you feel alone in it.

We'll look at the lives of biblical leaders who faced resistance, rejection, and ridicule, and still moved forward. You'll discover how pressure doesn't have to derail you. In fact, **it can refine you**.

The real test of transformation isn't what you do when things are easy. It's what you choose when the heat is on, when the crowd is quiet, and when you have every excuse to give up, but you don't.

So, as you wrap up this chapter, pause and reflect: Where has your faith already brought you? And are you willing to trust it to take you through the fire, not just around it?

You're not alone. And you're not done.

Let's move forward with boldness, because the next chapter will show you how to stay grounded, stay faithful, and keep walking strong, no matter what comes.

Chapter 14: Staying True Under Pressure: Faithfulness in the Journey

I. Introduction

I remember a time when everything looked like it was falling apart. Business slowed down. People I trusted walked away. The momentum I had been building for months felt like it evaporated overnight. And right in the middle of it all, that little voice crept in: "Maybe this just isn't going to work."

I've felt that pressure. The kind that doesn't shout but whispers with authority. The kind that tempts you to compromise, to back down, to shrink into a version of yourself that feels safer, smaller, more acceptable to people who never saw your vision in the first place.

Pressure reveals what you're made of. It doesn't create your foundation; it exposes it.

And here's what I've learned: **faithfulness matters more in the dark than it ever does in the spotlight**. When everything is going well, it's easy to appear committed. Easy to look bold. But real faithfulness shows up when no one's watching, when the accolades disappear, when obedience means discomfort.

This chapter is about that kind of faithfulness, the kind that holds firm when every excuse to give up is right there in front of you.

Staying true under pressure is what separates those who dabble from those who are truly called. It's where purpose gets proven. It's where shallow roots get exposed and deep roots get strengthened. You can't fake resilience, not for long.

We're all going to face moments where the easiest thing to do is to quit. The most logical choice might be to retreat. But logic doesn't build legacy; **faithfulness does**.

Pressure can come from everywhere: external circumstances, inner doubts, unexpected delays, even the opinions of others who think they know what's best for you. But pressure isn't the enemy. It's a proving ground.

When your commitment is tested, it's not because you're doing something wrong; it's because you're getting close to something right. And the resistance you face is often a signpost that you're on a meaningful path.

Look at any person of impact, whether in business, faith, or leadership, and you'll find a common thread: they didn't quit when it got hard. They stayed faithful when the doors didn't open. They kept walking when their emotions screamed, "Turn back."

In this chapter, we're going to unpack what it really looks like to **stay faithful under fire**. We'll explore what it means to stand when the pressure rises, to stay aligned with your values and your calling, even when everything around you seems unstable.

You'll see examples from scripture, people who stayed the course when it cost them everything. You'll hear stories of men and women in modern times who refused to bow to pressure, who kept building when no one believed in them.

And most importantly, you'll walk away with practical tools for standing firm. Because this isn't about white-knuckling your way through storms. This is about building the kind of inner fortitude that thrives under pressure because it's rooted in something eternal.

Faithfulness isn't flashy. It doesn't get all the headlines. But it's the bedrock of a life that matters. And when you look back over your journey, you'll realize something powerful:

The pressure didn't break you. It built you.

So, if you're feeling the heat right now, don't run. Don't bow. And don't believe the lie that says pressure is a sign to quit. It's a sign you're being prepared.

Let's dive in. It's time to discover what faithfulness really looks like and when it counts the most.

II. Understanding Pressure and Opposition

If you're serious about change, you're going to face pressure. Not maybe. Not if. You will. It's baked into the process of transformation. And the deeper the calling, the heavier the resistance tends to be. That's not punishment, it's preparation.

Let's break it down. There are two main sources of pressure that threaten to pull us off course: **internal** and **external**.

Internal Pressure: Doubt, Fatigue, Discouragement

The first kind is the kind nobody sees, the pressure inside your own head and heart. It shows up as self-doubt. That quiet question that pops up right after you take a bold step: "Who do you think you are?"

It's the fatigue that settles in when you've been consistent, but the results haven't caught up yet. You're showing up, doing the work, and nothing seems to be moving. That's when emotional exhaustion sneaks in and whispers, "What's the point?"

Discouragement is sneaky. It doesn't always shout. Sometimes it just erodes your confidence in small doses, until you wake up one day wondering if this dream of yours was just a fantasy. That kind of pressure is brutal because it feels personal. It doesn't come from your haters, it comes from yourself.

But here's what you've got to remember: **doubt isn't the enemy, quitting is**. Fatigue isn't failure, it's feedback. And discouragement? It's just a detour, not a dead end. You can feel all of it and still stay faithful.

When you anchor yourself in purpose and truth, you can let those thoughts pass through without letting them define your direction.

External Pressure: Criticism, Slow Progress, and Resistance from Others

Then there's the pressure that comes from outside. This one's easier to point to, but just as dangerous if not handled properly.

Criticism is one of the most common forms. It can come from strangers online or people close to you. And the harshest critiques often come from folks who aren't building anything themselves. They just don't get it, and they try to protect you from disappointment by encouraging you to shrink your vision.

You'll hear things like:

"Isn't that too risky?"

"That's not realistic."

"You've changed."

Yes, you have changed. You're supposed to.

Then there's the pressure of slow progress. You're showing up, putting in the reps, and trying to stay consistent, but the breakthroughs aren't showing up on your timeline. The temptation is to change the plan, second-guess your strategy, or worst of all, water down your calling just to make something happen faster.

But lasting transformation isn't microwaved. It's marinated.

Faithfulness is staying the course even when the results don't validate you yet.

And let's not forget opposition from others, people who actively resist your growth. Sometimes it's subtle: eye-rolls, silence, or disengagement. Other times it's direct: pushback, confrontation, or sabotage. Whatever form it takes, it's rooted in discomfort. When you level up, it can threaten the comfort zones of others. Don't take it personally. Take it as confirmation.

Growth creates friction.

You're not doing something wrong just because it's hard. You might be doing something right and the resistance is proof that you're pushing against something that needs to move.

In Scripture, almost every person used by God faced opposition. Moses had Pharaoh. Nehemiah had Sanballat and Tobiah. Jesus had the Pharisees. Paul had prison, a shipwreck, and more. What didn't they have? A guarantee that everything would be easy.

Still, they kept moving. That's the difference.

So, whether the pressure is internal or external, whether it's coming from your own insecurities or from people who don't see your vision, don't be surprised by it. Don't be shaken by it. And definitely don't let it decide your next move.

You weren't called to ease, you were called to impact. And impact requires perseverance.

So, ask yourself this: Will you bow to the pressure? Or will you rise with the purpose that got you started in the first place?

The next section will give you the strategies and perspective you need to keep showing up, no matter what's pressing in.

III. The Call to Faithfulness

Faithfulness isn't flashy. It won't always get applause. It rarely makes headlines. But when it comes to walking out your purpose, especially under pressure, faithfulness is everything.

Let's define it clearly.

Faithfulness means showing up with consistency, choosing trust over fear, and staying obedient even when you don't feel like it. It's not about perfection; it's about direction. It's not about hype; it's about heart. Faithfulness is the quiet, steady decision to keep going, even when no one else understands why you haven't quit.

We live in a culture that glorifies outcomes and ignores the process. But God values the process. In fact, He often hides the promise inside a process to see who will be faithful enough to unlock it.

Let's look at a few biblical examples of what faithfulness under pressure really looks like:

Daniel: Faithfulness in Conviction

Daniel was taken from his home, brought into a pagan culture, and pressured to conform. Yet even in the face of political power, peer pressure, and the threat of death, he remained consistent in his devotion to God.

He prayed daily, even when it was outlawed. He refused to eat the king's food, not out of arrogance, but out of conviction. He stayed committed to his identity, and as a result, God elevated him to positions of influence he never could've reached by compromising.

Daniel didn't just survive pressure, he was promoted through it. And that promotion came after the lion's den, not before. His faithfulness opened the door for favor.

Job: Faithfulness in Suffering

Job lost everything: his wealth, his children, and his health. His friends didn't comfort him. His wife told him to curse God and die. But Job, though broken, held on. He wrestled with God. He questioned. He grieved. But he didn't walk away.

What does that tell us? Faithfulness doesn't mean pretending everything is fine. It means clinging to God when it's not. It means refusing to let go, even when the answers haven't come.

In the end, Job's story wasn't one of defeat; it was one of restoration. God gave him double what he had lost. But that only came after a season of pressure that tested every ounce of his faith.

Faithfulness doesn't always change the situation immediately, but it always changes you.

Esther: Faithfulness in Assignment

Esther didn't ask to be queen. She didn't go looking for influence. But when the moment came, and her people were under threat, she had a choice: stay silent and safe or speak up and risk everything.

Her famous words still ring out: "If I perish, I perish."

That's what faithfulness looks like when it meets purpose. It's not about what's comfortable. It's about what's right. Esther understood that her position was not about luxury; it was about legacy. She risked her life to fulfill her assignment.

And because of her faithfulness, an entire nation was saved.

Faithfulness isn't about being perfect. It's about being present, willing, and anchored, not to outcomes, but to obedience.

It's easy to start strong. It's easy to show up when you're inspired or when people are cheering. But the real test comes when the crowd is gone. When the lights are off. When the breakthrough is delayed. That's when faithfulness either takes root or falls apart.

And if you want to fulfill your calling, faithfulness isn't optional; it's essential.

So, here's the call: Stay consistent in the small things. Trust when the results are unclear. Obey when it's inconvenient. That's faithfulness.

Because your destiny doesn't depend on how you perform when it's easy; it depends on how you respond when it's not.

Let's keep going. The next section will give you tools to stand firm while the pressure is rising.

IV. Standing Firm in Your Identity

When life applies pressure, one of the first things it tries to shake is your identity. That's not an accident, it's strategic. The enemy isn't just after your peace or your progress. He's after your perception of who you are. Because if he can distort that, he can derail your purpose.

Graham Cooke says it best: "God is never working on your behavior; He's always establishing your identity." In other words, God is far more interested in who you're becoming than in the external image you're trying to maintain. And trials? They tend to reveal whether you're building your identity on truth or performance.

Pressure has a funny way of exposing what's been buried. It brings to the surface all the lies we've believed: "I'm not good enough. I'm falling behind. I must've missed it Maybe I'm not called." Those lies don't come from God. They come from fear. And fear loves to disguise itself as logic during tough times.

You are not your results. You are not your current season. You are not the opinion of others. You are who God says you are, period. That doesn't change based on how much you've achieved or how much you've lost.

Standing firm in your identity doesn't mean ignoring hard circumstances. It means facing them with the right lens. You walk into the fire like Shadrach, Meshach, and Abednego, not because the fire isn't real, but because you know it can't redefine you. They said, "Our God is able to deliver us... but even if He doesn't, we will not bow." That's identity. That's faithfulness. That's courage rooted in conviction.

When you know who you are in Christ, you stop negotiating with fear.

This isn't about hyping yourself up with positive affirmations. This is about reminding yourself of what God has already said about you.

- **You are chosen**. (1 Peter 2:9)
- **You are more than a conqueror**. (Romans 8:37)
- **You are God's workmanship, created for good works**. (Ephesians 2:10)
- **You are seated with Christ in heavenly places**. (Ephesians 2:6)

Your job during times of pressure is not to reinvent yourself, it's to remember yourself. Who you truly are. Who you've always been in God's eyes, before the struggle and after the breakthrough.

Now, let's get practical.

When you feel the heat rising, when the discouragement kicks in, or the delays tempt you to give up, here's a simple but powerful practice:

Pause. Breathe. Speak your identity aloud.

Something like:

> "This pressure doesn't define me. God defines me. I am a person of purpose, faith, and resilience. I've been called for this. I am equipped for this. I'm not shrinking back, I'm standing firm."

Do that until your internal atmosphere shifts. Because sometimes the storm around you only calms after you calm the one within you.

And remember this: **Jesus was affirmed by the Father before He ever performed a single miracle.** Before He preached one sermon. Before He went to the cross. God said, "This is My Son, in whom I am well pleased." That's identity. And that same approval is spoken over you, not because you've done everything right, but because you belong to Him.

So, when the pressure comes, and it will, don't collapse under the weight of trying to prove yourself. Return to who you already are.

Faithfulness isn't just about showing up. It's about showing up with your identity intact. The real you. The one who knows they're backed by heaven, even when earth feels shaky.

V. How Pressure Refines and Strengthens

We often see pressure as something to avoid, something that signals we're off course or under attack. But what if pressure is actually a gift? What if it's God's forge, a process He uses to refine us, not break us?

The Apostle Paul lays it out clearly in Romans 5:3–5:

> "We also glory in our sufferings, because we know that suffering produces perseverance; perseverance, character; and character, hope. And hope does not put us to shame…"

That's not religious poetry; it's divine process. Pressure isn't punishment. It's preparation.

Think about that.

We pray for strength, and God gives us opportunities to build it. We ask for clarity, and He allows resistance that reveals what we truly believe. We cry out for transformation, and He walks us straight into the kind of pressure that makes us choose between staying small or stepping up.

Bob Proctor once said, "Pressure is the fertilizer of potential." It forces what's dormant to wake up. The same way a seed has to break open before new life can spring out, your growth will often begin at the breaking point, not the breakthrough.

The refining process isn't glamorous. In fact, it's usually uncomfortable and inconvenient. But ask anyone who's come through the fire and they'll tell you they're better for it. Stronger, sharper, and clearer.

Pressure reveals the cracks in our foundation, and that's a good thing, because you can't fix what you're unwilling to face.

One of the biggest lies people believe under pressure is, "If I were doing it right, this wouldn't be so hard." But that's not how growth works.

Gold is refined by fire. Diamonds are formed under pressure. Muscles are built through resistance. In every area of life, the very thing you think is slowing you down is the thing that's shaping you up.

If you're feeling stretched, tested, or pressed right now, consider this: **Maybe God is trusting you with pressure because He's preparing you for more**.

You don't strengthen your faith when everything's easy, you strengthen it when everything's not. That's when you dig deeper. That's when you decide whether your convictions are built on convenience or commitment.

Pressure also humbles us. It strips away pride and self-reliance. It reminds us we're not in control, and that's exactly where faith finds room to grow. When you hit the edge of your own ability, you begin to draw on God's.

The most refined people I know are the ones who've endured something without losing their identity in the process. They didn't come out bitter, they came out bolder. They didn't shrink, they expanded. That's the gift of pressure.

So, how do you embrace the refining process instead of resisting it?

1. **Recognize the purpose in it**. Don't ask "Why is this happening to me?" Ask, "What is this growing in me?"
2. **Stay connected to the Word**. Romans 5 reminds you this process has an end result, hope. And hope never disappoints.
3. **Let God do the heavy lifting**. You're not responsible for perfecting yourself. You're responsible for staying surrendered.

Every ounce of pressure you're feeling is shaping your character. Not just for this season, but for the assignment you haven't even stepped into yet.

God is playing the long game. He's not just developing your skills, He's cultivating your spirit.

So, breathe. Don't rush the process. Pressure isn't proof that you're failing. It's evidence that you're becoming.

Let it refine you.

Let it strengthen you.

Let it prepare you for what's next.

VI. Staying Aligned with Purpose Under Fire

Pressure doesn't just challenge your endurance; it challenges your alignment. When you're under fire, emotionally, spiritually, or financially, it's easy to lose sight of why you started. The vision gets blurry. The path feels foggy. And if you're not intentional, you can start drifting, not because you don't care, but because you're tired.

I've lived that. I've had times where I was crystal clear on my purpose, on fire with passion, then life turned up the heat. Suddenly, I wasn't questioning my goal... I was questioning me. Do I have what it takes? Is this still worth it? Did I miss God?

It's in those moments that you've got to go back to your "why." You've got to remember the reason behind the work. Because when pressure comes, it doesn't just test your actions, it tests your motivation. Are you doing this for applause or because it's what you're called to do?

Jim Rohn said, "Discipline is the bridge between goals and accomplishment." But under pressure, discipline becomes more than a bridge, it becomes an anchor. It holds you steady when emotions want to pull you off course. It's the daily decision to stay faithful to your assignment, even when the feelings fade.

Staying aligned doesn't mean you don't feel the fire; it means you don't let it burn away your calling.

You remind yourself that you're not here to please people. You're here to fulfill a purpose.

That's what separates those who dabble from those who finish. It's not talent. It's not luck. It's alignment. It's the ability to come back to your core, to what matters most, when everything around you is screaming for compromise.

Pressure can bring seductive shortcuts. Opportunities to quit quietly, to tone it down, to conform, coast, or play small so you don't rock the boat. But here's the deal: when you shrink to avoid heat, you trade your destiny for comfort.

Purpose isn't a convenience. It's a covenant.

It's the agreement you made, between you and God, to live a life that means something.

And you can't afford to forget that when the pressure comes.

This is why spiritual alignment matters so much. When you know whose you are and why you're here, you stop letting circumstances dictate your consistency. You show up because you're rooted. You stay the course because you're not doing it for a result, you're doing it from a revelation.

That's what Jim Rohn was really getting at. He wasn't just talking about grinding harder; he was talking about staying aligned. He knew that people lose their way when they lose their why. And trials have a way of making us forget.

So, what do you do when the fire comes?

You reconnect with your purpose.

You revisit the promise.

You remind yourself that God doesn't start what He doesn't intend to finish, and if He brought you to it, He's faithful to bring you through it.

Take time to journal your "why" again. Speak it out loud. Declare it in prayer. Let your spirit hear it until it starts pushing back against the pressure.

Because pressure doesn't get the final say, purpose does.

And the more you align with your purpose, the less the fire can intimidate you. You start seeing it not as a threat, but as a confirmation that you're walking the path worth protecting.

So, stay aligned, stay anchored, and trust that the same fire meant to break you... will be the fire that brands your purpose on the world.

VII. Practical Strategies to Stay Faithful

Faithfulness isn't a vague spiritual quality; it's a practiced lifestyle. When life gets loud and distractions pile up, staying faithful to your purpose, your identity, and your calling requires strategy. You need anchors. You need rhythms. And you need to guard your gates, what you hear, what you see, and what you let into your heart.

Let's start with your **daily anchors**. These aren't just routines for routine's sake. They're spiritual tools designed to help you stand firm when the pressure comes.

1. Prayer

This isn't about reciting the same lines every day. It's about real conversation with God. When you feel the temptation to drift, prayer brings you back to center. It reminds you that you're not doing this alone. It's where you offload the weight, the fear, the fatigue, and receive strength, wisdom, and direction. Sometimes faithfulness means praying when you don't feel spiritual. Especially then.

2. Reflection

We live in a culture that moves fast. If you're not careful, you'll be too busy to even notice when you're veering off course. Daily reflection, whether through journaling or quiet meditation, forces you to slow down and see yourself clearly. What did you do well today? Where did you waver? What does God want to show you about this moment? This habit keeps your spirit sharp and your motives aligned.

3. Truth-Telling

Be honest with yourself and with God. Faithfulness doesn't mean perfection; it means walking in truth. If you messed up, admit it. If you're tired, say it. If you're scared, bring that to the Lord. He's not asking you to fake strength. He's inviting you to walk in real strength. And that starts with authenticity. Pretending you're okay when you're not doesn't make you faithful. Pressing forward with God's help despite your weakness? That's faithfulness.

Now let's talk about **controlling your inputs**. One of the easiest ways to lose your footing is by consuming the wrong things, mentally, emotionally, and spiritually. Pressure always amplifies what's already inside. So, if you're constantly feeding yourself negativity, comparison, fear-based news, or drama-filled conversations, that's what will bubble up when life squeezes you.

What You Hear:

Faith comes by hearing. So does fear. So be intentional about what you're listening to. Worship music, uplifting messages, and podcasts that build your faith; these aren't just for Sunday vibes. They're fuel for the battle. Don't underestimate how one anointed word at the right moment can recalibrate your whole spirit.

What You Read:

Your daily reading habits shape your perspective more than you think. The Word of God is your anchor in chaos. That's not a cliché; that's spiritual reality. Reading Scripture daily reminds you who God is, who you are, and what truth actually sounds like. When the world's narrative gets loud, you need a louder truth inside of you.

What You Say:

Your words either reinforce your faith or erode it. Watch your self-talk. Watch your declarations. Are you speaking life or reinforcing doubt? When pressure hits, your mouth will often reveal what you really believe. Start rehearsing truth out loud. Speak God's promises. Say your "why." Declare your next step in faith. Your mouth steers your direction.

These strategies aren't just about keeping you spiritual. They're about keeping you stable. When the storm hits, the unprepared drift and the anchored remain. You don't have to be perfect. You just have to be consistent. And with these practices in place, you're not just reacting, you're building a foundation strong enough to carry the weight of your calling.

So, if you're feeling shaky, don't panic. Go back to the anchors, guard your gates, and walk it out, one faithful step at a time.

VIII. Support Systems That Sustain You

No one finishes the race alone. If you're trying to be faithful through life's pressures without community, you're carrying more weight than God ever intended for you to carry. Even Jesus had His circle: Peter,

James, and John. He leaned on them in Gethsemane, and if the Son of God valued spiritual support, how much more do we need it?

Faithfulness is forged in the fire, yes, but it's sustained in the context of godly relationships. When you're under pressure, the enemy will try to isolate you. He'll whisper that you're the only one struggling, that others won't understand, or that asking for help is weakness. Don't buy it. That's how people fall away, not because they didn't love God, but because they tried to do it all by themselves.

Let's talk about three support pillars: **mentors, spiritual leaders, and accountability partners**.

Mentors

Mentors aren't just people with more experience. They're people with wisdom. A mentor has walked through fire and still kept their faith. They've fought battles you haven't fought yet and carry insight that could save you years of confusion or delay.

One of the most impactful times of my life came after I started listening, really listening, to a mentor who had no agenda but to see me become the person God called me to be. They didn't sugarcoat things. They called out blind spots. They reminded me of my identity when I was ready to quit. And sometimes, just their presence alone reminded me that I wasn't crazy for believing big, even when everything around me looked small.

A mentor won't do the work for you, but they'll remind you why the work matters. Don't wait until you're falling apart to find one. Seek out someone who lives at the level you're aiming for, and be teachable.

Spiritual Leaders

Your pastor, spiritual coach, or small group leader can be a lifeline when the pressure hits. These leaders are often graced to speak directly into the storm with spiritual authority. They carry insight from Scripture, experience in shepherding others, and a burden to help you stay grounded.

But here's the key, you have to show up. You have to stay connected. The people God sends to strengthen you can only do so if you allow them access. Don't ghost your spiritual leaders when things get hard. Press in. Let them know where you're struggling. Let them pray with you, speak truth over you, and remind you of God's promises.

Accountability Partners

Accountability gets a bad rap sometimes. It sounds rigid or performance-based. But true accountability is rooted in love. It's not about judgment, it's about alignment. It's someone who knows what you're committed to and won't let you forget it when life gets messy.

Sometimes your accountability partner is a friend who texts you every week to check in. Other times it's a group chat with like-minded believers, reminding each other to stay the course. The key is honesty. No masks, no posturing. Just real people helping each other stay faithful when life tries to pull them off track.

Testimonies That Inspire

I've watched people walk through unimaginable pressure and come out stronger, not because they were superheroes, but because they leaned on the right support system.

I think of a friend who lost their business and their marriage in the same year. They were tempted to disappear. But instead, they pressed into their church community, let their mentors speak into their pain, and leaned hard on God's Word. Today, they're not just restored, they're helping others walk through their storms.

Faithfulness doesn't mean you never feel weak. It means when weakness comes, you reach out, not pull back.

You weren't made to walk this path alone. Let your support system do what it was designed to do: hold you up, speak life, and keep you walking in truth. When pressure comes, people matter. And the right people make all the difference.

IX. Redefining Success Through the Lens of Faith

In the world's eyes, success is all about outcomes: bigger numbers, larger platforms, more influence, more income. And sure, results matter. We all want to see fruit from our labor. But if we only define success by what we accomplish, we set ourselves up for constant anxiety, discouragement, and comparison.

Faith uses a different standard. In the Kingdom, **obedience is the win.**

God's not impressed with metrics. He's moved by the posture of your heart. He's not asking, "Did you hit your goal?" He's asking, "Did you trust Me? Did you obey? Did you stay faithful when it would've been easier to quit?"

When you're walking through pressure, it's easy to think you're failing just because you haven't arrived yet. But faithfulness isn't about arrival, it's about direction. It's about waking up each day and choosing to move forward, even when the results don't come as fast as you hoped.

In Matthew 25, Jesus tells the parable of the talents. The master didn't praise the servant who made the most money. He praised the ones who were faithful with what they were given. "Well done, good and faithful servant." Not "good and successful." Not "good and efficient." Faithful.

That shifts everything.

When you judge yourself by worldly standards during times of pressure, you'll feel like a failure. But when you use the lens of faith, you start to realize that **showing up is a win. Staying true is a win. Obeying when it costs you something is a win.**

Obedience Over Outcomes

Obedience isn't always glamorous. Sometimes it looks like keeping your commitment when no one's watching. Other times, it's saying no to shortcuts that could have brought faster results but would've compromised your values.

One of the biggest breakthroughs in my own journey came when I stopped measuring success by how many people joined my team or how many sales I made and started asking: Was I obedient to what I felt God told me to do today?

If the answer was yes, I gave myself permission to celebrate. If the answer was no, I didn't beat myself up. I realigned, repented if I needed to, and got back on track. That's what faithfulness looks like in real life.

Celebrate Progress, Not Just End Results

We live in a highlight-reel culture. Everyone's showing off the big wins, the breakthroughs, the flashy numbers. But very few are posting about the ordinary days of faithfulness that led there, the days where they felt unseen, the days they wrestled with doubt and chose to press on anyway.

Those are the days that count most.

If you've been obedient, if you've persevered, if you've shown up when no one else clapped for you, that's success in the Kingdom.

Take time to celebrate your own progress. Reflect on how far you've come not just in results, but in your resilience. Maybe six months ago, pressure would've knocked you flat. But now? You're still standing. You're still praying. You're still believing. That's growth. That's faithfulness.

And God honors that.

Remember Galatians 6:9: "Let us not grow weary in well-doing, for at the proper time we will reap a harvest, if we do not give up."

Faithfulness Is the Fruit

Here's the thing most people miss: You don't just walk through pressure with faith, you grow fruit from it. Staying true under pressure produces a harvest of character, maturity, and clarity that can't be formed any other way.

In the end, success isn't just about where you arrive. It's about who you become on the journey, and whether you stay in alignment with who God called you to be.

So if you're in the thick of it right now, take a breath. You're not falling behind. You're being refined. You're building spiritual muscle. And every step of faithful obedience is writing a success story Heaven celebrates, even if the world doesn't notice.

You're not just surviving pressure. You're mastering the art of living by faith.

X. Practical Exercises and Reflection

Pressure doesn't usually show up with flashing lights. It creeps in quietly, through delays, discouragement, distractions, or self-doubt. That's why one of the most powerful tools for staying faithful is awareness. When you can identify the pressure points, you can prepare for them. You can build spiritual muscle in advance, instead of getting caught off guard.

This section is about more than journaling or tracking, it's about training. Think of it as spiritual conditioning. When life pushes hard, this is how you push back with intentionality and faith.

Exercise 1: Your Pressure Journal

Start keeping a simple "Pressure Journal." You don't need anything fancy, just a notebook, a doc on your phone, or a few blank pages in your planner. The goal is to notice your pressure patterns.

Here's what to track:

1. When pressure hits.

Write down the times you feel overwhelmed, tempted to quit, or pulled off course. Is it in the morning before you've grounded yourself in truth? Is it late at night when fatigue kicks in? Is it after conversations with certain people?

2. What triggers the pressure.

What's happening around you? Are you comparing yourself to someone else's results? Did you receive criticism? Are you facing slow progress?

3. How you usually respond.

Do you push harder in your own strength? Shut down? Procrastinate? Overthink? Numb out with distractions?

319

4. What a faithful response would look like.

Now reflect: How could you respond in faith? What promise could you anchor to? What action aligns with who God says you are?

Over time, this journal will reveal patterns and give you power. You'll stop being reactive and start being prepared. You'll recognize the enemy's strategy before he strikes. That's wisdom in action.

Exercise 2: The Faithfulness Tracker

Consistency under pressure doesn't happen by accident, it happens by design. That's where the Faithfulness Tracker comes in. This simple habit helps you focus not on doing everything right, but on doing the right things consistently.

Here's how it works:

Create a weekly chart with columns for key faith habits and rows for each day of the week. These are your anchors, the disciplines that ground you when everything feels shaky.

Example habits to track:

- Morning prayer and surrender
- Scripture reading or meditation
- Speaking truth declarations out loud
- Journaling your "why" or vision
- Checking in with a mentor or accountability partner
- Encouraging someone else (getting out of your own head)

Then each day, mark off what you completed. This isn't about perfection, it's about presence. It's about showing up with intentionality, even if you miss a day here or there.

After a week or two, review your tracker. What habits are helping you stay anchored? What tends to slip when pressure rises? Where do you need to reinforce your foundation?

You're not trying to earn favor here. You're building faithfulness through structure. You're training your soul to stand firm, not just when things are easy, but especially when they're not.

Reflection Prompts

Take time to sit with these questions. Don't rush through them. Let them draw something deeper out of you.

1. When do I feel the greatest pressure to compromise, quit, or shrink back?
2. What lies do I tend to believe during those moments?
3. What does God say about me, and this time, when I'm under pressure?
4. What would it look like to respond in faith rather than fear?
5. Who can I lean on for support when I feel weak or weary?
6. What small, consistent habits will help me stay rooted this week?

Remember: you're not trying to eliminate pressure. You're learning to thrive through it. Faithfulness is forged in the fire. These exercises are your training ground.

XI. Chapter Summary and Preview

If you've made it this far, you've been tested. You've felt the pressure. Maybe you've been tempted to give in, give up, or compromise. This chapter was about what happens when the emotional high fades, when momentum slows, or when life pushes back, and what it truly means to stay faithful anyway.

We explored the nature of pressure from all sides: the inner doubts and emotional dips, the external pushback and delays, and how faithfulness, real faithfulness, isn't flashy, but fierce. It's not about never feeling tired or discouraged. It's about choosing consistency over comfort and obedience over outcome.

We defined faithfulness as a spiritual backbone: a combination of identity, trust, and discipline that holds you upright when everything else feels shaky. The biblical stories of Daniel, Esther, and Job weren't about ease. They were about resilience. Steadfastness. And trust in a bigger picture.

You also saw how pressure doesn't just weigh you down, it refines you. It brings clarity. It forces you to reaffirm your "why." Like fire to gold, pressure can burn away distractions and purify your purpose. Romans 5 reminded us that perseverance produces character, and character produces hope, and not the kind that disappoints.

Practical tools like the pressure journal and faithfulness tracker gave you a way to face resistance with strategy and intentionality. We talked about setting daily anchors, prayer, reflection, and truth, and protecting your mind by curating what you consume, who you listen to, and what you say to yourself.

We discussed the value of mentors and spiritual support systems, those voices who walk with you, pray with you, and remind you who you are when you forget. And finally, we reframed success through the lens of faith. Not results. Not numbers. But obedience, consistency, and perseverance.

Now you're ready for the final chapter.

Preview of Chapter 15: Your Personal Roadmap to Lasting Success

Chapter 15 is where we tie it all together. It's where the rubber meets the road, not just in mindset or theory, but in a framework that can carry you for the rest of your life.

This chapter will help you design your own success map. Not someone else's plan, yours.

You'll revisit all the foundational principles you've learned: faith, discipline, identity, and mindset, and learn how to integrate them into a daily method of operation (DMO) that reflects your purpose and calling.

We'll talk about crafting routines that anchor you in your values, setting non-negotiables that protect your growth, and staying focused on the vision God gave you, without losing sight of today's responsibilities.

You'll build out your own framework for long-term alignment: a personal blueprint built on clarity, conviction, and consistency. And you'll learn how to check in, adjust course, and keep growing through every season.

This next chapter isn't just about sustaining change, it's about multiplying it. It's about becoming the kind of person who lives with purpose and leads from purpose.

You've been refined. You've been prepared. Now it's time to codify the vision and live it out with intention.

Let's finish strong. Your roadmap awaits

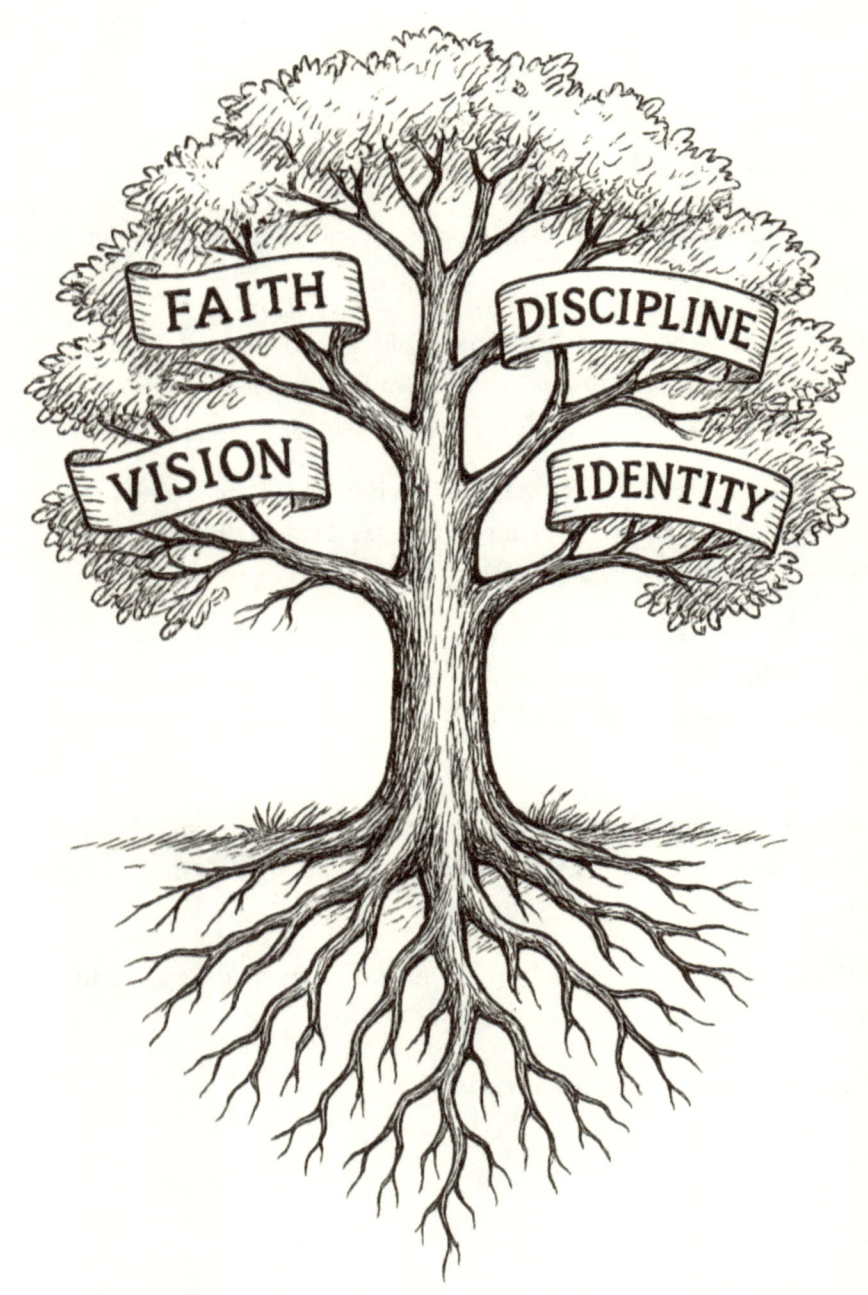

Chapter 15: Your Personal Roadmap to Lasting Success

I. Introduction

Reflecting on the journey through the previous chapters
The purpose of creating a personal roadmap for long-term growth and fulfillment

Take a deep breath for a second. Seriously, just pause and take one.

Now look at how far you've come.

You've made it through fourteen chapters of mindset, identity, discipline, faith, purpose, pressure, and personal transformation. If you've read with an open heart and applied even a fraction of what we've covered, you're not the same person who started this book. Something's shifted. Maybe it's subtle, maybe it's seismic. Either way, you've begun the process of becoming someone who lives from the inside out, with vision, conviction, and alignment.

That's no small thing. In a world constantly trying to pull us in a hundred different directions, getting grounded in who you are and why you're here is a powerful act of resistance. You've chosen growth and purpose. You've chosen to believe that your life has meaning and that you can live it with intention.

But here's the thing: momentum fades and emotions settle. The world doesn't stop just because you've had a breakthrough.

And this is where most people stall out.

They feel the fire. They start strong. But without a structure to carry that fire forward, it fizzles. And when life gets busy or messy or hard (because it always does), they slip back into old patterns. That's not going to be you.

Not anymore.

This final chapter is where you get to turn all the lessons, insights, and transformations you've experienced into something solid, something that lives beyond inspiration and becomes your personal operating system. A clear, practical, repeatable framework that keeps you moving forward long after the excitement dies down.

Think of it like this: we've just spent the last fourteen chapters clearing the fog from your windshield. Now, we're going to chart your course. You're the driver. The road's yours. But your roadmap? That's what we're building right here.

You're not winging it anymore. You're not hoping for change. You're designing it.

This chapter is about integration, taking all the truths you've uncovered and translating them into systems, habits, and a vision that keeps you grounded and growing. Because real success isn't accidental. It's intentional, structured, and it's anchored in the deep work you've done to align your actions with your faith, purpose, and identity.

We're going to revisit what matters most. We're going to sketch out your unique daily method of operation. We're going to create rhythms that sustain you, non-negotiables that protect you, and a long-term vision that inspires you. And at the end of this chapter, you'll walk away with something concrete: a personal success roadmap, one that actually fits you.

So, if you've ever felt like you "start strong but finish weak," that ends today. This is where you shift from learning to leading yourself. This is where it becomes real.

Let's build your roadmap and make it stick.

Let's finish strong.

II. Reviewing Key Lessons

Brief recap of foundational principles: identity, faith, discipline, mindset
Why integration matters more than information

Before we map out your personal roadmap, let's hit pause and take inventory.

You've covered a lot of ground in this book, not just concepts, but shifts. You've peeled back layers, challenged old beliefs, and started building a foundation that's meant to last. So before we build your strategy for the future, let's remember the pillars it's standing on.

Identity

It all starts here. If you don't know who you are, everything else will be unstable. We talked about identity not as something you create, but as something you uncover, something already placed in you by God. You're not just a sum of your past or your performance. You're called, equipped, and deeply valued. When you operate from that truth, you stop chasing validation and start living with authority.

Faith

Faith isn't just a belief system. It's a fuel system. It's what keeps you going when you can't see the outcome yet. In this book, we've leaned into the biblical truth that faith is the substance of things hoped for (Hebrews 11:1). That means it has weight. It has structure. Faith gives you the strength to hold your ground, to take the next step, even when logic or circumstances say, "sit down." When you've got God's promises driving your process, you don't need perfect conditions, you just need trust.

Discipline

We busted the myth that discipline is about grinding harder or forcing yourself into rigid routines. It's not. Real discipline is a gift; it's what frees you from chaos and gets you moving in the direction of your calling. It's not about hustle. It's about consistency. It's about honoring your purpose with your schedule. When your habits align with your identity and values, discipline becomes a joy, not a jail sentence.

Mindset

And let's not forget mindset, the engine room of it all. Your thoughts create emotions, your emotions drive decisions, and your decisions create your results. You've learned how to interrupt toxic thought patterns, shift your self-talk, and take control of the inner dialogue that shapes your outer world. This isn't just positive thinking. This is truth-aligned thinking. And it changes everything.

Integration Over Information

Now, let me hit you with something that separates this chapter, and really, this entire book, from most of the personal growth content out there: **Information doesn't change lives. Integration does.**

You can memorize every quote from Jim Rohn or Bob Proctor. You can know every scripture, underline every principle, and have the cleanest bookshelf full of "success books" known to man, but if you don't live it, it won't help you. You'll stay stuck in the loop of knowing better but not doing better.

Integration means bringing what you know into what you do. It means aligning your habits with your beliefs. It means showing up on Monday morning the same way you do on Sunday morning when you're fired up from a sermon or a success video.

This is the game-changer. Most people stop at inspiration. Few ever move to implementation.

You're not most people.

You've seen how faith, identity, discipline, and mindset work together. You've been equipped with strategies, scripture, and stories to reinforce your growth. Now the invitation is simple: don't just know it. Live it, own it, and integrate it.

Because what you integrate, you become.

So, let's get practical. Let's design your framework, your DMO, and your daily rhythm, not based on hype, but based on the truth of who you are and who you're becoming.

Ready?

Let's go build it.

III. Designing Your Success Framework

Building your own blueprint using the principles in this book Practical template: Vision → Belief → Decision → Action → Review → Adjust

Now that you've taken in the core lessons and values from this journey, it's time to turn them into something that works for you. Not just something that sounds good or looks impressive on paper, but a framework you can lean on when life gets real, when motivation dips, or when the next big step feels intimidating.

You're not here to wing it. You're here to build it, intentionally.

This section is about giving shape to your growth with a success framework that reflects your unique calling, character, and capacity. And to do that, I want to offer you a simple but powerful template to structure your journey:

Vision → Belief → Decision → Action → Review → Adjust

Let's break it down.

1. Vision

Everything starts here. Your vision is the picture of the future that inspires you today. It's the reason you get up early, stay committed, and keep moving forward when things get tough. It's not just about what you want to achieve; it's about who you want to become.

Your vision should feel personal, energizing, and anchored in purpose. If your goals don't stir something in your spirit, they'll never be strong enough to carry you through resistance.

Ask yourself: What does the best version of my life look like? What does it feel like to walk in alignment with my calling?

Write it down. Let it breathe. Let it stretch you.

2. Belief

Once the vision is clear, belief becomes the fuel. If you don't believe it's possible for you, you'll sabotage the process, plain and simple.

This is where you deal with the inner work. We're talking about confronting limiting beliefs, replacing lies with truth, and getting aligned mentally and spiritually with where you're going. Remember: your feet won't go where your mind refuses to lead.

Feed your faith with scripture. Speak affirmations grounded in truth. Surround yourself with people who reflect possibility, not limitation.

3. Decision

Belief without decision is still just potential.

There comes a point where you have to decide that you're going to act like the person you're becoming. You draw a line in the sand and say, "No more delay. No more excuses. This is who I am, and this is what I'm doing."

Decision is about cutting off other options. No plan B. No toe-dipping. When you decide, things start to move. The fog begins to clear. Resources show up. Clarity increases.

Faith becomes action.

4. Action

Now we're in motion. But here's the thing, your actions don't need to be perfect. They just need to be aligned.

Are you taking steps every day that reflect the identity, purpose, and vision you're holding? Are your habits and priorities making room for your future self?

Don't get stuck in overplanning. Take the step in front of you. Make the call. Start the routine. Share the message. Do the uncomfortable thing that aligns with your growth.

5. Review

This is the part most people skip. But if you're serious about growth, you have to be honest with yourself.

Every week, every month, take a moment to review. What's working? What's not? Where are you drifting from your vision? Where are you out of alignment with your values?

Self-reflection isn't about guilt. It's about course correction.

6. Adjust

Based on your review, make small shifts. Adjust your schedule. Rethink a routine. Revisit a goal that's no longer serving you. You're not meant to build this once and lock it in forever. Life evolves. So do you.

The ability to adjust without losing your vision or identity is one of your greatest success skills.

This framework isn't complicated, but it's powerful. Vision. Belief. Decision. Action. Review. Adjust.

It gives you a repeatable system to move forward with intention, stay grounded in faith, and respond to life with clarity and strength.

You're not building a moment. You're building a movement, one rooted in who you truly are.

Let's keep going.

IV. Creating Your Daily Method of Operation (DMO)

Crafting faith-anchored, purpose-aligned routines
Morning and evening rituals, time blocking, and habit tracking

Let's get one thing straight: success doesn't happen by accident. It's the result of structure, not just desire. It's built in the trenches of your daily routine, not the mountaintop moments of inspiration.

Your Daily Method of Operation, or DMO, is the engine of your transformation. It's the rhythm that turns your values into actions, your purpose into productivity, and your goals into results. Without it, you're just hoping. With it, you're building.

But here's the key: your DMO isn't meant to be a grind. It should reflect your values, your vision, and your faith. It should nourish you, not drain you.

Let's walk through what that looks like.

1. Morning Rituals: Starting from Identity

Your mornings set the tone. Period.

Before you check your phone, your email, or the latest drama online, check in with God. Tune in to your source. Remind yourself who you are and why you're here.

Here's a simple faith-anchored morning ritual you can personalize:

- **Prayer & Gratitude (5–10 minutes):** Start with thanks. Anchor your heart in God's presence. Thank Him for breath, purpose, and progress.
- **Scripture or Devotional Reading (10–15 minutes):** Feed your spirit before feeding your mind. Pick a verse, a promise, or a short passage to carry with you.
- **Declarations (2–5 minutes):** Speak truth out loud. "I am focused. I am favored. I walk in purpose. I respond in peace."
- **Top 3 Priorities (5 minutes):** Identify your top 3 purpose-aligned tasks for the day. Not just busywork, impact work.

This isn't about perfection. It's about consistency. A morning like this doesn't just get you going; it gets you going in the right direction.

2. Time Blocking: Protecting What Matters

If it's not scheduled, it's not real.

Purpose doesn't live in your intention list, it lives in your calendar. Time blocking is about assigning specific blocks of time to specific activities so your day reflects your priorities, not distractions.

Start with this framework:

- **Faith Block:** Time for prayer, study, or journaling.
- **Mission Block:** Income-producing or calling-aligned work.
- **Relationship Block:** Intentional time with family, spouse, friends.
- **Health Block:** Movement, hydration, rest.

Don't just hope your priorities get attention, guarantee it with your schedule.

3. Evening Rituals: Closing with Purpose

Most people let their days end in chaos; scrolling social media, stressing about tomorrow, and mentally replaying mistakes. But when you end with intention, you set yourself up for a powerful tomorrow.

Try this:

- **Evening Reflection (5–10 minutes):** Ask, "Where did I stay aligned? Where did I drift?" No guilt, just awareness.
- **Gratitude & Release (3–5 minutes):** Thank God for what went well. Release what didn't. You're growing.
- **Plan Tomorrow (5 minutes):** Write out your top 3 intentions. When you sleep with purpose, you wake up with clarity.

4. Habit Tracking: Measuring What Matters

You've heard it said: what gets measured, gets managed. Tracking your habits helps you stay accountable without being obsessive.

Pick 3–5 keystone habits that reflect your values and goals. Things like:

- Morning prayer
- Reading 10 pages
- Drinking water
- Messaging 3 prospects
- 30 minutes of movement

Then simply check them off daily. You'll be surprised how motivating it is to see progress stack up, even in small wins.

Your DMO is your agreement with your future. It's the daily structure that tells your mind, "We're serious about this." It's not about hustle, it's about alignment. When your routine flows from your identity and your faith, it becomes a joy, not a burden.

This is how you become who you're meant to be, on purpose, every single day.

Let's keep building.

V. Defining Your Non-Negotiables

Values, faith practices, personal boundaries
What you must protect to stay aligned and productive

One of the fastest ways to lose momentum in life is to live without boundaries. And one of the surest ways to stay aligned with your purpose is to get crystal clear on what you will no longer compromise, your non-negotiables.

Non-negotiables are the personal standards that guide your behavior, filter your decisions, and protect your priorities. They are your internal compass. They keep your life anchored to your values, not tossed around by emotions, distractions, or outside pressure.

Let me tell you, without non-negotiables, your "yes" gets hijacked a hundred times a week. Your peace gets traded for urgency. Your faith gets sidelined by fear. Your purpose gets diluted by noise. So, this chapter is about drawing your line in the sand and saying, "This is who I am, and this is what I refuse to compromise anymore."

1. Get Clear on Your Core Values

Start here. What really matters to you?

Not what sounds good. Not what culture says should matter. What truly reflects your heart, your calling, and your walk with God?

Some common values to consider:

- Integrity
- Generosity
- Peace
- Faithfulness
- Growth
- Authenticity
- Excellence
- Service

Choose your top 3–5 values. These are your true north. When a choice comes your way, say yes only if it aligns with these. If it doesn't? It's a no, no matter how shiny it looks.

2. Establish Your Faith Practices

Your faith can't just be something you turn to when you hit a wall. It has to be part of the foundation you build on every single day.

So, what are the non-negotiable ways you nurture your relationship with God?

- Daily prayer time (even if it's just 10 minutes)
- Reading or meditating on scripture
- Listening to faith-building messages
- Weekly worship and spiritual community
- Journaling or quiet reflection

These aren't about checking a box. They're about staying rooted, so when life pulls, you don't snap. When storms come, you don't crumble. Faith practices are soul maintenance. Without them, your engine will eventually stall.

3. Define Your Personal Boundaries

If you don't protect your energy, your focus, or your peace, no one else will.

That means setting boundaries around:

- **Time**: Who gets access to you and when?
- **Conversations:** What kind of talk you allow in your space (gossip, negativity, drama).
- **Digital input:** How often you scroll. What you consume. Who you follow.
- **Work:** When you stop for the day. When you unplug. When you rest.

Here's the thing: Boundaries aren't walls. They're fences with gates. You can open them with intention. But if you don't build them, your life becomes an open field for distractions and chaos.

Protect your sacred spaces, your morning routine, your creative hours, your rest, your sabbath, your family time. These are holy. They are not for negotiation.

4. Guard What Fuels You

Ask yourself:

- What activities drain me?
- What environments uplift me?
- Who pulls me closer to God?
- Who constantly pulls me off course?

You've got to get ruthless about your inputs. What goes into your mind, heart, and spirit will always shape your outcomes. Protect your joy. Protect your focus. Protect your walk.

5. Write It Down and Review Often

Your non-negotiables should be written down somewhere you can see them regularly. They serve as a personal constitution, something you return to when decisions get hard, when you feel off-track, or when someone pressures you to compromise.

These standards don't make your life smaller. They make your impact stronger.

This isn't about being rigid, it's about being rooted. When your days are grounded in values, faith, and firm boundaries, you'll find yourself walking in more peace, more clarity, and more power.

So, let's lock it in. You've come too far to let little things shake what God is building in you. Protect what matters most.

VI. Long-Term Vision and Short-Term Focus

Setting big-picture goals with daily action plans
Balancing dreaming big with staying grounded in the present

If you've made it this far, you're already doing more than most people ever will; you're building a life with intention. But here's the next critical skill to master: holding a long-term vision while showing up fully for today's assignment. It's the art of dreaming big without drifting off into the clouds.

Long-term vision gives your life direction. Short-term focus gives it traction. And you need both if you're going to build something that lasts.

The Power of Vision

Let's talk vision first.

Vision is the picture of what's possible. It's the mountaintop you're climbing toward. Without it, you wake up reacting to life instead of leading it. Vision is what pulls you through tough days, dry seasons, and slow progress. Proverbs 29:18 says, "Where there is no vision, the people perish." That's not just poetic, that's practical.

But here's the catch: a compelling vision without grounded action becomes a source of frustration. It turns into fantasy instead of fuel. You keep saying "someday," but someday never shows up because there's no real plan.

So, if your vision is to build a six-figure business, transform your health, start a ministry, or break a generational pattern, it's going to require you to translate that vision into daily decisions.

Create Your Daily Bridge

This is where short-term focus steps in. What are you doing today to move that vision forward?

A big goal doesn't need massive effort every day. It needs consistent effort; focused, non-negotiable, small-but-purposeful action.

That might look like:

- One key conversation per day
- 45 minutes of uninterrupted creative work
- 20 minutes of prayer and journaling
- Sending two follow-ups
- Blocking distractions for two solid hours

These aren't glamorous. They don't feel like you're changing the world. But they are the seeds that grow your future.

Small steps executed consistently, day in and day out, compound over time. Jim Rohn put it like this: "Success is neither magical nor mysterious. Success is the natural consequence of consistently applying the basic fundamentals."

Reverse-Engineer Your Goals

One of the best strategies for balancing big vision with short-term focus is to reverse-engineer.

Here's a simple breakdown:

1. **Start with the End Goal**
   (e.g., "I want to earn $10,000/month from my coaching business in 12 months.")

2. **Break it Into Milestones**
   (e.g., "In 3 months, I want to have 5 paying clients.")
3. **Determine Monthly, Weekly, and Daily Actions**
   (e.g., "Each week, I'll book 3 discovery calls. Each day, I'll reach out to 5 people.")

This creates a pipeline between your vision and your calendar. No more guessing. No more waiting for motivation to hit. Your plan becomes the vehicle that gets you there, one short trip at a time.

Stay Grounded in Today

Here's the mindset shift: while your vision is out there in the distance, your responsibility is right here in the present.

It's easy to feel overwhelmed when you measure today against your future goal. But if you can stay faithful with the next step, the one right in front of you, God will multiply your efforts. Remember the loaves and fishes? Faithfulness feeds favor.

Jesus said, "Don't worry about tomorrow, for tomorrow will worry about itself." (Matthew 6:34). That wasn't a suggestion to avoid planning, it was an invitation to stay anchored in the grace that only shows up today.

Final Thoughts

Vision without action is fantasy. Action without vision is busywork. But vision + action? That's legacy.

Keep dreaming big. Keep planning smart. But never forget: the way you do Tuesday morning determines whether that dream becomes your reality.

VII. Accountability and Course Correction

**How to regularly check in with yourself and your mentors
Tools for honest self-assessment and redirection**

Let's talk about a game-changing principle that separates dabblers from doers: accountability. Not the kind that shames or micromanages, but the kind that protects your purpose, sharpens your focus, and helps you get back up when life inevitably knocks you off track.

Success isn't about never falling. It's about how quickly, and honestly, you course correct. And that comes down to two things: self-awareness and strategic feedback.

Check Yourself Before You Wreck Yourself

We all drift. We all hit points where motivation fades, distractions creep in, or our habits start slipping. If you wait for disaster before checking in with yourself, you're operating in recovery mode, not growth mode.

Build in regular checkpoints:

- **Weekly reviews** to assess what's working and what's not
- **Monthly reflections** to recalibrate goals and energy
- **Quarterly resets** to realign with your vision and core values

These aren't just rituals, they're recalibrations. They keep your inner compass pointed toward your true north.

Ask yourself:

- "Did my actions this week match my intentions?"
- "Where did I drift, and what caused it?"
- "What adjustments do I need to make immediately?"

342

Self-honesty is the bridge to breakthrough.

Invite a Mirror, Not a Micromanager

Self-assessment is powerful, but outside accountability adds another layer of clarity and momentum.

You need people in your corner who aren't impressed by your potential but are committed to your progress. Mentors, coaches, accountability partners, people who know your mission and aren't afraid to challenge you with love and truth.

Look for mentors who:

- Have already walked where you want to go
- Operate from faith and wisdom, not hype
- Will ask hard questions and expect real answers

Regular check-ins with these mentors create rhythm and reinforcement. They help you catch blind spots before they become breakdowns.

I can't tell you how many times I was ready to give up on something… until a mentor reminded me who I am and what I'm building. Sometimes, we just need someone to call us up, not out.

Tools to Stay Aligned

Let's get practical. Here are tools that can help you stay on track:

- **The 3Q Journal:**
  At the end of each week, answer:
    1. What worked?
    2. What didn't?
    3. What will I adjust?

- **Weekly Scorecard:**
  Rate yourself from 1–10 in areas like:
    - Faith connection
    - Discipline
    - Daily execution
    - Integrity to your vision
    - Energy and mindset

When you track it, you can tweak it. Awareness fuels improvement.

- **Mentor Check-In Sheet:**
  Before every call or meeting with your mentor, answer:
    - What am I celebrating this week?
    - What challenge am I facing?
    - What do I need feedback on?
    - What's one commitment I'll make before our next session?

This keeps conversations focused and fruitful.

Grace + Truth = Growth

Not every week will be a home run. Some weeks, you'll miss the mark. That's not failure, it's feedback. The goal isn't perfection, it's progress with awareness.

That's why you need both grace and truth in this process.

Grace reminds you you're still growing. Truth reminds you that growth requires action.

When you embrace both, accountability stops feeling like pressure and starts becoming fuel.

Final Word

Accountability isn't just about staying on track; it's about becoming who you said you would be.

And course correction? That's your superpower. It means you're still in the game, still listening, and still adjusting.

So don't wait for crisis. Build in regular reflection. Lean on wise mentors. And check in with the only person who can do the work, you.

VIII. Living from Identity, Not Circumstance

Graham Cooke's approach to staying anchored in who you are
Choosing to respond to life from strength and vision

One of the most transformative truths I've ever learned came from Graham Cooke. He said, "We don't live from our circumstances, we live from our identity." That line hit me like a lightning bolt, because most people are living reactively. They respond to stress, pressure, or disappointment based on how they feel in the moment, not based on who they are.

That's not sustainable. That's survival mode. And it keeps you on a constant emotional rollercoaster.

But when you learn to live from identity, not the noise around you, not the opinions of others, not the bills on the table or the messages in your inbox, you unlock something unshakable. Something God-anchored. And that's where real freedom lives.

Who You Are Determines What You Do

Your identity isn't defined by your past, your failures, or even your current level of success. It's defined by your Creator. It's wrapped in truth, not performance.

Graham Cooke teaches that identity comes from intimacy with God. The more time you spend with Him, the clearer your true self becomes. You're not just a business owner, coach, or parent. You're a beloved child of God, equipped and empowered to live with purpose.

When your decisions flow from that place, not from fear, scarcity, or ego, you show up with peace, power, and clarity. Even in chaos.

Circumstances Shift. Your Identity Doesn't.

Life isn't always fair. Sometimes things fall apart. People disappoint you. Opportunities collapse. Emotions flare up. But your identity? That's constant.

If you anchor your sense of self to external wins, then you're only as strong as your last good day. But when your identity is rooted in God's truth about you, you can weather the storm without losing your footing.

You stop reacting to setbacks like a victim and start responding like a leader.

You stop asking, "Why is this happening to me?" and start declaring, "How will I grow through this?"

Responding from Strength, Not Emotion

Living from identity means you've already settled who you are, so when life presses in, you don't panic, you pivot. You don't let fear dictate your next move; you let purpose lead.

Here's how that plays out:

- **Instead of complaining**, you speak life.
- **Instead of shrinking back**, you step forward in faith.
- **Instead of lashing out**, you choose patience and wisdom.

- **Instead of quitting,** you remind yourself why you started.

This isn't about pretending everything's okay. It's about remembering who you are when things aren't.

It's not fake faith. It's formed faith.

Identity First, Action Second

Before every decision, ask "Is this response flowing from who I truly am?"

If not, pause, re-center, then move.

Let your identity set the tone before your circumstances do. That's how you lead your life instead of being led by it.

Identity Anchoring Practices

Here are a few habits that help you stay rooted:

- **Start each day with a truth statement.**
  Example: "I am bold, favored, and faithful. Today, I live from purpose, not pressure."
- **Use identity-based journaling.**
  Instead of asking "What happened today?", ask "How did I show up as the person I'm becoming?"
- **Meditate on scriptures that affirm who you are.**
  Ephesians 2:10. 2 Timothy 1:7. Romans 8:37. Let them reshape how you see yourself.
- **Limit your exposure to voices that reinforce doubt or drama.**
  Your identity can't grow if you're soaking in messages that contradict it.

Final Word

Living from identity isn't a one-time decision; it's a daily discipline. It's choosing to show up as the version of you that God already sees, regardless of what the mirror, your bank account, or your inbox says.

The world needs more people who are steady in who they are. Not perfect, just anchored.

IX. Letting Your Life Speak

Becoming a walking example of alignment, faith, and transformation
How your lifestyle becomes your greatest testimony and influence

At some point in your journey, you realize the loudest message you'll ever preach isn't what you say, it's how you live.

Your life speaks.

Your habits, your peace, your posture in the face of adversity... all of it sends a message to the people around you about what you believe, what you value, and who you serve.

And the truth is, people are always watching, even when you think they're not.

They're watching how you handle pressure.

How you respond when things don't go your way.

How you treat people who can't do anything for you.

How you bounce back from setbacks.

How you stay grounded in your identity while others shift with the wind.

Letting your life speak is about alignment. When your words, actions, and values line up, there's power in that consistency. And that power doesn't need a platform; it shows up in your presence.

Your Lifestyle Is Your Legacy

Think about the people who've influenced you the most. Chances are, it wasn't just their advice that changed you. It was their example. How they lived and how they showed up, day in and day out.

Maybe it was the way they led their family with quiet strength.

Maybe it was how they carried themselves in business with integrity.

Maybe it was how they stayed faithful when others walked away.

When you live on purpose, with faith and alignment, your life becomes the message.

You don't have to convince people, your fruit does the talking.

Living Out Loud Without Saying a Word

One of the most powerful things you can do is become unshakably consistent in who you are. That's what speaks volumes.

You don't need a stage or a podcast or a best-selling book to influence others (though those things can help).

You just need to be someone whose daily life reflects the transformation you've experienced.

When your friends, family, or coworkers see the difference in you, it creates curiosity. They may not say anything right away, but they notice.

They see when you respond with grace instead of offense.

When you stay patient when others lose their cool.

When you choose gratitude over gossip.

When you keep showing up even after a setback.

That's not hype. That's holy. That's the influence of a life aligned with God.

Becoming the Message

You don't have to try to be perfect. But you do need to be real.

Let people see the journey, the progress, and the lessons learned.

Let your integrity do the heavy lifting.

Let your peace speak louder than your pride.

Let your purpose pull you forward when your feelings want to pull you back.

When people watch you live out your values consistently, especially under pressure, they begin to trust that what you have is real. And that opens doors for deeper conversations, for ministry moments, and for authentic relationships built on mutual respect.

The Influence of Transformation

True transformation is magnetic. Not because it's flashy, but because it's rare.

In a world full of fake and filtered, authenticity stands out.

So let your life reflect the inner work you've done in this book. Let the small wins, the daily disciplines, the mindset shifts, and the faith-fueled habits become visible. Let your life quietly challenge others to rise. Not by preaching at them, but by living in a way that makes them curious about what changed you.

Final Thought

Don't underestimate the impact of living well.

When you show up aligned with your values, anchored in your identity, and powered by your faith, your life speaks volumes. And that message may be the seed that changes someone else's entire path.

In the next section, we're going to put it all together: your daily method of operation, your personal success map, and your mission statement. This is where your transformation becomes a tool, not just for your success, but for your calling.

Let's build it.

X. Practical Exercises and Reflection

Create your personal success map and DMO
Write a personal mission statement based on everything you've learned

Now it's time to take everything you've walked through in this book, every mindset shift, every habit, every lesson rooted in faith, and put it into a living, breathing framework that you can use every single day.

This isn't about creating some rigid routine or trying to fit into someone else's mold. It's about you designing a roadmap that's built on the foundation of your values, faith, and purpose. Something that works in real life, not just on paper.

Step 1: Build Your Personal Success Map

Start with this simple yet powerful framework:

Vision → Belief → Decision → Action → Review → Adjust

Let's break it down:

- **Vision** – What are you moving toward? What kind of life are you building? Define it clearly, don't play small here.
- **Belief** – What do you need to believe about God, yourself, and your future to make that vision possible?
- **Decision** – What decisions must you make (and stick to) to support that belief?
- **Action** – What consistent behaviors and habits will turn that decision into momentum?
- **Review** – Schedule regular check-ins (weekly or monthly) to assess what's working and what's not.
- **Adjust** – Be flexible enough to make changes but committed enough not to quit.

Your success map isn't just a one-time project. It's a living guide. Keep it where you can see it; print it, post it, pray over it.

Step 2: Create Your DMO (Daily Method of Operation)

This is where the rubber meets the road.

Your DMO should be:

- Simple enough to stick with
- Specific enough to track
- Strong enough to move the needle

Here's a sample to build from:

Morning:

- Gratitude (3 things)
- Scripture + prayer (15-30 min)
- Review the top 3 goals for the day
- Speak 3 faith-filled declarations over your life

Work Block:

- Focused 90-minute work session
- 5-minute stretch and reset
- Check in with your accountability partner or group

Evening:

- Journal wins and lessons
- Prayer + reflection
- Prepare tomorrow's top priorities

You can customize this. But make sure it aligns with your vision, reflects your values, and honors your faith. That's the key to staying consistent even when life throws curveballs.

Step 3: Write Your Personal Mission Statement

Write a short, powerful statement that reflects the life you're committed to living. It should:

- Capture your identity in Christ
- Clarify your purpose and calling
- Inspire you when the fire fades

Here's a fill-in-the-blank template to start:

> "I am a [who you are], called to [your purpose], driven by [your values], and committed to living each day with [your anchor]. I lead with faith, serve with love, and build a life that reflects the goodness and purpose of God in every area."

Here's what mine might sound like:

> "I am a builder and a bridge, called to raise up leaders, restore purpose, and help people break through. I walk in integrity, lead with compassion, and grow by faith. My life is a reflection of God's grace, and everything I do flows from who I am in Him."

Now write yours. Speak it out loud. Post it somewhere you'll see it daily. Revisit it often.

Final Reflection

This moment matters. The fact that you're still here, reading, growing, and reflecting, means something.

You didn't just read another book. You started to build a new blueprint. One that's anchored in faith, aligned with purpose, and equipped for real-world execution.

So, take a deep breath. You've come a long way.

Now it's time to walk it out, with clarity, with boldness, and with God's strength carrying you forward.

Let's move on to the final section, where I share some final encouragement to keep you grounded, focused, and ready for whatever comes next.

XI. Final Words of Encouragement

A personal message to the reader from Ray
Invitation to revisit and recommit to the process often

Let me just pause right here and say this plainly:

I'm proud of you.

You didn't just flip through another self-help book or skim for a quick fix. You showed up for yourself, chapter after chapter. You took an honest look at your thoughts, habits, beliefs, and patterns. And you kept going, even when the truth hit hard or the changes felt uncomfortable.

That tells me something about you. You're not here for surface-level success. You're not chasing hype or hoping someone else will come along and do the work for you. You're building something deeper. Something sustainable. Something real.

And that's exactly why I wrote this book.

I've walked through the highs of momentum and the crushing weight of self-sabotage. I've seen what happens when you try to hustle your way to peace, when you chase goals that aren't aligned with who you really are. I've burned out. I've messed up. I've had to start over.

But I've also learned what it means to rebuild from the inside out. To anchor in identity. To let faith, not fear, be the fuel. And most of all, I've discovered that transformation isn't about arriving at some perfect destination. It's about becoming a little more each day, the person God created you to be.

So, if you take nothing else from this book, hear this:

You already have what it takes.

Not because you're always strong or always motivated. But because you've got the Spirit of God in you. And because you're willing to keep showing up.

When you fall off track (and you will at times), don't beat yourself up. Don't let shame have the final word. Just go back to your roadmap. Revisit your "why." Look at what you wrote in your DMO, your vision, and your mission. Let those reminders pull you back into alignment.

This journey isn't about being perfect, it's about being faithful.

Faithful to your calling, faithful to the process, and faithful to the One who planted the vision inside of you in the first place.

Life's going to test everything you've written down. You'll be tempted to shrink back. To settle. To forget who you are and what you committed to. That's why I want to challenge you to make **revisiting and recommitting** part of your rhythm.

Once a week, ask:

- Am I living aligned with my values and vision?
- What adjustments do I need to make?
- What's God speaking to me about this week?

Once a quarter, reflect:

- What progress have I made?
- What breakthroughs have happened?
- Where am I still resisting growth?

And every single day, wake up and remind yourself:

"Today, I get to walk this out. I don't have to be perfect, I just need to be present, faithful, and willing."

You're not walking alone. God is with you. And so are others who've chosen to live this way, people just like you who've traded temporary hype for real transformation.

So, keep building, growing, and becoming.

I'm cheering for you, and I truly believe the best is yet to come.

Let your life speak.

Let your choices reflect your identity.

Let your faith carry you when motivation won't.

You've got this. Let's finish strong.

— Ray

XII. Appendix and Resources

Tools, book recommendations, scriptures, and templates for continued growth

Transformation doesn't end with the last page of a book, it begins there. This appendix is your toolkit. It's the "now what?" answer for those ready to keep building, refining, and living from the inside out. These resources are designed to be simple, practical, and powerful; tools you can revisit often as you evolve.

1. Tools and Templates

Personal Success Map Template

Use this layout as your go-to blueprint:

- **Vision:** What does your ideal future look like?
- **Belief:** What must you believe to move forward?
- **Decision:** What bold decision do you need to make right now?
- **Action:** What small, consistent steps will get you there?
- **Review:** What's working? What's not?
- **Adjust:** What changes will you implement this week?

Daily Method of Operation (DMO)

Morning:

- Scripture/prayer (15 min)
- Review mission and top 3 daily priorities
- Declare who you are out loud

Evening:

- Gratitude journaling
- What did I honor today?
- What needs adjustment tomorrow?

Faithfulness Tracker

A simple weekly log:

- Did I honor my values this week?
- Where did I show up with courage?
- Where did I hold back, and why?
- What do I commit to next week?

2. Recommended Reading

These are books that have helped shape my journey, spiritually, mentally, and practically. I encourage you to read them slowly, reflectively, and with a pen in hand.

Mindset & Growth

- As a Man Thinketh by James Allen
- Think and Grow Rich by Napoleon Hill
- The Power of Awareness by Neville Goddard
- The Slight Edge by Jeff Olson
- Atomic Habits by James Clear

Faith & Identity

- The Way of Life by Bill Johnson
- The Nature of Freedom by Graham Cooke
- Victory Over the Darkness by Neil Anderson
- Spirit Wars by Kris Vallotton

Productivity & Purpose

- Living Forward by Michael Hyatt & Daniel Harkavy
- Essentialism by Greg McKeown
- The 5 AM Club by Robin Sharma
- Purpose Driven Life by Rick Warren

3. Scripture for Ongoing Growth

Here are a few anchors for your journey. Meditate on them. Memorize them. Let them recalibrate your focus when life feels off-center.

- **Jeremiah 29:11** – "For I know the plans I have for you…"

- **Proverbs 3:5–6** – "Trust in the Lord with all your heart…"
- **Romans 12:2** – "Be transformed by the renewing of your mind…"
- **2 Timothy 1:7** – "God has not given us a spirit of fear…"
- **Hebrews 12:1–2** – "Let us run with endurance the race set before us…"
- **Galatians 6:9** – "Do not grow weary in doing good…"
- **James 1:4** – "Let perseverance finish its work…"
- **Psalm 1:2–3** – "Meditates on His law day and night… whatever he does prospers."

4. Optional Resources to Create or Use

If you're building systems for yourself or others, here are a few resource ideas you can create or customize:

- **Weekly Check-In Worksheet** (to evaluate your alignment with values and purpose)
- **Mission Statement Builder** (a guided fill-in-the-blank template)
- **Habit Tracker Printable** (customizable by priority or goal)
- **Scripture Declarations List** (speak these over yourself daily)
- **Vision Board Worksheet** (digital or print version)

5. Next Steps: Your Journey Isn't Over

Come back to this book often. Reread the chapters where you feel stuck. Reprint your DMO when it feels stale. Revisit your mission statement quarterly. This isn't a one-time shift, it's a lifelong journey.

You're not just learning how to succeed, you're learning how to become.

And that's what changes everything.